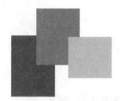

SOCIAL WORK CAREER DEVELOPMENT

A Handbook for Job Hunting and Career Planning

SECOND EDITION

By Carol Nesslein Doelling

NASW PRESS

National Association of Social Workers
Washington, DC

Gary Bailey, MSW, *President*
Elizabeth J. Clark, PhD, ACSW, MPH *Executive Director*

Cheryl Y. Bradley, *Publisher*
Paula L. Delo, *Executive Editor*
Marcia D. Roman, *Managing Editor, Journals and Books*
Jackie Rodriguez, *Editor*
Lou Goines, *Copy Editor*
Jeanne Haught and Cara Schumacher , *Proofreaders*
Leonard Rosenbaum, *Indexer*

Cover design byEye to Eye Design Studio, Bristow, VA
Interior design by Metadog Design Group, Washington, DC
Printed and bound by Port City Press, Baltimore, MD

©NASW Press

Library of Congress Cataloging-in-Publication Data

Carol Nesslein Doelling
  Social Work Career Development by Carol Nesslein Doelliing—2nd. ed.
  p. cm.
Includes bibliographic references
  ISBN; 0-87101-363-0 (pbk.)
  1. Social service—Vocational guidance—United States. 2. Job
    hunting—United States. I. Title.
  HV10.5.D63 2005
  361.3'2'02373—dc22   2004018036

Printed in the United States of America

Table of Contents

Acknowledgements

Social Work Career Development, the second edition, was written with the support and insights of colleagues and graduates of the George Warren Brown School of Social Work. In particular, I would like to thank Shanti K. Khinduka, former dean, for his encouragement and support for this project.

I appreciate the able assistance of the staff at NASW Press and NASW offices, especially Cheryl Bradley, Marcia Roman, Paula Delo, Heather Brady, Beth Ledford, and Katrina Alaman Murray for editorial services; Jessie Reed for advice on benefits; Carolyn Polowy for advice on legal issues; and Crystal McDonald for advice on professional liability insurance. I would also like to thank Stephanie Bardo and Sharon Foreman for research, Angie Fox Antoniak for insights on various sections, and Karen Hudgins and Kalyn Coppedge for administrative support.

Several people provided an array of information and support. NASW chapter executives offered views on the job market and recommendations of people to interview: Katherine Boyd, Vicki Hanson, Stephen Karp, Scott Manchester, Daphne Peterson, Tamitha Price, and Joel Rubin. The Social Work Career Development Group provided an arena to discuss ideas, Cindy Paydon shared details on negotiation, and Donna DeAngelis, Association of Social Work Boards, reviewed segments on licensure.

Associates with a number of policy groups, government units, national networks of organizations, professional societies, and large service providers offered insights on trends, recruitment, credentials and connections to resource people. Policy and program specialists in Washington, DC, provided details on career issues and expectations for working at the national level. These organizations included the American Public Human Services Association, the Center for the Study of Social Policy, the Child Welfare League of America, the Children's Defense Fund, the National Association of Child Welfare Administration, the National Latino Behavioral Health Association, the School Social Work Association of America, the Society for Social Work Leadership in Health Care, and the U.S. Department of Health and Human Services.

In particular, I would like to thank Mary Lee Allen, Evelyn Bonander, Linda Bowen, Kathleen Buescher, Pam Day, Madeline DeWoody, Frank Farrow, LaDeana Gamble, Janet Hartnett, Robert McKay, Shari Miles, Karabelle Pizzigati, Tess Scannell, Robin Scott, Toshio Tatara, Betsy Thielman, Carol Williams, Jake Terpstra, Rita Vandivort, and Joan Zlotnik.

The staff of several associations, as well as others, clarified questions on licensing, credentials, trends, and career development issues and suggested contacts. My thanks go to Corrine Anderson-Ketchmark, Linda Brandeis, Elizabeth Cole, Tonya Edmond, Steven M. Fishbein, Randy Fisher, Reed Henderson, Vivian Jackson, Stuart Meyers, William Pompos, J. Robin Robb, Marie Sanchez, Julie Evans Starr, and Toby Weismiller.

There were also individuals who shared their career paths and job search stories. Specifically, I would like to thank the graduates of social work programs and experienced social workers whose advice, job search stories, and career paths brought life to what would have otherwise been merely a to-do list for job hunters, especially Rosa Bautista, Stephanie Boddie, April Breeden, Gerald L. Byington, Melinda Cardin , Jaimie Carley, Charita Castro, Katie Eller, Gina Guillemette, Mary Lacey Hayes, Amy Gifford Hume, Karin Hess Hopkins, Lori Kushner, Jodi Lawton, Abraham Lee, Stacy Marini, Carole Mayholl, LuAnn McCormick, Cathy McDougall, Janis M. McGillick, Kristin Mease, Nisha Patel, Allison Zidel Meyers, Debra O'Neill, Ronald Pitner, Joan Sadoff, Nicole Stenke, Lisa Rahe Taylor, Ronald Thompson, Courtney Tierney, Michael Tinnin, April White, and Erika Wilson Young.

Special thanks for their patience go to my family—Denis, Christopher, Eric, and Catherine.

Introduction

*S*ocial Work Career Development, second edition, includes expanded sections on salary negotiation, interview questions, and outside-of-the-box career paths; and new résumé samples in addition to updated online services. The book remains a reference you can consult from time to time during your job search and throughout the course of your career. Looking for a job or thinking about a new career direction takes time, energy, and fortitude. It also takes information and ideas. When you need to expand your thinking about a search or career direction, revisit these pages.

The book is not meant to be read all at once. Skim the chapter headings and appendices, read the sections you need now, and mark pages for future reference. Take a look at the "Quick Tips" at the end of chapters 1–6. Use the contents as a springboard to get started or restarted, whether you are defining your next career step, looking for your first job, or seeking to expand your credentials. Note that throughout the book, BSW, MSW, and PhD are used to refer to all social work degrees at those levels.

Chapter 1: Setting a Direction for Your Search

The first chapter will help you make some decisions about your next career move, expand and warm up your vocabulary for a search, and prepare a concise message about your objective and qualifications. The chapter takes you through a series of self-assessment exercises to select the skills and knowledge areas in which you are most confident, identify your accomplishments, and consider what is important to you in your work. The exercises will enable you to write a résumé more quickly, focus the message of your correspondence and interviews more precisely, and evaluate an offer with greater confidence.

Chapter 2: Researching Market and Salary Information

You know it is difficult to solve a problem or assist someone else with a problem unless you first gather some information and assess the situation. The same is true of your search—this chapter helps you set the stage. How much you know about the big picture in your field of practice, particularly within your geographic boundaries, will affect what you look for, how long you look, and your ability to negotiate and make a decision on an offer. Think of researching the market as putting together your own resource and referral guide, database, or Rolodex. Instead of developing resource information for clients or constituents, you are preparing it for yourself. Chapter 2 discusses sources of information on potential employers, salary data, and network contacts. Appendices 1–4 provide detailed information on associations, employer directories, and questions you may want to ask about your field of practice.

Chapter 3: Preparing Résumés, Curricula Vitae, Portfolios, and References

Whether you are updating your résumé or curriculum vitae or starting from scratch with a new format, skim the information in this chapter and take a look at the samples in appendix 6. There are many possibilities for writing an eye-catching résumé. Select the style elements you like and create a résumé that best highlights your experience. If you are pursuing an academic career, review the discussion on the curriculum vitae and the sample in appendix 6. You will find the skills lists in appendix 10 helpful when writing or rewriting your résumé or curriculum vitae. Chapter 3 also discusses references and suggests how you can provide employers with samples of your work.

Chapter 4: Identifying Jobs and Pursuing Leads

You may believe that "who you know" is the best or only way to find a satisfying job. However, social workers have found satisfying jobs through other sources as well. When you need some additional ideas for sources of jobs, take a look at this chapter and at appendix 8. Chapter 4 suggests search strategies for those with a bachelor or master's degree in social work as well as those looking for an academic job, gives a detailed look at the job-search experience of some social workers, and discusses the value of several job sources for social workers. You will also find suggestions for following up on a job lead, including an outline for cover letters. Sample letters for several situations are in appendix 5.

Chapter 5: Interviewing Effectively

Chapter 5 recommends strategies for approaching the job interview as a two-way discussion between two or more people. When you are preparing to interview for jobs, review the suggestions for setting your agenda and packaging yourself, managing various interview formats, and fielding typical questions. You will find sample interview questions in appendix 7.

Chapter 6: Evaluating Job Offers

Deciding whether to accept a job offer can be difficult, especially when the employer wants a decision quickly. This chapter outlines a detailed process for evaluating and negotiating an offer. It may be helpful to skim this chapter early in your search so that you can anticipate the information you will need to make a satisfying decision.

Chapter 7: Career Management and Professional Development

Many insist that professional network is the key to a successful job search and career. Although "who you know" is an important element, keep in mind that "what you know" and "how you perform" are equally important in career management. Chapter 7 raises questions and gives examples for you to consider for managing a career change. You might read this section and the sample career paths once or twice a year to help brainstorm ways in which you might explore new options and expand your qualifications. The second part of the chapter details information on state licensures and certifications, professional certifications, postdegree training, and academic degree options. Appendix 9, which lists special opportunities, and appendix 11, which outlines recommendations for selecting graduate programs, complement chapter 7.

CHAPTER ONE

Setting a Direction for Your Search

Inside Chapter 1

Assessing Your Strengths
Deciding on Your Objectives
Making Transitions
Preparing Your Message
Moving On

Over the past 30 years the number of trade publications on career management has exploded. Some popular literature promises the reward of a dream job with minimum effort, if only you follow its flawless methods. Do not be frustrated if you are not finding that dream job. Some social workers, like people in other fields, find jobs that exceed their expectations, whereas others find positions that at least meet their highest priorities.

The job market is a complex environment. Your search will be influenced by the geographic target you set, the job requirements employers demand that you can or must meet, the economic and political factors that affect the financial resources of organizations, and the changing nature of practice. Professional decisions and personal factors—your presentation or ability to communicate, your resourcefulness and job-search skills, and your own personal commitments—will also make a difference.

The better you are at packaging and articulating your qualifications, the greater your chances—even in small, tight markets—of finding work that meets your needs. Preparing a well-thought-out, polished message for the varying circumstances of your search requires hard work, particularly if you are marketing your qualifications to organizations in which staffs have limited views of social workers.

Just as you would when working with any client, organization, or individual, you want to assess the situation and create a plan before you take action. Your assessment will help define what you want to do, sharpen your vocabulary, enable you to develop arguments for landing positions, and assist you in thinking about a strategy for your job search. One gerontological social worker described this as putting together her care plan. In this chapter you will begin to put together your care plan, starting with the following six exercises that will prepare you for writing résumés and letters and conducting interviews:

- create lists of your knowledge areas, skills, and other qualifications
- analyze the lists to select your best qualifications
- review work preferences that affect choices
- draft some objectives for your search
- outline your relevant qualifications
- compose brief and full introductions.

These exercises are organized into the four parts that make up this chapter. Part 1, "Assessing Your Strengths," guides you through a self-assessment of your strengths. Part 2,

"Deciding on Your Objectives," helps you identify your work preferences. Part 3, "Making Transitions," addresses the needs of social workers who are considering a move across job functions or fields. Part 4, "Preparing Your Message," helps you package your objectives and strengths into a statement that you will use throughout your search.

You will find it easier to spread the work of these exercises over a week or longer than to try to complete them in one sitting. It is also helpful to set time limits of 10 to 15 minutes for each exercise, particularly for each segment of exercise 1, which involves brainstorming. Do not spend extra time looking for the perfect phrasing. You will refine your message as you go through the process of looking for a job or deciding on a new career direction.

Assessing Your Strengths

The first part consists of two exercises. Exercise 1 entails listing your knowledge, skills, and accomplishments. Exercise 2 helps you select your greatest strengths from exercise 1.

Knowledge

It's helpful to list the subject areas that you have mastered or studied through education, experience, training, reading, and use of technology. This list can be especially pertinent if you are switching fields of practice, re-entering the workforce, are interested in weaving together two career histories, or are seeking an opportunity to do cutting-edge work. Before you begin brainstorming for the list, identify some categories. You might use the following:

- issues
- interventions
- theories
- policies
- populations
- settings.

If you are a student or recent graduate, do not assume that employers will grasp the range of knowledge you developed through your studies. Employers may know nothing about social work education, or what they know may be limited to social work programs from a different era. Unless

---

EXERCISE 1

ASSESSING YOUR KNOWLEDGE, SKILLS, AND ACCOMPLISHMENTS

First you will want to create a document on diskette or organize a notebook to compile and maintain lists of your skills, knowledge areas, and accomplishments. This is time-consuming work, especially if you are starting from scratch and have years of experience, but it is work that will pay off. There are several reasons you should find the discipline within yourself to initiate and maintain this file.

- You will build and refresh the vocabulary you need to articulate your objectives and qualifications succinctly in introductions to new contacts, correspondence with organizations, and telephone conversations and interviews with employers.
- From this material you will develop résumés and letters that establish why employers should hire you for particular positions. In this changing job market, you may need to find a job in a hurry. Even if you update this file only once each year, you will be able to mount a job search quickly and effectively.
- When you are rethinking your career direction, you can use this list to explore interests, identify themes, and identify transferable knowledge and skills. Your analysis will be part of any meeting with a career counselor or executive search consultant.
- When it comes time to write a cover letter or meet with a potential employer, this list will refresh your memory and help you pinpoint those elements of your background that are most closely related to the position.

Use this as a planning document as well as a record. As you brainstorm, you may identify goals and areas that you want to develop further. Ideas on what to include in your qualifications list fall into the categories of knowledge, skills, and accomplishments.

they are relatively recent graduates of your program or are actively involved in your school, they will not be familiar with the particular features of your education.

List your courses, specific topics you studied, and your papers and project topics. If you are a student, you can build your list as you go through the program. List the weekly topics from your course syllabi at the start of each semester. During or at the end of each semester, add papers and projects. Then mark those topics that you are especially comfortable discussing.

Creating your knowledge treasure chest gives you a head start for the next phase of your assessment. When you are creating a list of knowledge areas, you will often find that skills—those elements of how you apply that knowledge—are often mixed with knowledge. Try to separate your skills from your knowledge list in preparation for the next part of this exercise.

Skills

Your next step is to brainstorm a list of your skills and add them to the skill list you just created from your knowledge list. If you can think of categories for grouping items ahead of time, go ahead and use them. Considering functional areas such as advocacy, consulting, direct practice, supervision, program administration, management, community development, policy, research, and teaching and training—and these categories can be subdivided—might help you think of more skills. For example, do you have skills in evaluation methods or fundraising? After you have stated your skills in your own words, scan the list of skills in appendix 10 for more ideas. By using your own words first, you are more likely to think of those skills that you can truly "own" and substantiate.

With a list of skills and knowledge you are well on your way to assembling all the elements for making decisions about your search. Now is the time to add specific accomplishments to this skills treasure chest.

Accomplishments

When you attempt to convince someone you are qualified to do a job, you need examples of past performance that demonstrate your ability to put your knowledge and skills into practice. This exercise will help you brainstorm some additional skills and knowledge areas for your list.

First, think about and then list all the things you have done in jobs; community and professional associations; or courses, practica, and school activities. What problems have you solved or what projects have you coordinated? Have you earned one or more academic degrees or completed training programs? Have you held leadership positions, contributed to task forces or committees, received awards and honors, or met requirements for licensure or certification? Group your accomplishments according to these three areas.

When recording your projects, list project results as well as titles, and describe the role you played. Increasingly, social work agencies indeed, all not-for-profit organizations—are becoming more outcomes driven. However, few social workers are accustomed to quantifying or specifying results. It is surprising how many students write grant proposals during a practicum, complete the practicum before the funding organization has made a decision, and then a year later when discussing their qualifications, cannot say whether they have experience writing a successful grant because they never found out whether the grant application was funded. Likewise, if you are a member of a staff that is trying to lower the recidivism rate of clients, can you state how successful you have been?

Although those who are seeking leadership positions must present a history and theme of related accomplishments, individuals in direct practice need to think of their work in this light as well. Accomplishments can demonstrate a theme or direction for your work, a progression of skill building, an approach to self-evaluation, and recognition of your work by others. Think about your accomplishments not only from your perspective, but also from the perspectives of supervisors, colleagues, faculty, associations, and community groups. In other words, do not limit them to publicly recognized successes. You may or may not be asked directly about your accomplishments, but you will want to weave them into your responses to interview questions and clearly state them on your résumé. You may have, for example,

- rebuilt the agency's community resource directory
- delivered an in-service training class on prioritizing a caseload during a crisis
- received an excellent grade for an options paper discussing issues of collaboration for a statewide program
- increased by 25 percent the number of volunteers who completed the training program
- decreased, through intensive case management, four homeless families' repeated needs for emergency housing by one-third
- adapted a brief therapy model to work with depressed clients that met program requirements
- prepared a successful grant proposal to the Mountain Foundation for $100,000.

If you are in direct practice, you may not be used to tracking or stating results or even to encountering an interviewer who asks about them. Accountability, however, is becoming increasingly important in all social work environments. Even if you are in direct practice, including clinical practice, you will need to demonstrate an understanding of and an ability to work in an outcomes-driven environment. Although you may not have quantitatively evaluated your work, try to state an outcome for each accomplishment.

Deciding on Your Objectives

Now it is time to make some decisions about the type of work you are seeking. The second part of this chapter consists of four exercises. Exercise 3 presents a series of questions regarding your work preferences. In exercise 4 you will list characteristics that further define the type of work you want. Exercise 5 entails writing three objectives, and exercise 6 summarizes your best qualifications for one or more objectives.

Examining Your Work Preferences

In addition to identifying your key knowledge, skills, and accomplishments, you need to consider your work preferences. Knowing what you prefer will steer your search, enable you to judge the fit between you and work opportunities, and help you understand the dynamics of conflicts on the job and the sense of "needing a change." Think about what you would like at this time in your career.

EXERCISE 2

SELECTING YOUR BEST KNOWLEDGE, SKILLS, AND ACCOMPLISHMENTS

Step 1. Record where you developed each element of your knowledge and skills. These examples are important. You do not want to fool yourself by making assumptions and statements that you cannot back up with experience. For example, you might assume that, like many social workers, you are adept at working with diversity issues, but can you articulate where and how successfully you have done this?

Step 2. Qualify your level of expertise for each knowledge or skill item. Use the following notations: A = advanced, I = intermediate, B = beginning.

Step 3. Create a summary page of your best-developed skills and knowledge areas and sort your list. Add your most important accomplishments to this list.

It is easy to assume that how you felt, for instance, two years ago still holds true currently: "Well, of course, it's still important to me to become an executive director someday." Your preferences can change, however, as your needs and interests evolve. If you have been employed for some time, your current work preferences are likely to be quite different from those you held as a student. Do you still want to be an executive director or is your interest in direct practice? Have you discovered that you are more interested in thinking about the big picture and addressing policy change than in working in a one-on-one situation with the people affected by policy?

The following questions will help you think about your current work preferences. The idea is to sharpen your thinking about what you want in a position. The clearer your thinking, the better you can identify jobs and organizations that are going to be a successful match for you and the better you will be able to present yourself. Although you are not likely to find a job encompassing all your preferences, you will hopefully have at least two offers, each including some ideal elements. Look at "Deciding among Offers" in chapter 6. Each example describes how the individual weighed the strengths of each position against his or her preferences. (For a more extensive list of questions to consider, see appendix 2.)

EXERCISE 3

CURRENT WORK PREFERENCES

- How important is it that you work in an organization that formally recognizes the current NASW *Code of Ethics* (2000)?
- Do you prefer work focused on social change or services delivery?
- Do you prefer being part of large complex organizations or small, single-focus organizations?
- Do you prefer to work primarily with social workers or with an interdisciplinary team?
- Do you prefer to work with people who share your religious beliefs or cultural heritage?
- Do you prefer work settings that allow you to be a generalist or a specialist?
- Is your preference to work directly with people or to manage the resources that others need to work with people?
- Do you prefer that clients come to your office or do you prefer going out into the field (homes, schools, community centers)?

EXERCISE 4

CHOOSING ELEMENTS THAT FRAME YOUR OBJECTIVE

You will find it helpful to first outline some of your interests using the ideas you have generated about knowledge, skills, and work preferences. Start by jotting down some of your choices for each of the following:

Function or role (see exhibit 1.1):
Choice 1 _____
Choice 2 _____
Choice 3 _____
Field of practice (see exhibit 1.2):
Choice 1 _____
Choice 2 _____
Choice 3 _____
Issue area (housing, depression, substance abuse, and so on):
Choice 1 _____
Choice 2 _____
Choice 3 _____
Sector (not-for-profit, for-profit, or public arenas):
Choice 1 _____
Choice 2 _____
Choice 3 _____
Type of organization (see the list in appendix 4):
Choice 1 _____
Choice 2 _____
Choice 3 _____
Population (frail, older adults; homeless people; people with chronic mental illness; or other populations):
Choice 1 _____
Choice 2 _____
Choice 3 _____
Interventions (family therapy, case management, advocacy, and so on):
Choice 1 _____
Choice 2 _____
Choice 3 _____

Setting Objectives

The first question any contact or employer will ask you is "What do you want to do?" You also know from your own work that you are much more likely to be successful if you have a goal to motivate you. Your goal or job objective is the theme or mission statement that drives your job search plan. You will develop introductions, telephone conversations, cover letters, résumés, and interview agendas on the foundation of your objective. State your job objective in writing. The choices you listed earlier should help you. Do this regardless of whether you will use the objective on a résumé.

Stating an Objective

Your objective can include elements of the following: a generic job title, type of organization, applicable skills, and particular interests. Think of it as simply a statement of what you would like to do. Here are some examples:

- Seeking a clinical social work position in an outpatient setting
- Seeking a program management position in the area of developmental disabilities— interested in applying eight years of experience that include direct services, training, and program planning
- Seeking a clinical social work position in a pediatric health or mental health care setting working with children, adolescents, and families
- Seeking a position in fundraising that focuses on writing grants, researching prospective donors, and organizing special events for a not-for-profit organization— particularly interested in women and children's services
- Seeking a position in research and policy using experience in quantitative and qualitative analysis—particularly interested in health care, Medicaid, and AIDS.

EXERCISE 5

DEVELOPING THREE JOB OBJECTIVES

Unless the job market in your target community is unusually strong, prepare three objectives, one for your ideal job (a job for which there is intense competition), one for your best bet or most likely job (a job for which you have the qualifications and would be happy to take), and one for a fallback job (a job for which you are qualified or may be overqualified but one that would at least pay your dues and bills—this might be a job at an agency with a high turnover rate for staff, for example). Particularly if you take a fallback job, read chapter 7 for ideas on enhancing your position in the organization and other possibilities for developing your career.

The following exercise will help you begin packaging your qualifications for your objectives and others as you need them.

Step 1. At the top of a sheet of paper or a new document file, write one objective. Under the objective list the knowledge and skills important to the type of work you are seeking. If possible, divide the list into those qualifications that are required and those that are desirable. If you are using this exercise to prepare an application for a particular job, use the exact wording of the employer.

Step 2. Then review the summary list of best knowledge, skills, and accomplishments that you determined in exercise 2. How well does the list of requirements for the objective (step 1) match your best assets? You will find it helpful to write down your related qualifications across from or under each item in step 1.

SAMPLES OF KEY QUALIFICATIONS FOR AN OBJECTIVE

Seeking a clinical social work position in a pediatric health or mental health care setting working with children, adolescents, and families:

- had neonatal and pediatric intensive care experience
- had emergency room experience
- handled assessments with families
- provided individual and family therapy
- handled crises and made referrals
- designed a children's program at a shelter
- completed an MSW and certificate in play therapy
- studied and wrote on domestic violence, divorce and children, and crisis management.

Seeking an executive position with a social services agency focused on aging:
- have strong fundraising record, including several successful grants
- managed a department with clinical and research functions
- supervised multidisciplinary teams
- initiated and supported collaborative efforts across departments and institutions
- led a reorganization resulting in [insert dollar amount] savings
- directed a team in restructuring services and information management to meet requirements for outcome measures.

Step 3. Your answers to the following questions will help you fine-tune your objectives and qualifications:

- Do you need to learn more about what employers require and expect? How specific or extensive was your list for step 1? What do you still need to learn about this type of work? How is this work changing? What is known about the future of this work?
- If you do not have recent experience or credentials to cover all of the qualifications for your target position, what questions could the employer raise about your background? How can you compensate for those missing qualifications? If you decide to pursue this work, these missing items can be the basis of your response to the interview question, "What are your weaknesses?" (see "Difficult Questions" in chapter 5).
- What would people from other academic disciplines or with other training have to offer?
- What can you offer that others, particularly those from other academic disciplines, cannot offer?
- Does your objective entail a move across functions, fields, populations, settings, and so on?

If you are satisfied with the match between your objectives and qualifications, go to page 11 "Preparing Your Message," go to part 4 of this chapter to complete your message for employers. If you found that you have difficulty stating specific requirements for a position or that there is a gap between the job requirements and your background, read part 3, "Making Transitions."

Making Transitions

Your next career move may entail taking your skills and knowledge into a new arena. As the fourth part will show, you will need to learn about that new arena. A major transition will require careful consideration and a strategy. For a general overview of useful tools, see exhibit 1.3.

Educating Yourself on New Areas

Unless you want to make a lateral move within the same field of practice, you are likely to be pursuing a position in settings with which you need to become more familiar. This is especially important for those re-entering the field who need to update their understanding of the market and the changes in careers. Look over the work settings, job titles, associations, and questions listed in appendix 4 and the skills listed by function in appendix 10. These should help you expand your vocabulary and identify associations working in your interest area that you can tap for information—check with your NASW chapter office for names of its members or get the names of alumni from your alma mater. If you are near a university library or have access to interlibrary loan services, you will want to read the practice literature. Internet listservs are another way to educate you about other fields or issues. (See appendix 8.)

Information interviewing, popularized by Richard Bolles in *What Color Is Your Parachute?* (2004), is another education option. The purpose of information interviews is to give you an opportunity to explore a career field with a seasoned professional. You can gather information

---

---

on trends in services, particulars of the systems involved, political and economic factors affecting the work, and practice issues.

It is best to begin with someone you already know, who can then suggest other names. Alternatively, you can call an organization and ask to speak with the social services director, clinical director, program director, or a social worker. Introduce yourself. If you are a student, indicate that you are looking for information to help you target your studies and plan a career in social work. If you are a social worker, indicate the area in which you now work and say what your new interest is—for example, "I have been working in intensive in-home services for some time, and now I am exploring options. I understand that you work in domestic relations at the court, which is something I would like to learn more about. My reading in this area has prompted several questions. Would it be possible to arrange a time to meet with you?"

You might also be interested in learning more about preparing for a goal. For example, "My long-term goal is to be an executive director of a service for families and children. Right now, I need advice on how to build on my direct service and advocacy experience, add to my skill base, and position myself to compete for those opportunities. Jean Lowe suggested I contact you. Would you be willing to discuss this with me?" Or, "I have been involved in advocacy around family issues and domestic violence for several years. I am now thinking about a move into politics. Would you be willing to help me explore that idea?" Or, "I have been the executive director over several functions of a large research hospital for several years. At this point, I want to shift gears. I would like to remain in an executive role, but I want to work in a social services organization. Would you be willing to discuss this type of transition with me?" You can also send a letter requesting an information interview and follow up with a telephone call—do not ask the person to call you to arrange an interview.

Sample questions for a typical interview follow. If you are exploring advanced positions, you will focus on macro level issues. Use information in appendixes 4 and 10 to tailor your inquiries so that you can obtain the details that could help you decide whether to pursue this work.

- What are common titles for this type of position?
- What tasks do you perform? Or what work does this department do? Is this work handled similarly in other organizations or are there other models?

- What skills or abilities are critical to your success in this work? Might new trends require other skills?
- Do you work with a team? How does the team operate? With what groups or types of individuals outside your organization do you interact, refer to, or consult?
- What kinds of career paths are there in the type of work you do?
- What advice do you have for someone who is preparing to work in your field of social work? What are common mistakes people make in planning their careers in this field?
- Can you suggest other people to contact?

Moving across Functions and Fields: Transferring Skills and Knowledge

Look carefully at your list of knowledge and skills and compare it to the list of requirements for the work you want to do. Certainly there are shared knowledge and skills across the lists, but what are the unique aspects of your new direction and are they on the list? Do you know what they are? What will it take for you to build that second list to a level strong enough to compete for positions? Are there elements of your background—knowledge of evaluation, outcomes-driven practice, or technology—that would be an asset in the new environment or role? If you were in that new role, how would you think differently about management, policy, or practice? Do you know what the difference is? How well do you know the culture, issues, and language of the new arena? How well can you envision yourself in the next role, and can you present yourself as confident and knowledgeable—in other words, do you appear ready to assume that role? To help you analyze your readiness to make a transition, add the following category to exercise 6.

Transitions: Comparing and Contrasting Your Background with Your Goal

Go back to the end of exercise 6 and prepare an analysis divided into five headings: (1) skills, (2) knowledge, (3) technology, (4) culture and expectations, and (5) credentials. Under each heading list detailed statements under the subheadings of "comparable items" and "contrasting items." Your analysis of what your background and the new job goal have in common will result in comparable items, especially transferable skills. Those items in the job goal that you identify as different or perhaps missing from your background will result in contrasting items. Use the following questions to think through this process:

- What skills are required in the goal job that are part of your demonstrated skill list? What skills are different?
- What knowledge is required in the goal job that is part of your knowledge list? What knowledge is different?
- What technologies that are used in the goal job are part of your background? What uses of technology will be different?
- What work culture and expectations are part of the goal environment and parallel to your experience? How are these different?
- What legal or professional credentials that are required or desired for the goal job are part of your qualifications? What credentials may be different?

This step will help you determine how well prepared you are to make a case for your target job. The more definitive your statements, the more realistic your choice of a new goal will be. For a different perspective on working in nonprofit organizations, take a look at *The Harvard Business School Guide to Careers in the Nonprofit Sector* (Lowell, 2000) and *From Making a Profit to Making a Difference* (King, 2000).

What Will It Take to Make a Transition across Fields or Functions?

What enables people to change directions in their careers? A successful career transition calls for two things: motivation and a link from one job to the other.

To move from point A to point C, you need to find link B. You might think of this link as a stepping-stone or a bridge. You may already have a link or asset, such as skills, knowledge, credentials, or contacts, which would be of value to an organization outside your field. Look at your summary from exercise 2 and brainstorm other fields and settings that use similar skills, address the same issues or will need to address those issues in the future, or serve the same population. If you need ideas, visit a library or bookstore and browse through magazines and journals unrelated to your work or do Internet searches on subjects that concern you. You may discover something in your background that you can use to make a transition.

- Specialized skills such as a second language, a new practice method, ability to work with diverse populations, or experience with a particular computer package or program language might be the deciding qualification for an employer who is willing to train you in other aspects of the job. For example, an investment firm hired a social worker in the human resources department because she had the ability to work with diverse populations.
- Knowledge about a particular cultural or ethnic perspective, for example, or about diversity issues, aging, service delivery systems, or resource development may be the common factor that enables you to move across fields of practice.
- A new credential—a degree, professional certificate, or training program, for example—could strengthen your qualifications for another field and create the bridge you need.
- Your contact network itself may be the key to a transition. For instance, an information systems company that wanted to do business with state governments hired a social worker who knew administrators in many state social services departments.

If your review of your background or qualifications does not turn up a strong link, then pursue a new experience that will strengthen your case. You might volunteer for a special project at your present place of employment or in an association or get some training that would develop skills. You could make a lateral move in or out of your organization to a position that requires your primary skills but also enables you to stretch your experience in a new area. This could be the interim job or pivotal position that creates the link to your next major career move.

Can you identify the motivation or value that will sustain you through the transition? For the transition to succeed, your motivation—an intense desire or need to accomplish a goal (other than attaining a job) or to achieve some other value (money, prestige, freedom)—must be strong.

A major career change is difficult. The weaker the link and the motivation, the less likely the change will occur. You are more likely to succeed if you look at the areas most closely related to your current work or background strengths and make incremental moves, small steps outside your experience base. As you build new skills and knowledge and connect with associations and others in the new area, your identity will shift internally and externally toward a new goal. To learn more about making career transitions, read chapter 7.

Preparing Your Message

Now that you have listed your qualifications for your objective(s), begin preparing introductions. You will use these in telephone conversations, meetings with contacts, letters, and interviews. These samples are written for various audiences and circumstances. If a friend is introducing you to neighbors at a block party, your sound bite will be different from the one you would use with an exhibitor at a conference. Note that the introductions for Lisa Denton match sample letters in appendix 5 and sample résumés in appendix 6.

Brief Introduction

Take advantage of any opportunity to introduce yourself and tell someone what you are seeking. You can weave a brief message about your interest—a tag line or a sound bite—into a conversation almost anywhere. If you are already in the habit of doing this, great. If not, you will find it helpful to think precisely about a brief message that fits your job-search needs. Here are a few examples where the tag line follows the name immediately in a conversation, but this will not always be the case.

- *Hi, I'm Lisa Denton. I've just moved back to Dallas and I'm looking for a job as a clinical social worker.*
- *Hi, I'm Lisa Denton. I'm an MSW looking for a job. My experience is in health and mental health work with kids and families.*
- *Hi, I'm Lisa Denton. I'm moving back to the Dallas/Ft. Worth area in June and I hope to find a clinical social work position working with children and families.*

Full Introduction

You can add several sentences to your brief introduction to create a full introduction that states your objective and its related qualifications. This paragraph will become the basis for cover letters and responses to the interview questions, "Tell me about yourself" and "Why should we consider you for this position?" This message, which you will tailor for specific circumstances, will serve as a theme for your interviews.

- *Hi, I'm Maria Gonzales. I have a bachelor degree in social work and work experience, and I am looking for a case management position. My recent experience includes home visits, goal setting with clients, and assessments and referrals with emergency shelters, transitional-living programs, and homeless services. Before returning to school, I managed apartments—I worked with HUD guidelines, managed staff, dealt with tenant crises, and prepared budgets.*

- *Hi, I'm Lisa Denton. I'm moving back to the Dallas/Ft. Worth area in June, and I'm looking for a master's level social work position working with children and families. In May I will receive my master's degree from Mountain University, where I did two field placements. One was in medical social work in the neonatal and pediatric intensive care units; the other was in day treatment with a residential center. Before that I spent two years working with a children's program for a women's shelter in Dallas.*
- *Hi, I'm Lisa Denton. I'm returning to the Dallas/Ft. Worth area in June. I have nearly four years' experience working with children and families. I spent two years working as an advocate and volunteer coordinator for the children's program at a women's shelter in Dallas. I have recently had training in medical social work for neonatal and pediatric care units and day treatment at a residential center. Now I am looking for an opportunity to work with children and families in a health or mental health setting.*
- *Hello, I'm Caroline Denver. I am a doctoral candidate at Mountain University; I am looking for a tenure-track position beginning in the fall. My teaching interests are in gerontology and policy. My research interests center around the frail elderly population, caregiver stress, alternative care, and housing. By June I expect to defend my dissertation, which is on [name of subject]. I have had the opportunity to work with several faculty members on research projects and to teach as well.*
- *Hi, I'm Clayton Winter. I have been directing a multidisciplinary family outreach program at a large teaching hospital for nine years. The program encompasses an assessment center, parent training, counseling and family therapy, a school-based clinic, and pastoral care. Through grants and collaborative alliances, I have doubled the number of families served. Through my*

hard work, collaborative efforts, and fundraising, I have developed an interest in the work of foundations and resource allocations.

Moving On

You have assessed your background and set a primary and perhaps secondary objective for your search, or at least you have some ideas. With this focus you can begin researching your market, identifying leads, and pursuing opportunities. The next few chapters will help show you how.

References

Bolles, R. N. (2004). *What color is your parachute? A practical manual for job-hunters and career-changers.* Berkeley, CA: Ten Speed Press.

King, R. M. (2000). *From making a profit to making a difference.* River Forest, IL: Planning/Communications.

Lowell, S. (2000). *The Harvard business school guide to careers in the nonprofit sector.* Boston: Harvard Business School Publishing.

National Association of Social Workers. (2000). *Code of ethics of the National Association of Social Workers.* Washington, DC: Author.

CHAPTER 1 QUICK TIPS

Setting Your Direction

- Brainstorm five to 10 skills you want to use on a job, five to 10 knowledge areas you have, and three to 10 accomplishments you can discuss.
- Next to each skill and knowledge item describe where you used or learned that attribute.
- List two types of organizations you like to work for and two job functions you would consider.
- Write a sentence describing what you are looking for.
- Add four sentences to create a paragraph that concisely states what you would like to do and outlines key qualifications, skills, knowledge, accomplishments, experience, and credentials.

CHAPTER TWO

Researching Marketing and Salary Information

Inside Chapter 2

The Printed and Electronic Word:
What to Look for before Seeking Advice
The Human Element:
Building a Contact Network
What to Do if All You Hear Is Discouraging News

A man with a master's degree in social work and five years of experience in fundraising and political campaign management in California moved to Indianapolis to be with his fiancée. While juggling wedding planning with job hunting, he discovered an opening, applied, and was offered the job. It was a great job—he would work closely with a range of organizations in the local community. This experience would prove helpful when he was ready to change jobs or pursue some entrepreneurial ideas in the back of his mind. Of course, there was a catch. Accepting the offer meant a cut in salary. Efforts to negotiate did not close the gap.

The dilemma just described is a common one for social workers. When you decide to look for a job, you naturally apply for any appealing opening you come across. This makes sense—you certainly do not want to pass up an opportunity. If you also take time to become familiar with the market, you can make better-informed decisions and be more efficient with your time.

If you are able to anticipate a job search because you will be graduating, moving, or completing a project, consider yourself lucky and do some advance planning. For instance, if you are a student, designate an hour every week during your second-to-last semester to study your market. No matter how busy you are, you can find at least an hour each week to surf the Internet, clip items from newspapers, scan organization directories, or make some calls. Even if you lose your job suddenly, you can improve your chances of securing a good position by spending part of your time learning more about the market.

Researching the market is especially important for social workers who are relocating. The social work job market, especially for practitioners, is primarily a regional, if not a local, market (Barth, 2003). Employers generally select hirers from the local geographic area. Although the Internet has increased job information across locations, to be competitive and selective you need to understand your target market.

Research is also important for social work generalists and those who are re-entering the field or changing careers. To find a good match between your abilities and an organization's needs, you must know the details that affect organizations (see appendix 4). This information will help you tailor your message for the needs of the field and better compete against those with specific experience. Your goal for researching the market is to answer the following questions:

- What trends or events might present an opportunity or affect the market?
- Which organizations engage in the type of work I want?
- Who do these organizations hire? What skills do they need?
- How long should I expect to look?
- What is the salary range for the work I want?
- What organizations hire individuals with (or without) a license?
- Where can I get the supervision needed for a license?

In this research phase you want to gather information, not inquire about positions. Concentrate on two tasks: (1) compile information about employers, salaries, and licensure laws; and (2) seek advice from a network of contacts.

You may find this beginning step in the search fun, frustrating, or a good excuse for putting off decisions and actions. The suggestions posed in this section are not meant to overwhelm you. You need to have a realistic picture of the market, but you also may need to set limits on how much information you gather. If you can answer the questions in appendix 4, then you already know a great deal about your target market.

The Printed and Electronic Word: What to Look for before Seeking Advice

Before you seek advice from your network contacts, do some background research on your own. The more knowledgeable you are, the more specific your questions can be and the more productive your discussions with contacts will be. Here are some suggestions.

Update Your Memberships

If you are not a member of NASW, join. If you are a member who will be moving to another state, change your membership information as soon as possible so you can begin to receive the local chapter's newsletter and learn about social work in that state. Or review the NASW chapter Web site in the new state and ask for a couple of newsletters. There may be a small charge for this service, but it is worth it to learn of job opportunities and the names and activities of leaders in your new social work community. To change your NASW membership, call 800-638-8799 or go to http://www.socialworkers.org; have your membership username and password ready. Chapter addresses and telephone numbers are also available at the NASW Web site or by calling the number listed above. There may be other professional societies or organizations that you may want to join. Some societies list job openings in their newsletters, hold conferences and job fairs, maintain Web sites on the Internet, or offer referral services (see appendix 1).

Check Licensure, Certification, and Reimbursement Regulations

If you are interested in direct or clinical practice—particularly at the master's level—licensure, certification, and reimbursement regulations will affect your search. Find out what licensure levels or certifications exist in your target state and determine whether you qualify to practice there or even call yourself a social worker. You also will need to know about state regulations for reimbursement for your work—some states have complicated vendor laws regarding reimbursement. Will you be required to have supervision? From whom? How independent will you be? Will you also need professional certification for reimbursement at a particular level (personal communication with J. Robin Robb, PhD, private practitioner and past vice president for professional development, National Federation of Societies for Clinical Social Work, Arlington, VA, February 6, 2003)?

Request a licensure packet from the social work board for your target state. You will find links to state board Web sites at the Association of Social Work Boards's site, http://www.aswb.org. For an overview of state licensure and certifications, such as school social work certification, see chapter 7. In general, if you intend to provide direct services, you will need a state license or certification. Management and program administration positions in social services organizations may require or prefer a license. Policy and other macro positions, especially in organizations that do not provide social services, do not usually require licenses. However, it would be wise to put this on your list of questions to discuss with contacts in your field.

Compile a List of Target and Potential Employers

In any community, a finite number of organizations do the specific type of work you want to do. If you have not set geographic limits but instead are looking for a good opportunity to use your specialty, you can be more selective about choosing those organizations that match your mission, serve as models, have experts on staff, and are known for training.

Start by compiling a list of those organizations that do exactly what you want to do, bearing in mind the size of your geographic target, and expand your list from there. If your first love is pediatric social work and you are looking in only one community, children's hospitals will be the focus of your search. Unless your community has several children's hospitals and the job market is strong, you need to identify other potential employers. Conversely, an exhaustive list of children's organizations in a large city would take too long to compile and would contain agencies of little interest to you.

Break your list of employers into groups that do exactly what you want to do, those that address some of your interests, and those that do something related to your interests. Research these organizations through the Internet, directories, news publications, and your contact network. You may discover that some of the organizations doing exactly what you would like to do hire staff with credentials beyond yours, rarely have openings, or perhaps are merging with

other organizations. Or you may learn that an employer in your third-tier group has just received a grant to initiate a new project or has received a recognition award from a national organization. Your research efforts will allow you to reorganize your list into target, potential, and fallback organizations.

Locate Online or Printed Directories

Today many local community services directories are online. Check with the reference desk at your public library if you have difficulty locating such lists or do not have access to the Internet. The telephone book and resource information at your current agency or school's field education office are also good sources for local information. (See appendixes 3 and 8 for online and print directories.)

You may discover through networking that a local interest group has printed its own resource directory. For example, someone interested in working in AIDS services was making exploratory long-distance calls to Massachusetts. She discovered that an AIDS task force had printed a local resource guide on HIV and AIDS services. The contact person offered to send the job hunter a free copy.

For a search that covers several geographic areas, first try trade association Web sites, which often link to their member Web sites. You can try an Internet search, too, but not all types of employers are listed in online directories. In that case, try your public library—also, associations, publishing companies, and the federal government publish directories of programs, which are usually arranged by state. Examples include the Child Welfare League of America's *Directory of Member Agencies* at http://www.cwla.org; Alliance for Children and Families online directory of members at http://www.alliance1.org; and Congressional Quarterly's *Washington Information Directory* at http://www.cq.com. See appendixes 3 and 8 for a list of directories and associations. Look under the international heading for directories of organizations that work abroad.

Scan Publications and Web Sites Regularly

While visiting the Minneapolis/St. Paul area, one student noticed a series of newspaper articles on services for older adults; the articles named organizations and quoted professionals in the field. She asked a friend to save each week's article. The following year, six months before moving to the Twin Cities, she launched her search with information from the series and landed a job about a month after graduation.

Gather Information on Specific Organizations

As you compile a list of organizations, keep notes on information you come across and begin researching specific organizations. Always look carefully at the Web sites for your target organizations, as many have sites now. You can also request newsletters, annual reports, and brochures and speak with your contacts. You should look for the following basic information:

- who to contact (name, address, and tele phone number)
- purpose of the organization (for example, direct services, research, advocacy, educa tion, program planning, fundraising, community development, philanthropy, or organizing)
- types of services or projects carried out by the organization (primary or traditional services or innovative programs, for example)
- organizational setting (public, not-for-profit, or for-profit organizations)
- affiliation of the organization (for example, religious, university, or foundation)
- size of the organization's staff.

After obtaining these facts, you may want to check with your contacts and resources to get further information. Although it would be inappropriate to ask some of the following questions regarding particular organizations, keep the ideas in mind as you gather information:

- What are the organization's strengths? For what is it well known?

- Is the organization in a starting phase, a growing phase, or a well-maintained state, or has it become overgrown and stagnant?
- Who leads the organization? Does it have a strong leader, a capable management team, and a supportive and active board?
- Who makes up the management team? What are the different roles?
- What are the goals of the organization? How have the goals changed? How might they change in the future?
- Has this organization merged, downsized, or expanded recently?
- Considering the factors in this list, how does this organization compare with its counterparts?
- Do professionals and organizations with which this entity interacts respect its philosophy and staff?
- How do salaries in this organization compare with those of similar institutions?

If you have previously been part of a management team, you are familiar with accreditation standards and can assess the quality of a direct services organization. If you are not familiar with the accreditation standards for the types of organizations you are researching, discuss standards and their effects on agencies with people in your contact network. These are some questions you may want to ask about not-for-profit organizations:

- What are the funding sources and what proportion of the budget does each provide? Is the organization dependent on one primary funding source? Does the board raise money and, if so, how effectively?
- How heavily does the organization rely on volunteers and what roles do they play?
- Is this organization part of a larger umbrella organization? If yes, what is the relationship between them? Is the umbrella organization headquartered out of town?

You will want to know the following about public institutions:

- Does this public unit have a positive reputation among constituents or has it been a political "hot potato"?
- Compared with similar departments in other jurisdictions, is this department considered average, cutting edge, or behind the times?
- Is the political appointee heading the department interested in and committed to the agency's mission, biding his or her time, or possibly hostile toward the agency's work?
- Is the experience or education of members of the administration's staff related to the department's service?

Find out the following about for-profit organizations:

- Is the company publicly held?
- What is the size of this organization in terms of number of clients, revenue, number of facilities, and number of employees?
- How does it compare with its competitors?
- Does this company have a parent company or subsidiaries?
- Where is each located?

For an example of an applicant using research in an interview, see exhibit 2.1.

Collect Salary Data

Of course, you will have to consider salaries and the cost of living when you are searching for a job. Look at these variables carefully—in many cases they will affect your decision to take a position.

Set a Salary Goal

People in human resources and career development generally advise that you plan on spending one month seeking a position for every $10,000 you wish to earn. This formula assumes that you have the qualifications to compete for your preferred job; that the job market in your target community is at least moderately strong; and that you conduct an aggressive, efficient search and present yourself well. If you are switching fields or functions, lack familiarity with your target community, or cannot meet the criteria mentioned in the previous statement, you should plan on a longer search.

Think carefully about the salary you think is appropriate for your qualifications, about your expenses, and about the salary figure you are willing to accept. Salaries will be influenced by the following six factors:

1. *Geographic location*. Salaries and the cost of living on the eastern and western seaboards are higher than in the central part of the country. If you are comparing job opportunities in two communities, you will find the following Web sites and reference books helpful: http://www.data masters.com; http://www.salary. com; *ACCRA Cost of Living Index*, published by the American Chamber of Commerce Researchers Association; and *American Cost of Living Survey*, published by Gale Research.

EXHIBIT 2.1

Using Research in an Interview

I think what made my interview stand out the most was the fact that I had researched the company before I came in and showed them I was very interested in their company. Also, I spent a lot of time before the interview thinking about what I had to offer the organization that was different from what other people would have to offer. The most important thing I came up with was the ability to evaluate the programs and put mechanisms into place that could monitor the programs. I also expressed an interest in what the future held for their clients and employees. In the interview, we discussed various things that could be accomplished in the future. I believe this was helpful in putting the idea in the interviewer's mind that I was already a part of the organization.

2. ***Economic sector.*** In general, for-profit organizations pay higher salaries than do not-for-profit or public organizations. In the not-for-profit arena, organizations that do not have religious affiliations tend to pay higher salaries than those that do. Salary levels for not-for-profit and public institutions depend on the location, department, government level, and field of practice. NASW data from the Practice Research Network for 2002 indicate that public sector and for-profit members are better paid than their not-for-profit counterparts. NASW members with the federal government, including the military, report higher incomes than those employed at other government levels (O'Neill, 2001). For the federal government salary tables, go to http://www.opm.gov/oca/03 tables/html/kc.asp. For state government salaries, go to the Web site for each state's human resources office.

3. ***Field of service.*** The fields of child welfare, mental health, and health care usually pay better salaries than jobs in gerontology and school social work (O'Neill, 2001). Unfortunately, salaries in domestic vio lence, day care, and services for homeless people often reflect the low priority and poor funding that these groups receive.

4. ***Size of organization.*** Salary may vary according to the size of the organization. Salaries at a small, single-service not-for-profit organization are likely to be lower than those at a large teaching hospital, public school system, or managed-care company. Nevertheless, be aware that large size and wide reputation are not always indicators of higher salaries.

5. ***Job function.*** In general, management, policy analysis, fundraising, consulting, and tenure-track faculty positions pay better than direct practice jobs.

6. ***Qualifications.*** Academic degrees, licensure, certifications, experience, skills, and specialized knowledge all play a part in an employer's decision about salaries to offer.

Local Salary Data

Your best sources of salary information in your target location are the same people you will contact for a sense of the market: local social workers, not-for-profit managers, officers of local chapters of professional associations, and staffs of groups that study and fund social services. Once again, be sure you talk with several people; not everyone has up-to-date information on salaries around the community. Of course, you would not ask someone what his or her salary is; instead, you would ask what salary range you might expect. Some schools of social work routinely collect employment data on recent alumni and may be willing to give you salary ranges for particular types of services over the telephone. Be sure you know how recent the figures are.

Sometimes cold calls to employers work well. One person who was looking for a position working with older adults, including medical social work, called the human resources offices at several hospitals; some of those offices provided her with salary ranges for someone at her level of experience.

National and Regional Salary Data

Various groups collect salary data that may be useful to you. Often their reports are published and can be purchased. If you find that an organization does not make its report available to the public, perhaps people in your network will be willing to share information they receive as members of the society or association. These reports come from several sources:

- Some professional societies, including NASW, collect national and regional salary data; state chapters may also have membership-based salary information.
- Associations to which organizations belong, including the Alliance for Children and Families and the Child

Welfare League of America, also collect salary data (see appendix 8).

- Not-for-profit management assistance centers, United Way offices, regional think tanks, universities, and state departments of labor and economic development also may collect salary data.

National data are valuable but very broad—you should look at compilations carefully. For example, data classified by area of practice include those in entry-level positions as well as experienced directors, unless otherwise stated. The data may or may not reflect geographic differences, economic sectors, or academic degrees. Often distinct job types or titles, such as executive director, identify salary levels, but at lower levels many titles are less clear. The size of an organization can also affect salary; in a pool of executive directors you will find those running operations with budgets of $100,000 as well as those with budgets of several million dollars. Four good sources for national salary data in 2004 are the following:

- The Baccalaureate Education Assessment Project, a project of the Association of Baccalaureate Social Work Program Directors, includes nationwide data on first-time social work employment for those with a bachelor's degree in social work. Project coordinators are Vicky V. Buchan, Grafton H. Hull, Jr., Jannah Mather, Cathy K. Pike, JoAnn Ray, Roy W. Rodenhiser, John Rogers, and Marshall Smith. (For information on this project, visit http://www.rit.edu/~beapin dex.htm)
- The NASW Practice Research Network, a research program that collects and analyzes data on social work practice as well as a variety of social work services delivery issues, provides data on a representative sample of NASW members. These data include income by years of experience, gender, ethnicity, primary practice area, type of organization, primary auspice,

and principal role. NASW members can access these data at http://www.social-workers.org/naswprn/default.asp.

- The MSW Job Market collects salary data on new graduates of MSW programs; however, only a small number of MSW programs are participating at this time. Coordinators are Carol Doelling of Washington University in St. Louis, Barbara Matz of Bryn Mawr College in Pennsylvania, Susan Freidmark of Case Western Reserve University in Ohio, and Jennifer Luna-Idunate of University of Texas at Austin.
- *Statistics on Social Work Education in the United States* is an annual publication of the Council on Social Work Education (see Lennon, 2004); it includes data on faculty salaries by rank, geographic region, program type, gender, and ethnicity.

The Human Element: Building a Contact Network

Although you will find some useful information in print, people in your target community or specialty area are your best sources of information about your market. Like composing a list of potential employers, creating a list of contacts with whom you can network is a valuable step in the preparation process. Seeking advice from some of these contacts is the next step.

Create a List of Potential Contacts

Write down or use the computer to compile a list of possible names for a contact network. You will use the network to seek advice and job leads for your search. To get started, brainstorm a list of people who are knowledgeable about your field of social work, potential employers, and target community (if you are looking at a specific location). Remember also that people in your current location may have information on contacts, employers, professional societies, and advocacy groups in your new target community. To create your list, start with people you already know—coworkers, fellow committee members, classmates, practicum supervisors, former professors, friends, and family members. Check your address file, the resource referral list you use on the job or in practicum, your alumni directory (often online), and membership directories from professional associations. Do not overlook leaders of the social work community and others who work closely with professional and community issues, particularly if you are looking at the market for community development, advocacy, policy, or management positions. Consider contacting the following people:

- officers of local, state, and national professional associations (NASW, for example, or the American Association for Marriage and Family Therapy)
- staff at United Way offices and other organizations that consult with or study not-for-profit organizations (one executive director suggests that you consult United Way for the number, demographics, size, scope of services, and history of private agencies)
- volunteers and staff of civic groups (such as the Urban League) or researchers at regional think tanks
- facilitators of local collaborations, task forces, or coalitions
- faculty and staff at schools of social work
- individuals whose work you have read or heard about
- state legislators who are particularly interested in your field (contact them when the legislature is not in session)
- chairs and participants of NASW committees, agency networks, and so on.

Seek Advice from Key Contacts

Identify three to five people in the field who can give you advice about conducting a job search in your target community or a national job search in your specialty area. This step is especially important if you are moving to a new location, are inexperienced in job hunting, are unclear about the strength of the market, or have not looked for a job in a long time.

Think of who might have good overview of the field, services, and the local community or market you are exploring. If you are a doctoral student planning an academic career, you will want to meet with your adviser, members of your dissertation committee, and other faculty members to talk specifically about a nationwide academic search.

This conscious effort to seek advice for a search is pertinent for those who hold either a BSW or MSW degree. For instance, a student interested in program planning for children wished to relocate to Boston. Six months before graduating with a master's degree, she called three agencies in Boston and asked to speak with the program directors. Although she was able to reach only one person on the first try, he scheduled a time she could call to get his ideas on looking for a program-planning job. When you seek advice, keep these specific purposes in mind:

- get thoughts on your list of potential employers
- learn of any trends, legislation, or events that could affect your search
- build relationships with a few key advisers who can be consulted about your search when necessary
- make your name and professional interests familiar to others involved in your field.

Guidelines on Contacting People for Advice

After you have identified key contacts and before you pick up the telephone to seek advice, think through your approach.

Determine What Information You Need

Do your homework first. Learn about the community from print and online sources. Write down questions you want to ask, including broader issues that could affect your search.

Some ideas follow. (See appendix 4 for questions specific to broad areas of service.)Ask yourself,

- Is there a task force addressing my interest area that I should know about and get involved with—for example, a communitywide collaboration on family violence?
- Will recent public policies affect my job? Are the licensure laws changing? Is there a referendum on taxes being discussed?
- Who are the individuals in this community who know the most about services, new developments, and policies in my field—for example, aging, home health, children's advocacy?
- Are there state or local regulations that make services here different from those where I now work? For example, are all school districts required to have school social workers?
- What organizations have merged recently or may merge? What has been the impact on social work jobs?
- With what professional and advocacy groups do social workers or those specializing in this field affiliate? Who is the contact person?
- What organizations hire individuals with my level of experience? (Be familiar enough with your list of potential employers that you can recognize or mention names of organizations. For example, you could say, "I have a list of five treatment centers for adolescents, which are [state the names of the centers]. Are there any others I should add to that list?")
- What salary range is realistic for someone with my level of education and experience?

Prepare a Concise Introduction

Be sure you know how you are going to introduce yourself. If you do not already know the person you are asking for information, explain how you got his or her name. Explain the purpose of the call or letter (see sample letter 1 in appendix 5). Ask whether he or she has a few minutes to talk or find out when it would be convenient to talk in person or over the telephone.

Start with People You Know

Even if you are moving to an area where you have no contacts, start talking with people in your present community. They can give you advice on your next career move, and they may know social workers or be familiar with organizations in your target community. Of course, you will want to be selective in making contacts (for example, you may not want coworkers to know that you are looking for a new position).

Start your efforts with people you know to prepare you for contacting those you have not met. You need to be prepared for all of these calls and meetings, but you especially want to be prepared for a conversation with someone you do not know. The higher the position the person holds, the less time you are likely to have with him or her and the more precise your questions need to be.

Focus on Advice, Not Job Openings

During this research phase, the focus of your networking should be advice on how to go about finding the type of social work position you want in that community. In the course of a conversation someone may tell you about an opening, but do not use these conversations to specifically identify openings. At this point you are introducing yourself to other professionals and getting ideas on appropriate job-search strategies in your market.

Keep Your Call or Visit Brief

Part of a successful network effort is pacing your conversations. Strive to limit telephone calls to five minutes and visits to 15 minutes. However, be prepared to spend more time should you encounter a particularly conversant contact.

Remember Propriety and Protocol

If someone says, "I can refer you to Ms. Jones, but I want to call her first," be sure to respect your contact's wishes. When someone refers you to a colleague, always ask whether you can use his or her name when you follow up with that contact.

In some cases, if a potential contact is located in another community or is at an executive level, you may want to write a letter introducing yourself and indicate you will be calling. (See sample letters 1 and 6 in appendix 5.)

Record Detailed Notes from the Conversation

Be sure to take some notes during your conversations—immediately after the conversation, record as many details as you remember.

Thank Your Contact

Immediately after your conversation, send a brief handwritten or typed thank-you letter (see sample letters 7 and 8 in appendix 5). Do not send a résumé unless the person asked for one. Again, keep this initial contact focused on advice. Later, after you have assimilated the pieces of advice you solicited and you actually begin pursuing leads, you can write to particularly helpful contacts a second time. (See the section "Contacts and Networking" in chapter 4.)

What to Do If All You Hear Is Discouraging News

As you research your target market, you may find that people in the field discourage you from looking for the job you really want. If this happens, ask yourself these questions:

- Have I talked with a variety of people in not-for-profit, public, and, if applicable, for-profit settings?
- What is their information based on? Have they come into contact with many social workers with my experience who are looking for the same type of job? Have they been frustrated in their own work or in attempts to change jobs or careers?
- Do I have a comprehensive list of employers for my primary and secondary interests?

- Do I know which organizations are likely to hire someone with my background?

In other words, be certain that you have covered all the bases to obtain a balanced picture of the opportunities. It is not uncommon to encounter someone whose personal experience makes him or her overly negative; your background and experience with the market could be very different.

Yet the community of your choice may indeed be saturated with qualified professionals—this often happens in college towns and popular cities. Nonetheless, you may find a position if you extend the length of your search, expand your objectives, or take a position that will allow you to keep in touch with your goal, professional associations, and community while you are working. Vigorous networking is be the key in this situation. For example, if you are a new MSW graduate, your chances of finding a job with an employee assistance program (EAP) may be slim. You may decide to take a job in a substance abuse treatment center to get a few years of experience while earning your clinical license and substance abuse certification, and eventually become a member of the Academy of Certified Social Workers. You can simultaneously become involved in the professional community and network with individuals in EAPs. Then you will be better positioned to look for your preferred job.

References

American Chamber of Commerce Researchers Association. (quarterly). *ACCRA cost of living index.* Louisville, KY: Author.

American cost of living survey. (Biennial). Detroit: Gale Research.

Barth, M. C. (2003). Social work labor market: A first look. *Social Work, 48,* 9–19.

Lennon, T. M. (2004). *Statistics on social work education in the United States: 2001.* Alexandria, VA: Council on Social Work Education.

O'Neill, J. V. (2001). Members' median income is $45,660. *NASW News, 46,* 8.

U.S. cost of living comparisons for 399 U.S. job markets. Available: http://www.datamasters.com/cgi-bin/col.pl.

Researching the Market

- Obtain licensure or certification information from your target state.
- List five to 10 organizations doing the work you want to do. Consult printed directories and online information.
- List five to 10 organizations doing some type of work related to what you want to do.
- Brainstorm a list (no more than five) of people you know who could give you advice on your search and current issues in your field of social work.
- Talk with the NASW chapter and fellow alumni in your target area or make "cold" calls to organizations to determine the salary range for the type of position you are seeking.

CHAPTER THREE

Preparing Résumés, Curricula Vitae, Portfolios, and References

Inside Chapter 3

Some social workers find jobs without résumés, but chances are that you will need one sometime during your job search. Even if you use your résumé only once, the process of composing your document is a good exercise in recalling your accomplishments, clarifying your career direction, refining your presentation skills and knowledge, and setting goals for the future. You may sometimes hear the term "vita" or "curriculum vitae" (CV). Generally speaking, a CV is the academic version of a résumé. CVs are used primarily in academic and research environments, whereas U.S. agencies and businesses usually ask for résumés. CV is used in place of the term résumé in the international arena. A portfolio, which is a compilation of materials that demonstrate your knowledge and skills, might also prove useful in your search; it could include published or unpublished papers to which you have contributed, a videotape of a presentation that you made, or other evidence of your accomplishments. No matter what form your submission to a potential employer takes, be sure that you can back it up with references if you are asked to provide them.

Résumés

There are as many ideas on effective résumés as there are career counselors, interviewers, and job hunters, and any library or bookstore is likely to have several texts on résumé writing. More difficult to find are specific suggestions for social workers, which is what this chapter will provide.

Before You Start

Everyone has a unique set of credentials and personal goals, and your résumé should be individually designed to reflect yours. Compose your own. You might be tempted to use a résumé template—a preformatted layout—from your computer's word processing program or purchase résumé software. Be aware that templates do not offer the flexibility of simple word processing, which allows social workers to highlight their unique mix of work, training, and public service assets. Also note that résumés written by professional résumé writers or friends often do not use social work language accurately, nor do they highlight your job-related strengths. They are likely to focus on generic skills and lack content specific to social work. To help outline a strategy for presenting your best qualifications, answer the questions in this section; then complete exercises 1, 2, and 5 in chapter 1 or follow the instructions in the section "Comparing Your Objective with Your Qualifications".

What Is the Purpose of This Résumé?

Will you use the résumé to look for a job, to apply for graduate school or training programs, to explore consulting or speaking opportunities, to update your employer or board on your professional activities for public relations purposes, or simply to keep your own records organized? The format and qualifications you choose for the résumé will depend on your answer. If you are applying to graduate school, you might emphasize your research assistantship. If you are keeping a record of your experiences, you should probably use a chronological format.

Who Is Your Audience?

Are the people who will read your résumé in your field or are they trained in other disciplines? The language you use in your résumé depends on your readers' background. You should be careful about language; as one employer cautions, "Some language, such as 'facilitate implementation,' is too fuzzy." What criteria will your audience use to review résumés? Do you know what your audience is looking for?

What Is Your Goal?

Regardless of whether you state your objective on your résumé, you should write a sentence about what you want for yourself. What are you looking for? This theme statement will help you organize your information. Of all the elements in your background, which are the most relevant to your goal? The answer to this question will help you formulate a strategy for drawing the reader's attention to your best qualifications for your current goal.

Comparing Your Objective with Your Qualifications

At the top of a sheet of paper marked "worksheet A," write your job objective or a statement of what you would like to do. Under the objective, list the knowledge and skills important to the type of work you are seeking.

On a second sheet marked "worksheet B," list all of your key experience, degrees, and accomplishments, including those not related to your objective. Then prioritize those items as they relate to your objective. The items high on the list will be the ones you emphasize on your résumé. In other words, you have identified the best cards you have to play.

Compare worksheets A and B. Do the high-priority items on worksheet B address the knowledge and skills listed on worksheet A? If you do not have experience or credentials to cover all of the qualifications on worksheet A, you can anticipate what questions an employer could raise about your background; review all of the items on worksheet B to find out whether some of your skills and experience might compensate for those missing qualifications. Let your qualifications and those elements that are important to the work you want to do determine the format you choose for your résumé.

Choosing a Format

Both one- and two-page résumés are acceptable in most social services organizations. Even longer résumés are used for high-level positions. The important issue is that anyone skimming your résumé should be able to pick out your key qualifications. Regardless of whether your résumé is one page or two, it must be a stand-alone document—do not count on a cover letter to fill in missing information. You could be in a situation in which you simply hand the résumé to someone without an opportunity to include a cover letter, or the résumé might be copied and distributed to a search committee or staff without a companion letter.

Résumés are usually chronological or functional, or some combination of those forms. The format you choose depends on your personal preference and the nature of your qualifications. A chronological résumé lists all employment and unpaid experience in reverse chronological order. A functional one outlines experience according to skill areas and states an objective; this format is sometimes used when changing careers, because it highlights abilities rather than particular job titles or dates. (If you prefer to use a functional résumé, you should also prepare one with a chronological format, in case an employer requests it.) A combination format includes elements of both chronological and functional résumés according to personal preference, and often includes an objective and a section called qualifications, accomplishments, or skills.

You may need to prepare more than one résumé. For example,

- you may need résumés crafted for different purposes
- you may prefer to write a résumé for a specific opening
- you may be looking at more than one type of job
- you may be sending or posting résumés that require different formats and phrasing.

Résumés for Different Media

Ask yourself how you will be using your résumé. Will you be handing it to contacts, sending it through regular mail, sending it by fax or e-mail, or entering it into a database, perhaps on the Internet? In most cases you will use a résumé that stresses action and accomplishments through verb phrases (see appendix 10 for examples). However, if you know that your résumé will become part of a database in a human resources department or professional association career service or entered in an Internet résumé database, you will need a résumé that focuses on nouns (see sample 13 in appendix 6). When employers search a résumé database, they use certain nouns, or key words, such as policy analysis, project management, or case management to narrow their search for qualified applicants.

The use of technology for a job search also affects the format you choose. If you are sending your letters and résumé electronically, you must format them differently than if you send them through the mail. In general, if you plan to send your résumé file to an employer via e-mail, you must save your résumé file as a text document, which removes any special formatting (italics, bullets, and so forth), edit it, and test it by send-

ing it to yourself or a friend. If you learn that an organization will be scanning a printed résumé into a database, print it without bullets, italics, boldface, and other design features, which some scanners are not able to read. To learn more about electronic résumés, visit *The Riley Guide* at http://www.dbm.com/jobguide, which provides details on preparing such résumés (Dikel, 1994–2004).

Format Strategies for Different Stages of Experience

Whether you are a new graduate, career changer, or experienced social worker does not determine which format you use. In general, however, those with more experience are in a better position to use the functional and combination formats, simply because they have more to say. The following notes will help you determine how you might organize your material using the headings described later in this chapter.

New Graduates

Your most important credential is your degree. Therefore, put the education section at the top of the résumé after your objective, if you choose to use one, or after the summary or qualifications section if you are using a combination résumé. For a new graduate without job experience, your practicum will be your second key credential. A section on professional development that describes your leadership, affiliation, workshops, and so on can be used to demonstrate additional accomplishments and commitment to the field. If your extracurricular activities, volunteer or part-time work, or college honors are significant in terms of skill development or levels of responsibility, describe them. See appendix 6 for sample résumés.

Career Changers and Social Workers Re-entering the Workforce

If you are a career changer, you want your mental shift—a commitment to your new career—to be evident on paper. You will want to state your objective and probably use a qualifications summary. Emphasize your social services experience, and put it early in the résumé. Without diminishing your accomplishments, streamline information about your previous career. Retain the major elements of your work—such as "supervised 25 people"— and those elements related to your new goal— "coordinated team-building exercises to reduce stress" or "experience with analysis, communication, and problem solving." If community and social work professional activities are your strong suit, they should dominate your résumé. Take a look at your draft. If you were an accountant, homemaker, volunteer, lawyer, or teacher and are just beginning your social work career, what gets the most attention on your résumé? Your first occupation or the experience related to your new career? To which audience does your résumé speak?

If you are taking your traditional social work experience into a nontraditional arena, you also will need to demonstrate a commitment and potential for success in your new target career. In this case, you will convert specific social work language into terms commonly used in your new field. You will also add to your résumé those elements that may not have special relevance to your current social work career, but are important in your target arena. If you are looking at government opportunities, public service might be one of those items.

If your recent career stage entailed stopping for a period of time to manage family and personal responsibilities or pursue other interests, you will want to demonstrate your renewed commitment to the field and your recent skill set. Some social workers choose to treat their stop-out commitments as positions and list them chronologically in the experience, community service, leadership, and other sections of the résumé. You have recent knowledge, skills, and accomplishments; describe how they contribute to your new direction.

Experienced Social Workers
Your postdegree experience and license (if appropriate) are now your most important qualifications. In a chronological format, professional experience should precede academic degrees; practicum experience will diminish in importance, if indeed you mention it at all. Professional development should focus on recent and major career accomplishments. Only outstanding college and graduate school awards and activities, such as Phi Beta Kappa or president of the student council, should remain, if at all. For clinical social workers and other direct practitioners, licensure and certifications are very important. In this case, add LCSW (licensed clinical social worker or your state's equivalent) and ACSW (Academy of Certified Social Workers) or any other professional credential you have behind your name if appropriate for the work you seek. It is not uncommon for someone at the executive level to have a résumé several pages long.

Sections and Sample Headings
Résumé content can be organized in many ways. A sample list of section headings and ideas for each follows. Select those sections that are most appropriate for your unique background.

Objectives and Summary Statements
There are a number of optional devices that you can use to alert the reader to your goals, interests, accomplishments, and skills. These techniques enable you to convey your message, rather than leaving the interpretation of your background to the reader. The following sections show some of the choices you have.

Key words. A summary paragraph of key words or terms is recommended if your résumé will go into a database. See sample 13 in appendix 6.

Objective—job or career. A statement of your objective is optional if you are using a chronological format. However, it is helpful to use it or a qualifications summary in functional or combination résumés to explain your purpose. Write a brief objective. In one or two sentences you can include a job title, type of organization, skills to be used, and a particular interest area (see "Deciding on Your Objectives" in chapter 1).

If you have easy access to a computer and wish to use an objective, tailor your résumé each time you need it. If you do not have easy access to a computer but have a specific job objective, write one résumé using the objective. At the same time, prepare a general résumé as a backup that can be used for unexpected opportunities that do not fit your objective. If you don't have a specific objective in mind, write a general résumé without a job objective and incorporate your job objective in the cover letter. (See samples 2 and 4 in appendix 6.)

Professional summary, qualifications, special accomplishments, or professional accomplishments.

Select three to five statements representing your key accomplishments, experiences, or skill sets that highlight your background and convey your message. (See samples 6, 10, 11, and 12 in appendix 6.)

Skills. You can use this heading with any résumé format. Use it to highlight skill sets or to list those skills not stated elsewhere ("fluent in Spanish" or "computer skills," for example). When used in functional résumés, divide the skills section into two to four subheadings, such as direct practice, clinical social work, administration, management, program planning, research, or fundraising. Under each subhead describe your relevant experience in concrete terms. (See samples 5, 8, and 10 in appendix 6.)

Education

Education is a standard heading, although some social workers combine it with professional credentials. If you choose this combination, be sure that your credentials are easy to find. Employers skim résumés, so put your highest degree first. You can use initials (for example, MSW, BSW) or spell out the title of the degree. If you are

moving, think about whether the name of your university or the name of your particular school of social work is more likely to be recognized and list them in that order (for example, Boston University, School of Social Work; or Ringel Institute of Gerontology, School of Social Welfare, University of New York at Albany).

If you are a student, do not list courses unless you need to show a connection between what you studied and the position. For example, you may be applying for a position that is not usually held by social workers and need to stress your knowledge of budgeting, statistics, policy analysis, and program evaluation. You may or may not choose to state your concentration or academic emphasis.

Experience

You have a number of options for listing your paid, training, and volunteer experiences. Using the questions at the beginning of this chapter or the work you did in chapter 1, select the heading that works best for your background mix. In addition to the headings below, you may be able to use descriptive headings, which tell a story and get attention, like those in sample 9 in appendix 6. This works best for people whose types of experience fall into neat chronological sequences.

Professional experience. If you have full-time experience in the field, list it in this section, which will go at the top of the résumé if it is postdegree experience and after the section on education if it precedes the degree. You might use the heading "professional experience and training." This arrangement will work if your recent field training is more closely related to your job goal than your previous experience. A combined section of "professional and volunteer experience" is a practical choice when your volunteer positions are stronger than or equal to your work experiences or you are a student whose work and volunteer experience is important but secondary to accomplishments gained in your practicum experiences.

Related experience. These headings are alternatives for people whose experience does not fall easily into another, more descriptive heading. If you use related experience, your résumé should have an objective or summary. The word related must refer to something, and in this case it is the objective.

Professional training. If you are a student without prior full-time work experience in the field, your best card to play, second to your degree, is practicum training. You can use a section entitled "professional training," and place it after the section on education. This section should describe each field placement as if it were a job, and it should dominate the page. Use descriptive titles such as "social work intern" or "medical social work intern." Many graduating students list field placements as professional experience; however, some employers prefer to see practicum work separated from full-time postdegree experience. The choice is yours as long as you make the context of the experience clear through position titles or headings.

Community service or volunteer experience. Volunteer experience can be an important asset in your search. You need to assess its importance, like that of all other information, to the position you are seeking. If you founded an organization, served as an officer or on the board, had responsibility for a major project, or coordinated a team effort, you will probably want to describe these activities in detail, similar to the way you describe your jobs if they are equal to or more important than your work experience. If you have extensive community work, consider the heading "community activities" or "public service." Like titles for internships, use descriptive terms such as "special events volunteer" or "volunteer tutor," especially if you combine volunteer work with other experience.

Leadership and Professional Development

For some social workers, professional and community leadership roles and other professional activities are among their most important assets.

Here are a couple of alternatives for presenting them.

Professional development. This heading is good for grouping additional items that indicate commitment, particularly to the profession. Use subheads such as presentations, publications, leadership, research, grants, affiliations or memberships, training, licensure or certification, language or computer skills, and community or volunteer work. These sections must be brief. If you have many presentations or publications, put them on a separate sheet.

If you are a direct practitioner, probably you have attended many in-service training sessions, workshops, and continuing education seminars. Do not list each of these on your résumé. You might give a very brief statement listing the topics, such as "2001–2003 attended workshops on ethics, family-centered practice, and interventions with blended families." If you completed an extensive training program by a recognized organization or expert and you have space, give the title, date, and location.

Leadership. If a type of experience is extensive, it may warrant its own section on the résumé. Leadership is one example. If this is the case, you might consider using "leadership" as a key section or add it to the heading "professional development" and lead this section off with your leadership roles. The same can be done with other subheadings under professional development. (See samples 2 and 3 in appendix 6.)

Describing Your Experience

Regardless of which format or headings you choose, keep the following points in mind when describing your experience, including leadership positions and major community or professional activities.

Include Your Major Job Functions (Counseling, Training, Data Analysis) and Major Accomplishments

State specifically how you contributed to each project, service, program, or outcome. Use brief, uncomplicated verb phrases for résumés that will be read and not scanned. A verb phrase is a statement without a subject. Write "organized local chapter," not "I organized the local chapter." Depending on your purpose, include specific experience with and knowledge of

- populations (for example, older adults, young children, homeless families)
- issues (for example, job training, eating disorders, budget cuts, mergers)
- methods (for example, group work, community organizing, advocacy).

Write for Your Audience

To convince a supervisor that you would make a good clinical therapist, use clinical social work terminology as, for example, psychosocial assessments, DSM-IV rev. (American Psychiatric Association, 2000), treatment planning, brief strategic therapy, cognitive behavioral therapy, treatment evaluation, and so forth. Or, to get the attention of the assistant superintendent reviewing résumés for a school social work position, use such terms as multidisciplinary team planning, group work, parent and teacher relationships, prevention programs, at-risk children, and so forth.

If you are looking at positions not usually held by social workers, adopt the language of the role and organizations that you are considering.

Consider Knowledge You Gained on Policies, Cutting-Edge Issues, Funding Streams, Political Feasibility, and Use of Technology

For some individuals, sometimes what was learned in a position is more relevant to the objective than what was done. Always consider how each experience contributes to what you want to do now. For example, as a student maybe you had a job as an administrative assistant for a nursing home where you learned about insurance, regulations, and issues facing older adults and families. Try using a learn statement, for example, "learned about alternative

care options for older adults." Or perhaps you learned new computer skills such as data analysis or SPSS and other computer packages while working on projects.

Quantify Your Accomplishments in a Way Appropriate to the Job You Are Seeking

Many authors of résumé books stress the importance of quantifying accomplishments, for example, "increased sales by 60 percent." This approach is important for administrators of programs, managers of social services, and fundraisers. Quantifying accomplishments in direct practice can be difficult, however, even though there is now a greater emphasis on outcomes. Handle accomplishments in direct practice differently by shifting the emphasis: for example, "follow-up interviews indicated that interventions were still effective after three months" or "chose evidence-based interventions when possible." Note that it is likely that even those in direct practice will increasingly need to be able to quantify results in the future.

Put All Experiences within a Section in Reverse Chronological Order

The examples in appendix 6 list dates close to the content to emphasize content and minimize distraction. If you keep short-term or part-time jobs at all, condense information into one statement: "1999–2003 held a variety of part-time, temporary, and summer jobs as a cashier in a retail store, assistant in a library, and data-entry clerk for an insurance company." Do not list this information unless you need to demonstrate responsibility, account for time, or have limited experience.

Content Details

Keep the following details in mind as you prepare your résumé (or résumés):

- Type your name in capital letters and boldface (unless you are sending the résumé by e-mail or it is being scanned for inclusion in a database, where boldface will not be recognized). Be sure that your telephone number is listed, as well as an e-mail address if you have one.

- Do not use unimportant data, such as the word "résumé" at the top of the page, high school information, and hobbies unless they spark conversation and you have space.
- Do not include reasons for terminating employment or personal information such as marital or family status, gender, or age.
- A statement indicating your references and writing samples are available upon request is not necessary. If interviewers want them, they will ask. (The section below entitled "Letters of Reference" suggests some options.)
- If you are concerned about listing politically sensitive subjects on your résumé, consider creating two résumés, or do not list these items at all.
- Do not include street addresses and names of supervisors. If they agree to be references, this information can go on a separate reference page independent of the résumé.

Final Preparation

Before you seek several opinions on your résumé, be sure that the content and visual presentation is balanced. Relevant experience should be the focal point or dominant section. After you prepare your draft, look at the amount of space you have allotted to each item. Do your related qualifications stand out more than the less-related position in which you spent more time?

- Ask someone who has not seen your résumé to scan it in 30 seconds. Then ask him or her to summarize the key points. Are those the points you wanted to get across?
- Check and recheck for spelling and grammar. Do not rely on your computer program's spell check feature.
- In addition to capitalizing and using boldface type for your name and headings, try doing the same with job titles or names of

organizations. Don't overuse boldface, however—use it only for items that deserve emphasis. (Note: boldface should not be used for electronic or scanned résumés as mentioned above.)

If your descriptions are too wordy, do the following:

- turn phrases into adjectives modifying nouns—"a teen pregnancy program" instead of "a program addressing pregnancy among teenagers"
- break up long sentences (use phrases, not sentences)
- delete information on lower-level skills and minor functions of the job
- remove in-house titles of programs and replace them with generic terms.

Do not feel you must purchase a computer or camp out at a computer center to tailor every résumé. Many social workers find jobs with one résumé duplicated on quality paper. Start with a small number of copies on 8-1/2 x 11-inch paper in a conservative color (white, ivory, tan, or light gray). As you use these, you will find items that you will want to change.

Curricula Vitae

The curricula vitae, or CVs, are detailed accounts that stress teaching, research, grant awards, publications, and presentations. If you are planning a career in academia, you will use a CV instead of a résumé. Sometimes the CV is also used for research positions in nonacademic institutions, but a résumé is often preferred.

Before You Begin

Before you begin writing or revising your CV, think first about its immediate purpose and your strengths. Are you applying for tenure, looking for a job, or recording your work? Your answer to that question will determine how you organize your material and the tone you set.

Applying for Tenure

If you are submitting your CV as part of your package for tenure, organize the sections according to the criteria for tenure. For many faculty members, those criteria would call for grants and publications to immediately follow education in the front of the document.

Looking for an Academic Job

If you are looking at tenure-track positions, what are the priorities of the faculty at those institutions? Do they focus on teaching and community service or on research and teaching? The priority you give to teaching in your CV may be higher in the former situation than it would be in the latter. How important is practice experience for the positions? If practice experience is important and your experience is varied, you may want to use subheadings such as clinical practice and program development. The level of detail you use to describe experience and skills should reflect the priorities of the positions and institutions that interest you. If you are having difficulty writing the CV, think again about the fit between each position and institution and your strengths.

Also for a tenure-track position, you will want personnel committees to be able to determine the following from your CV:

- theme linking your research, publications, and presentations
- strong dissertation related to a faculty project (doctoral students)
- teaching interests and experience
- names of faculty and colleagues you have worked with
- level of your research skills.

Recording Your Work

The CV is a handy tool for keeping track of your work and providing others, such as funders, conference sponsors, or public relations staff, background on your accomplishments. If you are using the CV for public relations, keep education, honors, and awards up front and place long lists of publications and presentations toward the back. If you are seeking funding, your emphasis will be on grants, research, and publications.

Doctoral Students: Converting Your Résumé to a CV

Like the résumé, your CV conveys the theme of your work. Unlike the résumé, which presents the highlights of your theme-related experience in usually one or two pages, the CV describes all of your experience and has no specified or recommended length. You will use the CV document itself to keep track of all your accomplishments.

In the résumé, practice experience related to your goal dominates the page, and professional development experiences such as presentations, publications, teaching, and research projects play supporting roles. These roles reverse in the CV. Those items that once were listed together under the single heading "professional development" become their own sections, often with subheadings.

Use every opportunity to convey your knowledge areas and skills. Do not assume that personnel committees will recognize your level of ability through position titles alone. For example, unlike experienced faculty members, you will want to include details that describe your role in research projects.

Brainstorm a list of strengths of your academic program, which in turn will expand your thinking about what you have to offer.

Format and Headings

Once you have selected section headings and subheadings, list each item under the headings in reverse chronological order. Then order the sections to fit the interests of your readers and highlight your strengths. If you have received grant awards and know that this track record is important for your purpose, then place the grants section early in your CV. If you are looking for your first academic position, you will probably put your teaching and research interests on the first page.

Tailor headings to fit your material, and use subheadings if you have many items for a section. Keep like items together. Although you may have several subsections on presentations, do not mix them with sections on grants and publications.

Unless an item has two distinct components, it should appear only once on the CV. An exception is a paper that you both published and presented. Or perhaps you were selected for an honor associated with your job. In one case, a doctoral student had been selected to be an executive on loan to United Way while working for a corporation. Because this distinction was related to social work, she listed it in the community service section.

Sections and Sample Headings

Education. This will be your first heading. Under it list each degree, program title, institution, city, state or country, and year, beginning with your doctoral degree and working backward. If you are in a doctoral program, include your dissertation title and adviser's name. If you have completed your requirements for candidacy, indicate "advanced to candidacy" and an anticipated date; otherwise, state that you are a doctoral student.

Honors. Set off all academic honors, fellowships, and dissertation awards in one section. Include the name of the award, sponsoring institution, and date. Add a brief descriptive phrase if the honor is not self-explanatory. List papers selected for recognition here, unless they are listed elsewhere. If you were selected among others to attend a conference, include a descriptive phrase, particularly if the program is not widely known—for example, "one of 12 doctoral students selected nationwide to participate in the symposium." If you have one or two honors, consider listing them under the degree in the education section. Other headings you might use are "academic honors," "academic fellowships," "academic honors and awards," "scholastic honors and awards," and "honors, fellowships, and awards."

Grants. When listing grants, state the funding source, project title, names of investigators, dates, and dollar amounts. A listing in this section should not include fellowship or dissertation material, which are in the education and honors sections; unless it is specifically a dissertation grant. Other headings might be "grant development" or "funded research."

Teaching interests and research interests. You will probably want to create separate sections using each of these titles. These sections speak directly to the immediate interests of the institution's personnel committee members, who are looking for a good fit between prospective faculty members and the school. Particularly if you are seeking your first teaching position, list every course area in which you have taught, assisted, and developed a knowledge base or for which you have an interest. Make it easy for the personnel committee to identify the subjects you can teach—instead of the specific course title used at your institution, use language that parallels the accreditation standards of the Council on Social Work Education on curriculum content. Under research interests, simply list your subject areas.

Professional experience. Organize your experience into teaching, research, and practice. Depending on how much practice experience you have and on what you want to emphasize, you may divide your practice items into like categories. For instance, if you wanted to stress your clinical practice experience, you would create a section just for that work.

If you worked in another country, explain the U.S. equivalent of job titles and other terms in parentheses. For example, a school principal in one country may be the equivalent of a dean in another country. A U.S. reader who is not familiar with another country's terminology may not fully appreciate the impact or value of a position you held.

Teaching experience. If you were a teaching assistant, list in reverse chronological order each position you held, along with the name of the professor you assisted and the course title, name of the institution, location (city and state or country), semester, and year you taught. If you taught several courses at the same institution, just name the university, city, and state or country once and then list the course information underneath. You may also find it helpful to organize teaching experience by position titles: part-time faculty, lecturer, or teaching assistant, for example. Headings you might use include "teaching experience," "teaching and curriculum development," "courses taught," and "lectureships."

Research experience. When presenting your research experience, include the sponsoring or funding organization, project title, principal investigators, and your project title. If you are a doctoral student, describe your role in brief verbal phrases: "designed a questionnaire" or "coded, entered, and analyzed data." Briefly state the purpose of each research project, without giving an abstract, when project titles are not self-explanatory. Projects you conducted independently can also be listed in this section. If you are a student and sought advice from a faculty member on a project, you can state, "consulted with Jan Doe, PhD" at the end of the description.

Practice experience. For each direct practice, administrative, or management position, include the name of the organization or institution, city, state or country, position title, and dates. Describe your principal tasks, skills used, and accomplishments. Begin each descriptive phrase with a verb to give your work a vivid, active voice. If you held more than one position with one organization, list the agency, city, and state or country once; under that information list each position title and put the dates next to the title. For practicum experiences, put the word "intern" in the title or designate the experience as a practicum. Some headings you might consider are "professional experience," "clinical social work experience," "administrative experience," "management experience," and "program experience."

Previous career experience. If you were employed full time in a field other than social work, list this experience if it is relevant to your current work or if it accounts for a significant period of time. Include brief descriptions of primary accomplishments and contributions, particularly if they are pertinent to your knowledge and skills.

Publications. List all published and unpublished manuscripts, using the American Psychological Association (2001) style manual for the format to use. If a paper is accepted but not yet published, list it under "journals" and state that it is in press or forthcoming. Unpublished finished manuscripts can go into a manuscript subsection. Some people also list work in process, but others caution that it is better to list only finished work. If you are a doctoral student who has a paper nearly ready to submit to a journal, then consider listing it. This is important if you, like many doctoral students, have not yet had material published.

Use subsection headings to draw attention to your work and to make it easy for the reader to identify types of publications. Some subheadings you might use are "books," "chapters," "journal articles," "monographs and final reports," "book reviews," "peer review publications," "papers under review," "manuscripts," "service to journals and publishers," and "papers or work in progress." If you need a briefer CV for some purpose, consider using "select papers" or "select publications" as subheadings.

Presentations. List all presentations. For each include the title of the paper, coauthors, sponsoring organization, city, state or country, and date. Do not overlook presentations that you have made at your institution, such as one in a colloquium series, particularly if you are beginning your career. As in the publications section, you may want to use subheadings in this section, which might include papers presented at conferences, oral presentations, poster presentations, and workshops or in-service training.

Additional training. This section is another opportunity for describing your knowledge areas and skill sets. If you completed a certificate program or participated in an intensive, well-recognized training program, give specifics: title, sponsor, city, state or country, and dates. If you have attended several one-session workshops or lectures that supplemented your formal education, you can summarize them in a paragraph; for example, "between 1998 and 2003 attended training sessions on family preservation, grant writing, clinical supervision, and managed care." Possible headings or subheadings are "continuing education," "supplemental training," and "certificates."

Community, professional, and university services. Briefly list all your community and professional activities, including elected and appointed leadership positions, board positions, consulting, guest appearances on radio and television, and task force appointments or memberships. List the name of the group or professional society, your role, and dates. If you have done consultations or had contract jobs—for example, to conduct a program evaluation—you can list them under community service or practice experience. Include any university committee or task force on which you have served and responsibilities you have had for advising or field education liaison work. University work demonstrates commitment, contributions, and knowledge of teaching and campus life issues. Headings you might use are "consulting," "media appearances," "community service," "professional service," "university committees," and "community and university service."

Skills. Although it is better to show than to tell, you can use a skills section to summarize sets of skills, draw attention to skills, or list skills not covered elsewhere. This section is particularly important for doctoral students and those early in their careers. Do not assume that readers will review other sections of your CV to discover all your skills. For example, this section is where you want to state the specific computer packages you have used. If you are bilingual or fluent in a second or multiple languages, list

them. Headings or subheadings might include "computer skills," "languages," "research skills," and "special skills."

Visa status. If you are from another country, you might choose to state your visa status on the CV. It is legal for employers to ask you about your visa status.

Memberships. Give names of organizations to which you currently belong. Dates of membership are optional. This section can go toward the end of the CV. Headings you might use are "professional associations," "professional memberships," "professional affiliations," and "organizations."

References. Prepare a reference sheet that can be attached to your CV; put your name, address, and telephone number at the top. Tailor the reference sheet to the position.

Final Details

Be sure that you are not overlooking any of your experiences, especially if you are in the academic job market for the first time. Have you been an academic adviser, consultant to an agency on program evaluation, clinical supervisor, statistics workshop instructor, or study group leader? Have you reviewed manuscripts, moderated panels, led training on interventions or discussions on the integration of theory and practice? Have you provided consultation to faculty members on a computer package? Keep in mind these details:

- Put your name in bold letters at the top of page 1, followed by your address, e-mail address, and telephone numbers—place your name at the top or bottom right corner on each succeeding page.
- Although some people put CV at the top of the first page, it is not necessary.
- Number the pages, except for page 1.
- If you update your CV regularly or create different versions, footnote a date in small print at the bottom of the last page.
- Do not list personal information such as birth date, social security number, marital

status, number of children, or citizenship—put visa status on the last page if you wish.

- Ask two people to review your document, one who knows your work and one who does not—they will help you identify missing items, inconsistencies, and confusing elements.
- Proofread several times.

CV as Professional Development Tool

Update your CV at least once each year or, better yet, add each new accomplishment as it occurs. Review the organization of your material annually and think about what you would want to see on the CV in the coming year. Maybe the theme of your work is shifting. Is your new direction evident? Perhaps you've developed new curriculum and teaching techniques and then trained others. Do you need to reorganize the sections or add new material under special skills to reflect your current efforts?

Portfolios

You have heard of portfolios used by artists to demonstrate their skills—social workers can do the same thing.

What Is a Portfolio?

A portfolio is a set of materials that make up a sort of three-dimensional résumé. The contents of your portfolio demonstrate your clinical, writing, research, analytic, creative, and problem-solving skills. You can assemble samples and use them individually or organize several pieces in a file or use an attractive cover with your name and address on it.

Just about any item you have worked on that demonstrates your knowledge and skills can be included in a portfolio. Sample material might include reports, academic papers, white papers, program or curriculum outlines, program brochures, published articles, and presentation papers or outlines. Some people include electronic material. If you consider your Web site to be a product, you could include a printed page.

Develop the habit of building your portfolio: As soon as a project or phase of work is completed, put at least one copy in a file. If you collect a large number of pieces, select items for the portfolio that are most relevant to your audience.

Refamiliarize yourself from time to time with all the items in your portfolio. Also, you should practice presenting your portfolio by preparing a one- or two-sentence statement about each piece.

How to Use a Portfolio

You might use a portfolio as part of an application for a job or fellowship, or you might take it with you to show an interviewer or send it as a follow-up to an interview—increasingly, social services employers are requesting writing samples. Or, if an employer expresses concern or doubt about a particular ability—your writing skill, for example—you can pick a good example from your portfolio, send a copy, then follow up with a telephone call. The portfolio also might be useful when you meet with contacts to seek advice about career choices. Obviously, however, you must exercise good judgment. If you have only 15 minutes to spend with a contact, you might show one sample, but you are not going to focus on the portfolio.

A portfolio is always reused. Usually, you show it in person and take it with you when you leave. If the employer asks to keep it, make specific arrangements to pick it up or provide a self-addressed, stamped envelope. If you drop off a portfolio, make sure you get it back.

Important Considerations for Portfolios

The following considerations are essential:
- You must be certain that you are not breaking confidentiality by using a particular piece.
- You must be certain that you have permission to use an item you developed for an agency.

- You should take note that using electronic samples poses certain confidentiality issues and that equipment can be impractical. However, for interviews for upper-level positions that might involve making presentations, an electronic piece may be useful. Note that you should have release statements from subjects.
- If you choose to put material on a Web site, just remember that it is visible to the world.
- All portfolio materials must be your work or demonstrate parts of an effort for which you were the responsible team member.
- Items for your portfolio should reflect your best work. If a document has a misspelling, correct it or leave it out.
- Ideally, printed materials should be on agency letterhead or carry the name of the agency and should include your name whenever possible.

Letters of Reference

Employers often ask job candidates for references. You have three options:

1. *List of references.* The simplest option is to keep a list of names, titles, addresses, and telephone numbers of those people who have agreed to be references. Then give the list to employers when requested, or contact the individuals yourself when necessary. As on your résumé, your name, address, telephone number, and e-mail address should be at the top of this sheet.
2. *References on the résumé.* You can put the same information at the bottom or end of your résumé. However, you may not know when a reference is being contacted or by whom.
3. *Generic letters.* Another option is to ask your references to write nonconfidential "to whom it may concern" letters. You can make copies for employers. Then if you lose contact with a reference, you will still have a letter outlining his or her comments. You will have the security of a written statement and the option of asking the reference to tailor the letter for a specific employer. A supervisor in a children's health care center recommends using general letters to avoid the off chance that a reference might say more than you wish.

If your school offers a reference service that holds letters of reference and compiles reference portfolios at your request to send to employers on your behalf, take advantage of that opportunity.

Timing

Regardless of which option you choose, make certain that you have either a letter or a current address for each person who knows your work. Although you may not need a recommendation in the near future, in several years it could be very important.

The best time to get a letter of reference, especially for students, is shortly before or after a job, volunteer project, practicum, or class is completed. Recommendations written at this time will be stronger and more detailed because the information is fresh.

Choosing References

Choose your references carefully. When asking someone to write one, ask directly whether he or she can write a positive statement. This person should be up-front with you if there are any reservations about your work. If you have any doubts, reconsider.

Discuss your goals and experience with your references. Give them a current résumé for more information; it's especially handy for them to have when talking to employers or graduate schools on the telephone. Those people who provide recommendations usually appreciate your thoughts on what to include in the letter. If you want references to emphasize something, such as knowledge of grant writing, skills in family therapy, or your academic record, ask them to do so. Sometimes you will be asked to draft the letter.

If you think a particular employer will contact references soon, alert them. Keep your references informed of your progress—they are often good contacts and advisers.

Content of a Reference Letter

A letter of recommendation should contain the following:

- name of the candidate
- how and for how long the writer has known the candidate
- description of the work, project, or class in which the candidate participated
- specific contributions or accomplishments of the candidate
- candidate's skills and knowledge areas, work habits, and personality characteristics
- candidate's readiness for a position or graduate program
- summary statement.

Some reference letters also include a statement of areas to be improved or learned.

Confidential Letters

Some recommenders prefer to write confidential letters, meaning that you will never see the recommendations. Do not take this to mean that they do not think well of your accomplishments and work habits. It may simply be a personal preference regarding the integrity of a reference; some feel that a letter of recommendation that is not seen by the subject of the letter is more powerful. Others will automatically send you a copy of the letter for your own file. If you have any doubts about what someone might say in a letter, request a copy; if the request is refused, choose another reference.

References to Avoid

If you have had a negative experience with supervisors, coworkers, or faculty members—it is not an uncommon occurrence—you do not need to offer them as references.

When you are applying for a position, ask the employer about the process and timetable.

Employers do not usually check references until shortly before or after making an offer. If you advance in the selection process, you may need to explain why you do not have a particular reference. It is essential that you present your explanation in a professional manner. Keep your statements as positive and as brief as possible. If there was a personality conflict or difference in approach, say so and leave it at that. For example, you might explain the situation thus:

- My supervisor and I had different approaches. Although we maintained a working relationship that did not affect services, the situation was never entirely comfortable. That is why I asked the director of the agency to be a reference.
- Our staff accepts and uses a variety of approaches. It happens that my direct supervisor and I have different clinical styles. Although we respect each other's work, I think there are other members of the staff who can give you a better picture of my abilities.
- Unfortunately, I was in over my head in this particular practicum, but I didn't want to admit it. A situation arose in which I used poor judgment and did not alert my supervisor. In short, I was let go. It was a difficult but important learning experience. Two semesters later I completed another practicum without any problems. In fact, it was quite successful.

When References Are Not Available

For legal reasons, some organizations have policies that prevent staff from providing written or verbal references. In this case, the organization's human resources office provides confirmation of the dates of employment. You might also face a situation in which you have lost contact with a reference for one reason or another. Keeping complimentary memos or letters, performance reviews, and field practicum evaluations will enable you to fill the gap should you be missing a reference.

References

American Psychiatric Association. (2000). *Diagnostic and statistical manual of mental disorders* (4th ed. rev.). Washington, DC: Author.

American Psychological Association. (2001). *Publication manual of the American Psychological Association* (5th ed.). Washington, DC: Author.

Barth, M. C. (2003). Social work labor market: A first look. *Social Work, 48,* 9–19.

Dikel, M. F. (Ed.). (1994–2004). *The Riley guide.* Available: http://www.dgm.com/jobguide.

CHAPTER 3 QUICK TIPS
Résumés, Curricula Vitae, Portfolios, and References

- Make a list of three to five of your most important assets or qualifications (particular experiences, licenses, degrees, and so on) and put them in rank order.
- Select a sample résumé in appendix 6 or another style you like and follow that format for your own document.
- Draft your résumé or CV and ask someone to review it. Read it carefully for errors and initially make only five to 10 copies on good paper (to allow for future changes).
- Ask three people who know your work to be references.
- Select two or three items (reports, seminar outlines, papers) of no more than three pages each that represent your work, are not confidential, and would be suitable for showing a prospective employer.

CHAPTER FOUR

Identifying Jobs and Pursuing Leads

Inside Chapter 4

Job-Search Strategies
Sources of Jobs
Pursuing Leads
Cover Letters

The easiest way to get a new job is for an employer to call you. Maybe an employer will see your work and recruit you. It does happen, but you can't count on it. If you are like most people, you need to use several sources to identify job openings. This chapter outlines sources of jobs and evaluates their usefulness for a job search in social work, and goes on to suggest how you can screen job leads and compose cover letters targeted for specific openings.

We do not yet know a great deal about how social workers at all levels of experience find jobs. Many schools of social work survey their graduates on employment issues at least every few years. However, that information is not collected in a systematic way across institutions to give us an annual picture of the job market that new graduates enter. If you are looking in a geographic location where many of your fellow alumni live, check with your alma mater on the job sources reported by graduates.

The Association of Baccalaureate Social Work Program Directors sponsors a survey of graduates with the BSW degree. The Baccalaureate Education Assessment Project reports on salaries, types of positions and organizations, and length of job searches, among other employment details, as well as graduates' satisfaction with their education. Check the Web site http://www.rit.edu/~beap/index.htm or your BSW program office for the most recent data.

In the annual job market report on MSW graduates, Doelling and Matz collect data on job sources used by graduates completing an MSW. Unfortunately, most schools of social work do not collect such annual data. Although this project relies on aggregated data and the sample sizes for each year have been too small to report results, the responses did give indications about how some new graduates are finding jobs. Newspapers, networking, and practicum were the most commonly reported sources of jobs over the last few years (C. Doelling, director, Career Services, George Warren Brown School of Social Work, Washington University, St. Louis, and B. Matz, director, Career Development and Continuing Education, Graduate School of Social Work, Bryn Mawr College, unpublished data, 2002).

Job-search strategists recommend that you read or scan books on job hunting as you prepare and go through the search process. Most bookstores and libraries have well-stocked sections on careers and job hunting.

Many authors of job-hunting guides divide job-search strategies into two groups: traditional and what some people call "targeted" strategies. The traditional approach entails completing applications for personnel departments, responding to ads, and sending unsolicited letters and résumés in a widespread mailing campaign to employers. The targeted approach entails first researching potential employers and identifying those of particular interest to you;

second, using a network of contacts and printed resources to detail those problems in the organization that you can solve and to identify the person in the organization with the power to hire you; and third, in a face-to-face meeting convincing that person to hire you.

People do still get jobs using the traditional method, but many job-search experts now downplay that approach. In a competitive job market, authors encourage job hunters to use the more assertive targeted search. Many feel that this proactive approach increases the chances of a good job fit, greater job stability, and higher salary.

You can use elements of both methods. If convincing an employer—especially one that does not have an opening—that you should be hired based on your ideas and abilities to solve problems is an intimidating prospect, you probably do not want to put that strategy high on your list of approaches.

Job-Search Strategies

Job-search strategies need not be thought of as just traditional or targeted. The following six approaches are another way you might conceive of your job search (job sources for each approach are detailed later in this section):

1. Network and gain visibility through current contacts, professional and community associations, temporary and volunteer work, and position-wanted ads, for example.
2. Apply for openings identified through Web sites, newspapers, newsletters, job information services, and telephone calls.
3. Target organizations.
4. Use career services available through NASW and other societies, colleges, executive search firms, job fairs, online résumé databases, and registries.
5. File unsolicited applications, submit employer applications, get on government registers, and conduct a targeted mailing campaign.
6. Create an organization.

Job-Search Strategy for BSW Graduates

Like most social workers at any level of experience, the BSW holder needs to develop a message that highlights knowledge and skills and educates employers on the quality of the BSW degree (Boyd, 1996, and also personal communication, February 27, 2003).

Make a written list of your knowledge areas and skills (see chapter 1). Assume that you will need to educate others on what you know. One BSW graduate said to "sell" your degree—that is, your knowledge of service delivery systems, the systems and person-in-environment approaches, specific populations, and information about your internship.

- Think about trends and policy changes. Welfare reform and state budget crises will continue to affect state workers, who must work proactively with complex family situations. What do you have to offer in this changing environment? One BSW recommended working for a state government, where you can get good experience.
- Research your target geographic market well. Make an extensive list of all the organizations doing any work related to your interests. Call them to find out how they use BSW graduates. In 2002 the Baccalaureate Education Assessment Project reported that of the BSW respondents who had positions at graduation 46.9 percent found their first jobs in the nonprofit sector and 21.7 percent in the public sector (see Baccalaureate Education Assessment Project, 2002).
- Put yourself in situations, especially professional activities, that allow you to meet new people in the field (see "Contacts and

Networking" later in this chapter). Let everyone know what type of work you want to do, or at least educate them about your interests.

- Put applications on file and make cold calls to agencies to identify openings, and follow up.

- Be creative in your job search. BSW graduates have found jobs through summer work, field work, newspaper ads, professional activities, and tips from practicum staff and classmates; they have filed applications, performed volunteer work, contacted state employment security offices for listings, talked to neighbors, and sent unsolicited résumés and letters. Be persistent, start looking early, be prepared to relocate, and market your degree.

A BSW Graduate's Job Search

A student who would receive her BSW in May had been accepted for graduate school in a distant city where she had no social work connections; her family lived 30 miles away. She needed a full-time job while working on her MSW, so she made plans to conduct a search.

Phase 1. As part of her senior seminar she prepared a résumé. About five weeks before graduation, she requested that her college career center send a letter of reciprocity for services to the university career service center where she had been accepted for graduate school. As a result, the graduate school sent her a job list. She had also done her field placement at a social services organization with locations throughout the United States. She applied to the affiliate in her target location, but nothing came of the connection until midsummer, when the agency called her for an interview.

Phase 2. She moved to her target location in late May and began delivering her résumé to agencies by hand. Because her experience was limited, she thought at least introducing herself in person to the staff

would put her ahead of the competition. After three weeks of crisscrossing the town, she stopped. No one had responded, and staff did not have time to meet her or were unavailable; in any case, gas and parking were too expensive to keep up this effort.

Phase 3. Frustrated by her attempts to apply in person, she launched a mailing campaign, using a list of practicum sites from her future graduate program, the local United Way directory of community services, and classified ads in the newspaper. Over the next three weeks, she sent out 300 letters and résumés in response to ads or as unsolicited inquiries. It was not unusual for her to use a word processor to prepare and send 60 to 75 form letters in one day. She did tailor slightly the letters in response to ads, although she thought she lacked the experience to tailor the letters particularly well. The campaign yielded about a 10 percent response rate in the form of six or seven calls a day. This was encouraging until she discovered through a few interviews that most of the jobs did not pay a living wage.

Phase 4. That's when she began screening jobs over the telephone by saying, "since I know your time is valuable, as is mine, I thought I'd say up front that I will be unable to consider any position that doesn't pay a minimum of $24,000 a year." Employers appreciated her honesty. In the end, her screening process resulted in four opportunities that met her minimum salary requirement.

Phase 5. Two organizations, a circuit attorney's office and a homeless youth shelter, called her back for a second interview. In addition, a school system and a hospital notified her that they were interested in interviewing her again and would be in touch soon to set a time. Because she accepted a job before either contacted her, she told both she had already accepted an offer. She said that she appreciated their time, but believed she had found a position well suited for her. "They seemed happy for me and apologized for not having been able to move faster in the decision-making process," she reported.

Before going on second interviews, however, she met with a contact for advice. That person persuaded her that she was underselling her background, particularly her previous work experience. When she went to the second interviews, she detailed how her earlier work, education, and training fit each position. Before entering the BSW program, she had worked for 10 years as an apartment manager—collecting bills, dealing with evictions, making referrals to social agencies, dealing with situations of domestic violence, and consoling victims of crime and family members confronted with tragedies.

In her undergraduate program, she had completed several papers and projects on homelessness. The homeless youth shelter, which initially interviewed her for a position below her minimum salary requirement, called her back, this time to interview for a program director position that had recently opened. During the first interview the agency staff recognized that she had the skills to assume more responsibility. As it turned out, her experience working with tenants to collect rent matched their need to help youths with budgeting, her experience evicting tenants matched their need for someone who could do the tough job of turning away youths who did not fit the shelter's program, and her academic work on homelessness matched their need for someone who understood the issues. They also were interested in the fact that she was enrolling in a graduate program.

Although they had originally intended to hire someone with an MSW, they offered her the job, and she accepted. At the same time she knew the circuit attorney's office wanted to offer her a position working with victims; however, since their funding was not secure, they could not set a starting date. A week after she was on the job at the shelter, the circuit attorney's office called to offer her the job. They too liked her knowledge of systems and her previous experience in apartment management. Although the position paid more, she would have had to pay for parking and a professional wardrobe, which was not the case at the shelter.

Phase 6. With a second offer in hand, she spoke with the executive director of the shelter, explaining that she had undersold herself in the interview and feared she would resent her decision in the future, particularly because money would be tighter with this job. She said that she already felt invested in her job, however, and did not want to leave. She asked whether the agency could do anything to help her. Persuaded by her arguments, the executive director got approval to increase her salary by $2,500.

Recognizing and articulating what she had to offer was the first key to this graduate's search—her message, in other words. Early on, when she was preparing to move and look for a job, people told her that her work before she received her BSW was irrelevant to her search. She did not, therefore, approach the task of finding a job with confidence. It was not until well into the process that she began to link those earlier skills, as well as her BSW education, specifically to the opportunities she found. She did not rely on interviewers to discover the connections. She interpreted her background in terms of each position. "Initially, I was projecting confidence, pretending it was there. Later, I was sincerely presenting confidence in what I had to offer."

The second key was to identify those organizations that met her interests, and most of those offered only minimum pay. She dared to do something different—she screened for salary information when employers called. Handling this issue in a professional manner saved time for her and the employer.

When she moved to her target city, she went to a couple of chapter meetings of NASW, where she met supportive people in her field. They told her that a salary of $24,000 was appropriate in that community for a new BSW and gave her some job leads and advice. It was during these conversations that she began to think she was underselling her background.

Seeking advice on her search helped her target her message and salary goal. Of course, she could have used this technique initially to narrow the list of organizations she contacted, which would have saved effort, postage, and some frustration. Beginning at phase 3, her 300 applications generated 40 calls, four interviews in her desired salary range, and two offers. Much of the early work delivering résumés and mailing applications could have been eliminated through more research.

Like many job hunters, this BSW graduate found the job search process to be an emotional one. She had left a career paying much more an hour plus benefits, to do social work, which she wanted very much, but early efforts to find a well-paying job failed. Perseverance and advice seeking were essential to the success of her search.

Another Example

A second BSW student graduating in December describes her search as follows:

My heart was set on advocating for children. I started the job search late because I was so overwhelmed with the demands of my senior year. There was a particular organization that I had really wanted to work for. As I was mentioning my dream to a staff person at my college, I found out that she had a connection to the organization. She put me in touch with her friend, who I called early in January. I asked a million questions, which she graciously answered, and then she gave me the names of several people she knew at the organization. Although she didn't know whether they had any jobs, she suggested I send them a cover letter and résumé, making sure to mention her name. I had previously called the organization's job hot-

line, but none of the officially open positions met my qualifications or interests.

So I put together as attractive a package as I could, not even knowing if these connections had or knew of a job opening. In addition to the standard cover letter and résumé, I decided to add a photocopy of an award I had just received and a writing sample, even though I didn't know if one was required. I had learned through my college experience that what gets you ahead is going above and beyond what is expected of you. It's indeed why I am here today, as program assistant in a national advocacy organization, and with only a BSW. A week after I sent in the packets, I got a call from a staff member who set up an interview with me over the telephone. She offered me a temporary internship position (paid) for six months working on a specific grant-funded project. What made all the difference in the world for me for launching my career was my creation of a volunteer student organization while I was in college. This was the key to getting such a good job right out of school. As my internship was nearing completion, I started talking with people again . . . this time after developing a network of relationships with staff in the organization. By the time I decided to stay and postpone graduate school, I had four job offers, none of them published outside of the building.

Job-Search Strategy for MSW Graduates

Think broadly about looking for a job. Use a range of the job sources outlined in this chapter. Experienced social workers and new graduates can find jobs through many sources.

- Develop a presence in your target community; expand your contact network. If you are moving to a new community, get involved in a task force or committee, preferably one that gives you a broad overview of the field in organizations of interest to you. (See "Contacts and Networking" later in this chapter.)
- Look into licensure early. With the multiplicity of licensure and certifications regu-

lations, you may need more than one. One new graduate recommended, "If your state allows it, take the licensure exam ASAP. It will help keep you busy, and refreshing your memory will boost your confidence. It will also enable you to get it out of the way. It may be difficult for you to juggle studying and worrying about the exam with job searching. I think, though, that studying really is part of the job search, as it helps you refine your knowledge and build the confidence that you will need for the search." Note that passing a licensing exam is an asset that others might not have. If you have completed part of the licensing process, indicate that in your letters and on your résumé.

- Volunteer, particularly in communitywide advocacy, planning, and evaluation efforts, to gain visibility for your work. (See "Temporary or Volunteer Work" later in this chapter, and "Visibility" in chapter 7.)
- Bookmark and record Internet addresses for sites you want to check throughout your search—agency sites, job sites, government offices, professional activities, and salary data.
- File applications with select organizations, as the human resources staff often checks internal files when a position opens.
- Consider targeting organizations. You may or may not want to set up a meeting to discuss mutual interests and try to convince a manager that he or she should create a position to capitalize on your skills. However, the process of researching organizations and thinking about how you can sell your skill sets will definitely strengthen your search skills.

An MSW Graduate's Job Search
This is the experience of an MSW student who planned a final field placement overseas from January through March and a May graduation before relocating across the country:

In the preceding September, I began researching organizations in the Sacramento area. I knew I'd be moving to the area for personal reasons. I discovered this organization by doing an Internet search and sending e-mails to people I thought might be able to help me find micro-enterprise programs in the area. It took about five rounds of people responding with, "I don't know, but contact . . ." before I finally got in touch with someone at this small business development group. I set up an informational interview in October and we just seemed to think it was a great fit. They encouraged me to keep in contact and let them know when I returned from a scheduled trip to Nepal. I e-mailed them periodically, even while in Nepal. In April, after I was back in the United States, I went out to Sacramento for a formal interview and fortunately they were still interested in hiring someone. The position, enterprise development associate, was a newly created position.

I think a lot of it was luck—I got in touch with them at the right time. I think they hired me for several reasons. First, I had specific experience with individual development account programs. They had put their IDA program on the "back burner" because they were focusing more on other areas, but I happened to have experience and an interest in IDAs and micro enterprises. Second, they saw how assertive I was in contacting and meeting with them. I sought them out, I flew out there to meet, I showed a lot of interest, and so on. I think organizations don't really want to have to advertise and interview for positions, it's a lot of work. I made it easier for them, and by doing so showed that I was a "self-starter."

A second MSW student with several years of full-time experience was determined to find a supervisory position when she graduated and returned to her home state:

I knew the first job would set the tone for the rest of my career, so my plan was to conduct a long search and be very particular. My purpose was to find a significant experience, something I was interested in, something different that would stand out. I was fortunate to have maintained my relationship with the hospital where I had previously worked and filled in during school breaks. When I returned home, I worked per diem for the hospital, which gave me the flexibility for an extended search. Over a six-month period, I had 35 significant phone conversations to network and screen positions, 22 face-to-face job interviews, and 15 offers. I applied for positions broadly and never sent a cold letter—that is, I always made a phone contact first to screen for a fit in terms of philosophy and background. I finally found a challenging, strong fit as a supervisor in a private children and family services agency.

MSW job hunters offer the following advice:
- Call contacts first and ask whether you can send a résumé (they get so much mail that your material might be overlooked other wise); then send a letter and résumé right away so that they will recognize it when it arrives.
- Focus on your commitment to issues, not to a job function; various roles might fit your commitment.
- Use a name from a referral when contacting a new person, if possible.
- People are very busy, refine your message—when you reach a contact, get the important parts of your message across quickly (for example, that you have an MSW degree, you are bilingual, and you are new to the area and are researching it).
- If you say that you are bilingual, expect to conduct interviews in your second language.
- If the networking process seems to get bogged down, go back to earlier contacts for more advice.
- Make sure your confidence comes across every time you speak.

Another New MSW's Search

This is the job-search story of a May MSW graduate who planned to move across the country to the West Coast, where she was from. During her final spring semester, she juggled job hunting with two courses, a practicum, two part-time jobs, and research on a trip she wanted to take to Central America to refresh her Spanish language skills before starting a new job. To keep focused on her goals, she scheduled four hours a week for researching options for her trip and a job. Her full-time job for two years before graduate school had been in a town of 100,000, where it was easy to get into the action—that is, to see how agency boards operate and observe the politics. This experience gave her a broad view and increased her confidence.

November. She had not planned to start the job-search process until February, but a deadline for the school's career services' mailing to alumni encouraged her to begin earlier. She used community resource and national directories to identify community development organizations, then narrowed the list to those specifically doing employment training. She eliminated some agencies because their focus was on first-time home ownership and low-income housing development. She knew that self-employment training was the new trend and that money from the federal government was targeted toward it.

December. She sent letters to the organizations on her list to request information on their self-employment training taking place in her target city.

Winter break. She followed up with calls to the same organizations and met with an agency focused on housing and employment issues for women. The staff gave her a lot of information and mentioned one agency in particular. She had four contacts (one in person and three over the phone) with different agencies over the break.

January–March. She continued to follow up with more agencies. This included telephone contact with all agencies on her list and with those identified in initial research meetings. This was her introduction: "I am working in a micro enterprise in [city] and will be moving to [city] in the summer. I am beginning to investigate what projects are going on in [city]." Note that she had been working in micro enterprise development through a practicum and a part-time job.

In February, she spoke (a long-distance cold call) with a staff member of one agency, who spoke highly of the agency and recommended she talk with the director. For a couple of weeks she tried unsuccessfully to get in touch with the director for advice.

In late March, she talked with the career services director at her institution about her frustration with telephone tag. As a result, she sent a résumé with a letter stating that she was working in micro-enterprise development and giving the approximate date that she was moving to the city. She said that two contacts (from her earlier follow-up calls), whom she named, recommended the agency and that she would like to know more about the agency. She did not ask for an opportunity to seek advice, or whether they had job openings. A week and a half later, when the student called to follow up on her letter, the director was available on the first try.

The director, who had sent the letter to the agency training coordinator, said she would pass a message to the training coordinator to call the student. The training coordinator called back in 15 minutes and said, "We want to interview you." The student indicated that she would be at a conference in the region in late April. They arranged to interview at the conference.

April. The student met with the staff several times at the conference and later received an offer, which she accepted two days before graduation. (See chapter 5 "Example of an Interview Experience at a Conference" for a detailed description of her interviews.)

From the beginning, this MSW student defined herself as a professional. She treated her internships as professional experience. She marketed herself as a young professional with four years of experience (two years' work before getting her MSW, plus her field experience) and a master's degree. She determined what type of work she wanted first, rather than looking at what was available. She identified organizations, researched their work, and thought about the fit between their functions and her qualifications. Her research gave her leverage. She had done the homework, knew what was going on in the community, and where she could fit in. The research was like doing a needs assessment. She did not look at newspaper ads. She recommended that students initially do more self-assessment.

Job-Search Strategy for Experienced Professional and Other Specialized Searches

The basics of job hunting change little over time—many of the things you did to find a job when you were first starting out will be the same when you have many years of experience. Nevertheless, some elements of your job-search strategy are more important when you are a seasoned professional:

- Assessing your values and honing your message will take more time than before, because you have more work experience to filter, especially if you are moving across fields or functions. You will have more endearing experiences to let go of and synthesize for new audiences, particularly those outside traditional social work arenas.
- If you have focused on your work without building new skill sets or developing your contact network, you may need to spend more time in a preparation phase. (See chapters 1 and 7.)
- Your range of acquaintances, particularly at upper levels and in a variety of organizations, will be a key factor in your search. The reputation you have developed and

the visibility of your work will also affect the pace of your search.

- More than ever before, you will want to research your market and the target organizations that interest you. If you are staying in your field, you know what to look for in organizations. If you want to sell yourself in a new field, function, or industry, you will have considerably more background work to do.

- Take advantage of résumé databases and registries that professional and trade associations offer. They are usually focused on upper-level positions. (See appendix 1.)

- Contact executive search firms if you are looking for management positions. (See "Executive Search Firms" in this chapter.) If you are interested in positions at universities, read "Academic Job Search" in this chapter. If you have not looked for a position for a long time, use your support network. Job hunting can be an exhilarating experience if you have a strong support system.

- Expect potential employers to do a back ground check on you. They will speak with others in the profession and community; they may hire a firm to do this. At this level, expect employers to request supple mental materials, such as a very detailed résumé, samples of publications, a proposal for their project, responses to a list of questions they provide, and possibly psychological testing. For an executive position, such questions might address leadership, program development, accountability, and fund management issues.

Search for a Job in Policy and Research

This is the job-search experience of a doctoral graduate who began searching in the spring, defended her dissertation in late summer, and then moved to Washington, DC, to find a position in policy and research, preferably in health care.

First of all, my first contact here was a person who is "well connected," as they say in this town. That means that she knows lots of people who have authority, power, or whatever you want to call it, and she also knows what is going on in the government. I found this person through her daughter, who was a student in my social policy class and the first person who asked me whether I had considered locating in DC and doing research there. I also had a contact in a consulting firm, and I knew that a former faculty member was in DC. It turned out that both had changed jobs. This was not a problem, because at each place they told me where the people had gone and gave me a telephone number where I could reach them.

My original contact gave me about five names of people to contact; with some of them I could use her name, and with some I could not. All but one of these people had a background in child welfare. One was with the public health service and one led a division on health care research within the organization. These two contacts opened the doors of two different sectors: consulting firms and associations. There are possibilities in the public sector at the federal level—in the executive branch (Department of Health and Human Services) and legislative branch (House and Senate committees); in the private sector, there are associations (Child Welfare League of America, American Hospital Association, for example), consulting firms, and think tanks (Brookings Institution, Urban Institute, for instance). I pursued all but the legislative branch—I never got that far, although I added names from there to a list for cold mailings. The person with the public health service sent me a fax of his contractors, listing contacts' names and telephone numbers, and that is how I got to my job. One of my original contacts also sent me a long list of contractors that I was going to use as a source for blind calls, but I never got around to that, although I did get it on my computer, and I was trying to decide about the best time to send out cold letters.

Then I started networking, making phone calls to the people whose names I had. An amazing number of these people returned my calls. The approach I used on these calls was to call first and say that so-and-so had suggested I talk with them because they would know of openings or of other people I could talk with. After a while, I started asking whether the person had voice mail so I could leave a message—I didn't want secretaries or clerks screening me out. If they did have voice mail, then I left the pitch about being a new PhD. I emphasized that I had heavy methodological training and four-plus years' experience as a research assistant with a longitudinal study. Some people asked me to fax my résumé, although most people had me send my résumé, which they would pass around or keep in an open file. And they really did this. Although I thought that this might be a dodge, several people called me to tell me that so-and-so gave them my résumé; in one case, the person mailed a copy of my résumé to an organization that was looking for a research analyst. Several people explained about the timing of consulting work: The responses to federal RFPs [requests for proposals] generally are completed in the summer and then the contracts are awarded September 30. After the contracts are awarded, the firms know what their staffing needs are. Generally, only really big firms with more than 100 research professionals on staff hire on a regular basis. The smaller contract firms hire based on the contracts they have been awarded.

After my conversation with each person, I sent a thank-you letter with a copy of my résumé. The résumé (no one ever called it a "vita") would have been better as one page, but I couldn't get it edited down to that point. Some firms wanted a writing sample as well as the résumé, but I did not have one that I thought was appropriate—short (not more than 12 to 15 pages), sole authorship, and empirically based. I would recommend that people looking for research positions or other positions for which writing is important have something like this ready to send to those who ask for writing samples.

I also tried sending the résumé with an introductory letter saying so-and-so suggested that I talk with them and telling them that I would follow up in a week. I only did this with a few people, and it was fairly successful as far as I could tell. Actually, the success ratio for this type of job search is probably much higher than for the want-ad route. I did not hear from one firm to which I responded as a result of a want ad, other than the form letter sent out to acknowledge receipt of the résumé.

Most of the people I contacted were in the long-term health care area. I was just starting to get names from the maternal and child care segment of the market when I stopped searching. One thing that was apparent early on is that there are segments within segments, based on specialty. It appears to be pretty easy to get slotted into one particular area, and it is not clear to me how easy it is to move from one area of expertise to another.

There is no doubt that being in DC made a big difference in the search. It is so hard to do a search long distance, and it's expensive, too. Of course, it is scary to do it the other way—just pick up and go. The perfect solution would be to have someone to stay with while looking for a job, but I don't know too many people who welcome houseguests for months and months. In DC, people were astonishing in their willingness to refer me to people. A number of people went through their Rolodexes while we were on the telephone, giving me names and numbers and letting me use their names as door openers. I cannot say that it will be that way everywhere, and I know that it is not that way in all of academia. People here do not use their titles, do not appear to be into status; they are very open and giving of their time. I would not expect that everywhere. A lot of people work temporary assignments while looking for a job. It is tough to make all the telephone calls that way, but at least it puts some food on the table. As far as I can figure out, I spoke with approximately 100 people here, both before moving and after I relocated. It's hard for me to figure out how many names I have in addition. Most people did return my calls, even though some of this work was done in August, when many in DC take a vacation. My records do not indicate when I

Identifying Jobs and Pursuing Leads

made the first telephone call, but I remember I talked to [name of firm whose offer she accepted] at the end of April for the first time and faxed my résumé the next day.

The first interview with the firm was at the end of May. The second interview was at the end of July. I am convinced that the assigning [awarding] of contracts along with the September 30 timing has a lot to do with the quickness of getting a job.

An International Job Search

One MSW graduate, a program officer for an international organization, is working in Eastern Europe to strengthen a network of local non-government organizations (NGOs). He helps determine which projects his organization will fund, conducts outreach efforts, assists NGOs with organizational development and fundraising, plans and coordinates seminars and workshops led by outside experts, and monitors sub-grantee organizations, among other responsibilities. Earlier, he had been a volunteer with an NGO in a Central American country, a volunteer intern on a mental health team for an international organization working with refugees in Central America, and a volunteer with a second refugee service in Latin America. Contacts made through his work on the mental health team project led him to his current job.

In my opinion, and because of my personal experiences, I would have to say that it is difficult to find paid international work in the social work field. People with skills in financial management, construction, medicine, public health, agriculture, and engineering probably have a much easier time finding employment abroad. So I suggest that first-time international job seekers really review their abilities and consider what other skills they will need to become marketable. Some valuable skills are foreign language ability (especially Spanish, Portuguese, French, or Russian), project management, and other skills that are not readily available in the country where you're thinking about working.

Like any job search, connections and personal contacts are crucial for success. Try to get to know international NGOs and subscribe to publications that list job opportunities. A lot of this information is available on the Internet. Volunteering abroad is also a good way to get some work experience that will eventually help in locating a paid position. Apart from this practical advice, luck is a big factor in locating a job.

I hope this is helpful. It's really tough entering this field, but for me it was worth the effort.

A Search after Stepping Out of Social Work

If you are re-entering the social work market after stopping, for example, to raise children, care for parents, or a career in another field, you can apply many of the same job-search strategies noted in this chapter. You will need to spend more time organizing your thoughts about your skills, knowledge, recent experiences, and objectives. In addition to the exercises in chapter 1, think about how your recent experiences contribute to what you want to do now. The many fields of social work continue to change, so you will need to update your understanding about the field. Chapter 2 and appendix 4 should help you with this task. Rebuilding your contact network in the field and seeking volunteer opportunities to demonstrate your skills will be especially important.

Academic Job Search

The job market for social workers with doctoral degrees who are seeking academic positions is more competitive than it has been for several years. If you are in the academic job market, you are more likely than social workers looking for other types of work to find positions advertised, partly because it is a candidate's market and universities typically seek to recruit the best from a diverse pool of candidates. Although some academic programs hire master's-level faculty for teaching positions, the trend is toward all full-time faculty having doctorate degrees. Some characteristics of your search are listed.

- Chances are that your current environment is academic. This makes your research phase less complicated, at least initially. You have ready access to people and information about potential institutions.
- Background information on your potential employers is easy to obtain. Sources include Internet Web sites, including faculty profiles; reference material such as *Peterson's* guides; admission bulletins and brochures; alumni newsletters; and annual reports.
- You have the distinct advantage of being able to review faculty publications and attend faculty presentations at conferences.
- Be familiar with the accreditation standards of the Council on Social Work Education. Broaden your knowledge of academic programs, and tailor your message on teaching interests to the course content required of all schools.
- The academic world of social work is a close-knit one. If you are a doctoral student, seek the advice of your adviser and other faculty with whom you have worked. Your adviser and committee will be significant players in your search.
- Like all job hunters, research your market to identify those schools whose faculty and programs best match your teaching and research interests and whose cultures offer the best working environment for you. This process mirrors the one you followed in selecting a doctoral program.
- If you are a student, you will be competing for tenure-track positions at institutions whose academic programs are of similar quality or standing to your doctoral program. It is unlikely that you will compete effectively for positions in higher-tier schools.
- You will go through an extensive interview process, usually lasting more than a day. This will include a presentation, usually on your dissertation. (See chapter 5.)

- Your written and verbal communications must reflect the theme of your work and your ability and promise to produce scholarly work.
- If you are a doctoral student, your search is likely to begin 1½ to 2 years ahead of your projected graduation date. This is largely because of the academic calendar, the recruiting schedule of selection committees, the timing of conferences, and the competition for qualified candidates.
- In addition to your teaching, research, and practice experience, your products and products in process will be critical elements of your search. If you are a doctoral student, you may have a single-authored publication and some coauthored publications before graduation and other papers under review. Ideally, you will also make a conference presentation during the year that you are actively searching—this provides good visibility. Plan ahead: At least two years before your graduation, make a list of conference submission deadlines.
- In social work education, there are two focal conferences—the Annual Program Meeting of the Council on Social Work Education (CSWE) and the annual conference of the Society for Social Work Research (SSWR)—where school search committees typically conduct screening interviews. Both candidates and search committee members attend one another's presentations, and schools invite candidates to attend their evening receptions for an informal round of mutual scrutinizing. When you attend these meetings for the purpose of job hunting, you should be as ahead in your dissertation as possible.
- Participate in the CSWE Teachers Registry and Information Service or the SSWR Teachers and Employers Registry, which provide candidates with information on openings and school search committees with information on candi-

dates. (See the CSWE and SSWR entries in appendix 1.) Also, note that the *NASW News* and the *Chronicle of Higher Education* are widely used to post openings as well.

- In addition to the criteria you used when you were considering doctoral programs, inquire about the mission of the program; structure of the curriculum, including field education; expectations for teaching loads, committees, and community work; tenure process and timeline; faculty roles in field education, advising, admissions, and student services; relationship of the school to the community, including government units; the school's resources and track record regarding grant applications; and demographic composition of the faculty, including proportion of those tenured.
- Expect your expenses for travel to interviews to be covered by the institutions, but always confirm this.

An Example of Defining an Academic Search

One doctoral candidate initially followed through on all the contacts offered by her dissertation chair. Two recommended contacts resulted in job offers, which she turned down. Although the positions were at strong schools offering promising opportunities, she realized that her goal for a position was different from her chair's idea of an excellent tenure track opportunity. Although many people in her department questioned her decisions, she began to define and pursue her own goal. This process, in part, meant separating her work from her mentor's work—distinguishing her work. It also raised questions: How could she create a demand for her work? How could she further her work? Seeing her work in a broader context than the deep specialized arena of her mentor, she began identifying with scholars contributing to that broad context. This enabled her to identify institutions where her research agenda would not only fit, but also flourish.

A Detailed Example of an Academic Search

One doctoral candidate took a research position that would become a postdoctoral appointment after she defended her dissertation in December and would last until midsummer. This enabled her to postpone the search and concentrate on her dissertation. She began the search immediately after defending the dissertation. This timing gave her the advantage of giving a job talk on a finished piece rather than a work in progress, publishing two coauthored articles, and making presentations at several conferences. Few people, however, have the option of postponing a search until after the defense. She started by identifying a list of institutions that met her interests. Her sources were the *GADE Guide* (from the Group for the Advancement of Doctoral Education), which lists doctoral programs in social work, and recent articles that ranked social work academic programs, although she did not look specifically at the ranking. She also looked at announcements listed by her department, in the *NASW News*, and through the CSWE registry. (Note that the SSWR annual meeting is an equally popular site where schools identify and interview candidates. SSWR compiles a book of candidate profiles, which faculty search committees use to identify possible candidates.) She did not choose to have her information sent to institutions through the CSWE registry (although this is an important search tool for many, she thought it would complicate the process too much for her). To create the list, she set some geographic limits and decided that she wanted to work at a school with a doctoral program.

Once she had identified the institutions that best matched her interests, about 20 to 25 of them, she sent packets to each in December and January. In retrospect, this was too many schools—10 to 12 would have been adequate with her credentials, given the strong market. The packets consisted of a letter, which detailed her practice experience between the MSW and PhD degrees, her research agenda, a vita, copies of her two published articles, and a reference list.

Most schools asked for three to five references, so she listed five on the reference list. Some schools were also very interested in teaching evaluations. Before the packets went in the mail, she received a couple of calls from schools, one of which had gotten her name from a fellow doctoral student who knew faculty at that institution.

Before the Annual Program Meeting of CSWE that February, she exchanged several calls with institutions interested in setting up interviews at the conference. Over the course of two days at the conference, she had 13 interviews. This would have been a wild schedule for any candidate—she could have been more selective. After the conference, she narrowed her list of potential institutions. This entailed canceling some site visits, which had been offered during the initial interviews.

She visited nine institutions. The first visit was within two weeks of the CSWE meeting. This travel schedule was a logistical challenge that she would not recommend. Three to five site visits would have been adequate. By the week after her first site visit, she had received her first offer.

The site interviews typically consisted of dinner with faculty shortly after arriving, and then a series of interviews the next day and a presentation of her colloquium (job talk). The colloquium was scheduled to run between 45 minutes and 1 hours. Her typical colloquium followed this outline:

1. She described the steps that led her to these research questions, the theoretical and practice foundation for the study.
2. She presented the study, including two or three highlights or key findings.
3. She discussed the practice and policy implications—for this, she made it a point to talk in practice and policy terms.
4. She responded to questions from faculty on the study and its implications.

She found it helpful to summarize her points on PowerPoint (have overhead transparencies for backup); she summarized five points, and recommends not using more than seven points. On one occasion she was asked to tailor the talk to the institution, and she therefore focused about 10 minutes of her presentation on its interests. She thought specifically about how to address the needs of all faculty members with whom she met. That entailed speaking in broader or general terms with those who were not statisticians and using research terms with the quantitative/qualitative research faculty.

Individual and group interview questions during the visits covered the following areas:

- What could she teach and what had she taught. The faculty's teaching needs were of particular concern for next year.
- How did she handle various situations in class—the overly verbal student and the nonparticipant, confrontations with students, and the need to value diversity?
- Beyond the details of her research experience, what impact did she want to have on social work education and the field in five to 10 years and what expertise did she want to develop?
- Who did she work with on research projects and who was on her committee?

The timing of appointment offers was not ideal. Her first offer came between the first and second site visits and six weeks before the last interview. She decided to set her own deadline for a decision. She told the faculty from the institution making the first offer that the school was high on her list, which it was. In the end, she had five offers. She was fortunate that the school making the first offer was willing to wait until she had completed her interviews. Many institutions are not this flexible. She accepted this first offer. Her acceptance of the offer was based on the following factors:

- The institution had a doctoral program, and it appeared that she would be able to begin working with doctoral students fairly soon.

- She would be bringing a contribution to the faculty, both in terms of her substantive areas and her methodological interests.
- She would be able to teach in a couple of areas, namely, policy and administration.

This institution handled the selection process efficiently, and it effectively followed through. During the visit, the school arranged for a realtor to drive her around the community just to become acquainted with it, not to look for houses. Every week a different faculty member called to discuss a project or talk about textbooks she had used. They also sent the local newspaper. The school made an offer quickly after the site visit.

Beyond these positive aspects of the interview process, there were additional positive aspects:
- faculty was warm and open
- cost of living was reasonable
- geographic location was fine for her and her family.

If the market is good for applicants, you can be more selective in the number and types of institutions to which you apply. However, you need to be realistic about your chances of being hired by particular schools. You might select five that would be your top choices and five that would be satisfactory. Today, search committees at top-ranked schools look for doctoral students in the job market to have a first-authored article and at least a few coauthored publications.

The job searcher described above advises that it is a good idea to have a research project in process that is relatively pressing—in the analysis stage or with a publication deadline—so that your research agenda can continue to be a priority through your adjustment period on the job. Otherwise, your time might be consumed with course preparation, committee work, and the development of new relationships. Certainly that schedule of activities is important, but it also means a cold start for your research agenda.

Do not underestimate the time and energy necessary to keep a successful search organized.

Although you can put sections entitled "under review" and "works in progress" in your vita, you must have publications and preferably one sole authorship to be considered at leading schools.

Keep your lists of presentations and publications in balance. If you have many presentations that have not turned into publications, then simplify your list of presentations. If you do not have computerized reports, summarize comments from your teaching evaluations. Finally, do not wear yourself out by traveling with too much luggage: Pack light and carry everything on board if you can, but be sure to take extra copies of your vita and syllabi for the courses you have taught.

Sources of Jobs

"It's who you know" is a common refrain among job hunters. Although a contact network is a great asset to any job search, it is not the only way to find a job. Your strategy should include a number of sources, some of which are given in the following sections. Which resources you use depend on the sort of job you are seeking, your qualifications, and your research within the particular market.

Applications

Individual supervisors and human resources offices usually keep résumés and application forms on file for future reference. Particularly if you are applying to large institutions such as hospitals and school systems, send a résumé and letter to the director of social services and complete an application form for the human resources office (or personnel or employment office). For school systems, you will send a résumé to the student support services or pupil personnel services offices and an application to the personnel offices. This way, regardless of where the hiring process begins, you will have material on file. You may encounter a few organizations that charge applicants a fee. In that case, you may want to wait until you know for sure that an opening exists. Some human resources offices will mail you an application.

When filling out an application, use descriptive, detailed language, including social work terminology, to explain how your experience is directly related to the job you are seeking. For example, if you are a psychiatric social worker you will want to use DSM (*Diagnostic and Statistical Manual of Mental Disorders*, published by the American Psychiatric Association) terminology. If you do not have experience that is directly related to the position, then describe what you have learned and accomplished as it applies to the job. Often there is no space on application forms specifically for practicum or volunteer experience. Describe these positions like jobs in the work experience section. Include the words "intern" and "volunteer" in your title (for example, medical social work intern, research assistant intern, or volunteer fundraiser); in the salary box state "unpaid."

Applying in Person

The advantages of dropping off résumés are to know that your material arrived, to see the location and at least the external physical environment, and possibly to be able to talk with someone. Disadvantages are the amount of time and gas spent, perhaps not having all the information you need to complete the application, and the real possibility that the person making the hiring decision is too busy to see you. Going directly to an organization, particularly a large employer, may make sense if you are looking for an entry-level position or if using the mail would not ensure that your letter and résumé arrived on time; however, it is not appropriate for advanced positions. Generally speaking, you can use your time more efficiently. If you are going to personnel offices to complete applications, one student recommends taking a copy of a completed application with you so that you do not have to rely on your memory for details.

An exception is looking for positions on Capitol Hill. It is quite common for people looking for positions in congressional offices and on congressional committees to carry résumés by hand to offices.

Associations

Professional associations and national advocacy organizations provide several avenues for learning about jobs. Professional associations, such as NASW, are made up of individual members. Membership services may include a Web site listing state chapter contacts and job and résumé databases; they may also offer job fairs at conferences. If you are a student, be sure to inquire about student membership rates and any discount on registration for students who volunteer at conferences.

National advocacy organizations, also called trade associations, usually are made up of institutional members, although they may have individual members as well. The Child Welfare League of America is an example of a national advocacy organization. As a service to their member institutions, such organizations may offer a job database on a Web site; maintain a résumé database; and consult with organizations on their human resources needs, particularly at the executive level. Some national advocacy organizations also sell a directory of their member agencies. (See appendixes 1 and 8 for information on career services offered by specific associations.)

In addition to offering career or personnel services, associations provide a way to meet colleagues with interests similar to your own. Get involved in a committee or group concerned with your interests. This is the best way to develop long-term relationships and probably the most comfortable way of meeting people. Ask officers and committee chairs how to join committees.

Attend association conferences. (See appendix 1 for associations' meeting dates.) Local, state, and regional conferences are less expensive than national meetings and offer better opportunities to meet contacts in your target location. You usually will not find job fairs at these meetings, but you can find opportunities to expand your network. Contact the society's national office or state chapter for information. Details on hunting at job fairs are explained later in this section.

Colleges

Although many schools of social work, college career centers, and academic departments post job openings on their Web sites or send them to students via e-mail, some do post job openings on bulletin boards, which you can see by simply visiting the school. Although many institutions keep jobs in nonpublic areas of Web sites, some do not restrict access to the public.

Some social work programs offer job referral services, job listings, career planning and job-search workshops, a collection of community service and other directories, an alumni network directory, job or career fairs, and individual career counseling for students and alumni (Boston University, 1996). If you are a student, participate in programs offered by your college career services office early in your academic program, and definitely start working with the staff early in your last year. If you are part of a student social work organization or alumni association, talk with members about cosponsoring career information and job-search programs or services with your school and career center. If you are a graduate, inquire about alumni services.

Contacts and Networking

Contacts are considered a cornerstone of any job search but are particularly important for social workers seeking advanced positions, moving across fields or functions, or looking for work outside traditional social work settings and roles. You have already identified a list of people you know and others who are knowledgeable about issues and organizations related to your interests. (See chapter 2.) You have also sought advice from a few of these individuals. At this point, you want to let everyone on your contact list know that you are starting your search. When you contact people you know, briefly explain what types of positions interest you and ask whether they know of possible openings. In some cases you will want to give them a résumé. Selectively, call or follow up with a brief letter every three or four weeks to remind people that you are still looking, to inform them of any changes in your plans, and to see whether they have any additional suggestions. (For guidelines on contacting individuals, see chapter 2.)

Ask the people on your contact list for suggestions about whom else you should contact. In addition, begin thinking about functions you can attend and groups you can get involved with to meet new people.

International, national, regional, state, and local conferences for professional associations and collaboration groups, or special events sponsored by local task forces, can be productive meeting places. Ask your contacts about upcoming meetings. When you participate, make a conscious effort to meet people, including speakers, before and after workshops and while visiting conference exhibits, sitting at luncheons, attending receptions, and standing in line. You are more likely to make these efforts when your friends do not accompany you, so sit with people with you do not know when you attend a luncheon. If you are new to an association, attend any orientation sessions, receptions for new members, or training workshops specifically for beginners. Newcomers like you will be interested in meeting other new people. For more tips review *The Networking Survival Guide* (Darling, 2003).

Making the effort to get involved in committees can have added benefits as well. For example, a BSW graduate who was serving as a student representative on the school's self-study committee met some social work representatives from the community. When she saw a classified ad placed by an agency at which two committee members worked, she applied and mentioned her application to the representatives. As it turned out, both committee members were on the interview team for the position. The student had made a good impression in committee meetings; she received an interview and got the job.

Create an Organization

Through your research, you may have identified a service need that you can provide and thus create your own job. You might establish your own for-profit consulting or contractual business or a not-for-profit entity. You will have to study the environment carefully, create a business plan, have your own consultants in place, and probably begin on a part-time basis. If you want to consider this approach to creating a job, take a look at *Zen and the Art of Making a Living* (Boldt, 2000) and *The Practical Dreamer's Handbook* (Edwards, 2001). Books such as *The Not-for-Profit Handbook* (Grobman, 1999) will help you tackle the nitty-gritty of starting a new not-for-profit entity. Among helpful Web sites are http://www.sba.gov/starting and http://fdncenter.org/learn/faqs/starting_not-forprofit.html.

Current Organization

The work you do—your accomplishments on the job or in fieldwork—may result in an invitation to apply for a job or in a promotion. As you assess the potential of your current work setting for new opportunities, it may be helpful to talk with someone who has a broad or different perspective on your organization. Besides considering whether there is an opportunity for a promotion or full-time employment, is there a possibility for a transfer or for an interim position that could lead to something permanent? Look carefully at the needs and problems of your current employer. Could you propose the creation of a new position to address their problems? Could you propose a project, perhaps an entrepreneurial effort or collaborative project, with the potential for creating a job? Could you write a grant that creates a position to address a particular need?

Executive Search Firms

Like corporations, some public, not-for-profit, and for-profit health and social services contract with executive search firms to hunt nationwide for candidates for positions such as chief executive officer or chief operating officer, and occasionally for vice-presidential or middle-management positions. Large not-for-profit boards often hire search firms to locate executive directors, and large health care centers have used them to identify managers for psychiatric units. Search firms look for potential candidates by asking for suggestions from people in the field (for example, executive directors of similar agencies and professional and trade associations, as well as university deans). Your visibility and reputation could lead a colleague to suggest your name when an executive recruiter calls.

There are two types of executive search firms: retained and contingency. Retained firms have ongoing contracts with companies to consult on long-term and immediate hiring issues for only top-level positions. In contrast, contingency firm business depends on filling positions for employers as they occur. In addition to filling positions at the uppermost levels, some contingency firms locate candidates for middle-management positions. Note that executive search firms work for the employer. They are not in the business of locating jobs for individuals.

Although search firm business originates with employers and recruiters aggressively look for top-quality candidates, it is not unheard of for individual job hunters to initiate contact with executive search firms. To identify firms that have worked with health and social services organizations, do an Internet search or check your library reference desk for *The Directory of Executive Recruiters* (Fitzwilliam, 2002). You will find pertinent organizations listed by industry, function, and geographic region. If you choose to explore this source, check with the local Better Business Bureau and your contacts to be sure you are working with a reputable firm. When working with search firms, expect all fees to be covered by the hiring organization.

Government Registers

Regulations usually require public agencies at the local and state levels to use government registers to fill positions. A register is a list of applicants whom departments can consider for employment. This personnel practice parallels the one used by not-for-profit and for-profit agencies, whereby résumés or applications are kept on file for consideration for future openings. However, some government units allow people to register at any time, whereas others accept registrations only when there are openings. The formal registration process can be an effective tool for identifying openings, but networking among your contacts to learn about government openings is equally, if not more, important. When inquiring about public agency jobs, be sure to ask whether you need to live within that jurisdiction once hired, and find out how difficult it is to be considered for positions if you are not already living there.

In many states students can register with the state merit or civil service system before graduation; go to the state's Web site or state personnel office for applications. To learn about opportunities with state agencies, go online or call the state personnel office and the agencies themselves, which are listed in the telephone book. Look at the state's Web site or manual to learn about state departments and services; any public library will have a copy of its own state manual and possibly other government directories.

Visit the federal government's Office of Personnel Management Web page for openings at http://www.usajobs.opm.gov. Federal offices are no longer required to use the laborious SF-171 application form but instead can accept résumés. Expect to write knowledge, skills, and abilities (KSA) statements as part of your application. You will find helpful hints on writing KSAs at http://wflc.od.nih.gov/careers/ksa. Use the Internet and the *U.S. Government Manual* (Office of the Federal Register, 2003–2004), an annual you will find in most public libraries, and other publications to learn about federal government agencies.

Job Fairs

Associations, colleges, and some companies sponsor job fairs. Associations, such as the Council of Jewish Federations or the American Public Health Association, routinely or occasionally hold job or recruiting events at their conferences (see appendix 1). College consortia, individual colleges, and some schools of social work organize job fairs for their students. Sometimes a job fair open to the public is announced in the local newspaper. These public events, which may involve a fee, are usually for the technical, business, and health care fields.

Weighing the Cost of Travel

Job fairs held in conjunction with national conferences can be a good source of leads, particularly for social workers willing to relocate, but they can be expensive. Before you spend a lot of money to attend a national job fair, ask enough questions of the conference planners to know whether the trip is worth the cost. If a job fair is your sole purpose for attending the conference, get specifics ahead of time, such as the following:

- What is the structure of the event?
- Is it an exhibit format, in which you walk around introducing yourself?
- Do you submit résumés in response to jobs listed in a booklet you receive at the event, and then wait to hear from employers who want to interview you?
- Are on-site interviews arranged ahead of the event, so that you can judge whether the trip might be cost-effective?
- How many employers are expected to participate?
- What types of employers participate?
- What types of positions do employers list? Can you see the list in advance?
- Where are the employers located? Are most of these in the community near the conference site?

Surviving a Job Fair

People who have participated in job interviews at conferences can tell you that these are stressful experiences. When many job hunters are in a confined space waiting for an interview or a message from an employer, you can feel the tension. Here is some advice for increasing the benefits and reducing the stress.

- Approach the fair with a realistic attitude; do not count on it as your primary source of job opportunities but as one of several.
- Plan ahead—research the organizations and try to arrange interviews in advance.
- Take extra résumés with you, paper for writing quick notes, and paperclips.
- Do not spend all of your time around the job fair; go to the sessions, participate in other conference activities, go to your room for a nap, have coffee breaks with friends or read a good book, and leave the conference hall for meals and walks.
- Do not schedule too many interviews or back-to-back interviews—you'll wear yourself out.
- Pace yourself—it takes a lot of energy to be "on" all day.
- Get advice from others who have been through the process.

Job Hotlines

Although posting jobs online is common for many employers and associations, some employers still offer job information hotlines. You can check the telephone book or call organizations to see if this service is offered.

Listservs

If you are not already in regular communication with professionals in your field of interest, look for avenues to do this. Listservs, which are online discussion groups, are a good way to stay current on trends and to find some job announcements. You can go to the following location online for a directory: http://www.sc.edu/swan/listserv.html.

Mailing Campaign

Sending unsolicited letters with résumés can be effective in locating a job, if done selectively. Health and social services organizations often keep résumés on file and review these applications before advertising a job opening. Writing to employers who do not appear to have an opening can be productive for both local and long-distance job hunters, as part of an overall plan for direct practice positions, particularly at the entry level.

As a warning though, quality is more important than quantity. Do not send standardized letters with résumés to 100 employers. You will be wasting time, money, and paper. Review the list of employers you created. (See chapter 2.) Group them into three categories: your first, second, and third choices. Then select three to five organizations and write specific letters to each. (See appendix 5, sample 2.) Often letters of inquiry go unanswered simply because employers do not have the time to respond. However, if you follow up with a telephone call and contact the employer periodically, you may be remembered when a job that matches your qualifications opens up.

Newsletters

Several professional societies, publishers, colleges, and not-for-profit groups list job openings in newsletters and journals. The *NASW News* is an example. (See appendix 8 for a list of subscription newsletters.) Many groups offer an online version; students may find these available in their career centers. You may even find that one of your contacts will share recent issues with you. If you are thinking of subscribing, review publications before you purchase them.

Newspapers

Despite what you hear about the "hidden job market"—the view that only a small percentage of the available jobs are advertised—social services organizations are frequent users of classified advertising. BSW and MSW graduates find jobs through local newspapers, often online. Besides scanning the job announcements, read feature articles, news articles, announcements of grants, and the society column for information on changes taking place in the community and for names for your contact network.

For distant locations, first check the Internet for newspaper Web pages (see "Online Job Sources" in this chapter). Remember that out-of-town newspaper subscriptions will arrive several days later in the mail. Your alternative is to visit the library or look for a newsstand in your local community that has papers shipped to them overnight so you can purchase the Sunday editions on Mondays.

Social workers will find possible jobs under many classified headings or keyword searches, such as those in exhibit 4.1. (See also the job titles in appendix 4.)

Online Job Sources

Services include job listings, résumé databases, career information, and organization information. Services appropriate for social workers, particularly those in direct practice, are extensive, but can require effort to locate online. To get a sense of general online resources, take a look at the *Riley Guide* at http://www.riley guide.com (Dikel, 1994–2004). (Also see appendix 8.)

Though the Internet may seem expedient, do not expect the hiring process to be so. One person identified a job online in a distant city in February, but it took until May to receive an offer.

Résumé Posting Services

Some not-for-profit associations and for-profit companies offer a résumé posting service or résumé databank or candidate registry, which they make available to employers seeking candidates for jobs. Today most of these services are online. You can submit your résumé, which goes into a computerized database or on a registration list. You may or may not be charged a fee for participating. Among groups offering these services are NASW, Everett Jewish Job Finder, Employee Assistance Professionals Association, and CSWE. (See appendixes 1 and 8 for their Web addresses.)

Most online résumé databases emphasize high-volume technical and business fields. If you are looking for opportunities in business, you might explore these services. Ask how many requests come in for your interest area and talk with your network to find out whether anyone has heard of the service. Like all other aspects of your communications, you will want to carefully

---

EXHIBIT 4.1

Sample Job Classifications in Newspapers

- administration
- alcoholism
- analyst
- association
- BSW
- case management
- case manager
- clinical social worker
- community development
- community organizing
- coordinator

- counselor
- development
- director
- economic development
- education
- employment
- executive director
- fundraising
- health care
- international
- job development
- management

- medical social work
- mental health
- MSW
- not-for-profit
- planning
- projects
- research
- social services
- social work
- substance abuse
- training

tailor your résumé to the audience using that particular database. Remember that employers will use key words to search résumés, which means that you will want to use their language. Also note that you will need to prepare your résumé differently, depending on whether it will be scanned or entered online. Visit the online *Riley Guide* at http://www.rileyguide.com/eresume.html.

Telephone Calls

Although many people are uncomfortable making cold calls to agencies to inquire about openings, such calls do generate job leads especially at the entry level. If possible, ask for a program director, clinical director, medical social work director, or other title pertinent to the kind of organization you are calling. When talking with people at agencies, focus on networking. Find out whether they have openings and ask whether they know of openings at other agencies. When you need a job quickly, there is nothing faster than making calls to agencies and to people on your contact list.

Remember that, as in any phase of your search, you are making an impression. Be prepared for a brief, to-the-point conversation, and at the same time be ready to discuss your interests, experience, and abilities (see chapter 1). If there is an opening, this call could serve as a screening interview (see chapter 5).

Temporary or Volunteer Work

Working on temporary, contract, pro ata (or whenever necessary), postdegree internship, and volunteer jobs are good ways to get a foot in the door. If an organization that really interests you does not have a permanent opening and your situation is flexible, inquire about these short-term options. It is not uncommon for people to use this method in seeking work with national advocacy groups, legislators in Washington, DC, or international organizations. For instance, a BSW graduate, while working on a postdegree internship at a not-for-profit organ-

ization in Washington, met a volunteer who worked in the federal government. His contact told him about an opportunity for a caseworker handling correspondence at the White House. He got the position, and although it was not exactly what he wanted to do, it was a great position for learning about the executive branch, policy, and politics.

One of the great advantages social workers have is the ability to demonstrate their skills while volunteering. When you are between jobs, volunteer if you have the time and can make the commitment. Besides making a contribution, you will feel connected to the community, have a chance to exercise your skills, vary your daily routine of job hunting, and possibly learn about potential employers simply by being in that environment. When volunteering, take on extra responsibility, exercise good judgment, and get to know as much about the agency and the community as you can.

Pursuing Leads

When you hear about a potential job that you want to pursue, quickly gather some basic information, research the organization, and, if required, submit an application.

Screen Jobs

Because salaries and responsibilities vary greatly among social work employers, social workers often screen positions by first calling employers. Not everyone is comfortable using this technique, but for many it saves time. Talking with the person who will make the hiring decision is best; however, keep in mind that administrative assistants can also be helpful. When you call for information, be prepared to describe your qualifications briefly. Although you initiate the call, treat the conversation as a screening review. (See chapter 5.) Make the best possible impression on anyone you speak with at the agency. Through this conversation you will want to

- determine whether you are interested
- determine whether there is a possible match between you and the job
- request an interview if you are interested
- ask for a job description
- explore other potential options if the position is not of interest
- make a positive impression, regardless of the situation.

Gather basic information. If you want to pursue this job, find out the

- application deadline
- job description
- qualifications for the position
- contact's name, title, and telephone and fax numbers
- hiring timetable and whether there is an internal candidate.

The hiring timetable will tell you when they plan to interview candidates, if and when they will have second interviews, and when they will make their final decision.

Skip the Cover Letter and Go Directly to the Interview

Sometimes, if you are able to speak with the person doing the interviewing, you can set up an interview when you make that exploratory screening call. It will depend on how well your qualifications fit the employer's expectations, how effectively you present your qualifications over the telephone, and how soon the employer wants to fill the position. Although you may be able to bypass sending a letter with the résumé, take a résumé with you.

Explore options if the job does not fit your interests. If you discover the position is not what you are looking for, you can

- find out whether the position's responsibilities can be expanded
- ask to be considered for future possibilities related to your interests, and follow up with a letter and résumé
- ask for advice on seeking a more appropriate position in the field or community.

Should you apply even if you do not meet all of the qualifications? Yes, when the agency and type of work is of great interest to you and you meet most of the qualifications, go ahead and apply. In your letter state your interest in the organization and indicate that you would like to be considered in the future for positions appropriate for your background. It is possible that the current opening will be filled by a present employee, which may leave another position open that is appropriate for you.

Should you apply even if you are not available now? Yes. It can take an employer two months to fill a position, particularly during the summer and around the holidays, when many staff members take vacations. Indicate in your letter when you will be available, and state that if your availability and their timetable do not coincide, you would like to be considered for future openings. If you can start earlier on a part-time basis, say so in your letter. However, if it will be six months before you are available, file the information and contact the employer at a later date.

Research the Organization

Research the organization before applying by looking at the agency's Web site, talking with your contacts, requesting a brochure or annual report, and possibly picking up brochures at the site. When possible speak with clients, constituents, and colleagues associated with the organization. This information will enable you to tailor your letter and telephone conversations.

Also, look for Web sites and other background information on the Internet or try locating newspaper and magazine articles about the organization at the public library. This is especially important if you are applying for a position with a large or well-known employer (for example, United Way, American Red Cross, or a state child welfare departments). If your local or campus library has LexisNexis, an online information service, use it to locate articles. Even though you may not find articles written about the specific organizational unit, chapter, or site you want to research, you will get some ideas about the accomplishments and issues facing similar units; the organization as a whole; or a parent company, in the case of a for-profit organization.

Unfortunately, ideal circumstances that allow plenty of time to research the organization are often out of reach. You could meet someone today who tells you about an opening with an application deadline of tomorrow. You will be lucky if he or she knows the correct spelling of the contact person's name and the address. If possible, call the organization, confirm the fact that there is an opening, and ask for details.

When time is short, fax a résumé to the employer or send a letter and résumé through e-mail or deliver a letter and résumé in person. Include a formal letter with the fax. Call the organization to make sure the fax or e-mail was received. Also send a hard copy by mail.

Cover Letters

Sometimes an exploratory call to an employer will result in an immediate job interview. In most cases, however, you will send a letter and résumé as a formal application. Each cover letter must be written specifically to the employer, using the person's name and addressing the organization's interests.

As a social worker, you have three advantages in writing cover letters. First, you can express and demonstrate a commitment to your work that sets you apart from applicants educated in other disciplines. Second, your social work education encompasses both micro-level and macro-level knowledge, giving you a broad understanding of systems and the issues facing organizations. You can bring knowledge of services delivery to a macro-level organization or macro-level function and you can bring knowledge of policy and funding to direct services. Third, if you are a BSW or MSW student, you are likely to have more hours of specific, well-monitored training in the field and greater knowledge on multicultural issues than students with other backgrounds.

Plan a Strategy for Your Letter

A résumé is a summary of what you have to offer; a cover letter is a very selective statement interpreting your experience for a specific employer. You can prepare a few stock paragraphs for a cover letter, which can be adapted to various situations. However, the letter should always have a single, unique reader in mind. It should go beyond the surface facts of when you graduate (if you are a student), what experience you've had, and how you heard about the job.

To produce a letter that will interest employers, you need to know their needs. Your research on organizations may not reveal specific details, but you can work from your knowledge of common issues facing the field. Consider the following:

- What issues have an impact on this organization or service?
- What are the unique characteristics of this kind of service?
- What are the primary functions and skills of the position?
- How can your knowledge, skills, experience, and interests solve problems and improve services or operations?

Prioritize your qualifications according to the position's requirements and then select your best playing cards for your letter. Tying your background to the employer's needs is the initial step in persuading an employer to identify with you. (See sample letters 2, 3, and 4 in appendix 5).

Follow a Format

A traditional cover letter addresses four subjects: (1) why you are writing and how you heard about the position, (2) your related qualifications, (3) your interest in the organization, and (4) what you expect to happen next in the hiring process. In most cases each subject will have its paragraph. Limit your letter to one page.

In the first paragraph, state why you are writing and how you heard about the position. If you had a conversation with the employer or an assistant, indicate that you are following up the discussion. For example, "Following up our phone conversation on January 20, I am submitting a résumé for the clinical social work opening." If someone suggested you contact the agency, put that person's name in the first sentence (for example, "James Hill, professor at Mountain University's School of Social Work, suggested I contact you").

Summarize your related qualifications in the second paragraph. Emphasize your skills, knowledge, accomplishments, and what you can bring to the organization. Lead with your strongest qualification for the situation. That might be a range of experience, in which case you would open with a summary statement that sets the stage—for example, "My 12 years of experience include work with an inpatient hospital psychiatric unit, community mental health clinic, and family services agency." Or your strength might be experience with an organization known to the employer or a job performing the same function in a related area (see sample letter 4 in appendix 5.) Follow your opening statement with other highlights related to the opening. You might say, "At Baron Medical Center, I served as interim supervisor for six months." If your salary history or salary expectation is requested in an advertisement, many people in the field of career development recommend that you not give specifics. You can say that your salaries have been commensurate with the position and that you are seeking a salary consistent with the market and your qualifications. Or, you might state a range that is appropriate for that market. (See chapters 2 and 6.)

In paragraph 3 briefly express your interest in the organization. Take what you know about the organization or the field if you cannot locate specifics, and briefly indicate why you are interested or committed to that work.

Keep your statements positive and realistic. (See the sample letters in appendix 5.) You may know from your research that the last director left under adverse circumstances. You certainly will not mention that in the letter, but you will talk about your interest in the organization's work.

Paragraph 4 is an action statement. The action statement is often a request for an interview, but many candidates take the initiative themselves, saying that they will call the employer in a few days (with the intent to arrange an interview). If you are not certain that you will be able to follow up with a call, do not say you will in the letter. You can refer to the résumé you enclose in this last paragraph or in paragraph 1 or 2. If someone with a good connection to the organization is willing to put in a good word for you, mention the person's name in the final paragraph.

Other Important Points for Your Cover Letter

Use Column Format for a Specific Opening

You can replace the second paragraph with a list of requirements for the opening in a column on the left side of the page and your corresponding qualifications briefly stated on the right side. Each requirement should have a matching qualification. A social worker who has worked for several managed care companies found that this style worked well in her latest search. Note, however, that this format does not scan well.

Address a Specific Person

When you do not have the name of the person you need to address, call the organization and request the appropriate name and title. Occasionally, telephone calls and networking fail to produce a name. When all else fails, address the letter to the executive director, clinical director, director of medical social work, and so on. However, do not make this a practice: This should be a rare exception, not a rule, for your correspondence.

Edit Your Letters Carefully

- Use "I" in a limited number of sentences.
- Using a highlighter, mark the most important words on your draft, and then try to eliminate as many extra words as possible.
- It is very easy to overuse words—check to ensure that you don't.
- Be sure that your letter demonstrates enthusiasm.
- Look for negative statements and rephrase them in positive terms or delete them.
- Use a natural, conversational tone and vocabulary.

Follow Up Your Letter

If you are comfortable calling an employer, follow up your letter with a brief call. This call will be similar to the type of call that you would make to screen a job. Express your interest in the job and request an interview.

References

Baccalaureate Education Assessment Project. (2003, October 29). *Annual report.* At http://www.rit.edu/~ beap/index.htm

Boldt, L. G. (2000). *Zen and the art of making a living: A practical guide to creative career design.* New York: Arkana.

Boston University, School of Social Work. (1996). *Survey of career development services within graduate schools of social work.* Boston: Author.

Boyd, K. (1996). There is a job market for BSW graduates! *New Social Worker, 3,* 18–19.

Darling, D. (2003). *The networking survival guide,* New York: McGraw-Hill.

Dikel, M. F. (Ed.). (1994–2004). *The Riley guide.* Available: http://www.dgm.com/jobguide

Grobman, G. (1999). *The not-for-profit handbook* (national ed.). Harrisburg, PA: White Hat Communications.

Hefland, D. P. (1995). *Career change: Everything you need to know to meet new challenges and take control of your career.* Chicago: VGM Career Horizons.

Office of the Federal Register. (2003–2004). *United States government manual.* Washington, DC: Author.

CHAPTER 4 QUICK TIPS
Identifying Jobs and Pursuing Leads

Here are some suggestions if you must find a position quickly:

- Get on the pro re nata (whenever necessary) lists for hospitals and social work temporary agencies.
- Start the application process for the social services organizations that have the highest turnover rates.
- Update your contact network list and call everyone. Besides telling them that you are looking for full-time work, ask them about contract work. Ask yourself who you know or have met that does not know you are looking and contact them.
- Start calling every organization doing something related to your qualifications and every organization related to your interests.
- Find a job-hunters club. If you cannot find one through professional groups or your university, religious organization, or chamber of commerce, consider forming one.
- Put yourself on a strict schedule. When you are not calling contacts and organizations or replying to openings, research organizations, update your knowledge of developments in the field, and polish your message. Call search firms if you have management experience.
- Draft a letter, which you can tailor as needed, following the outline of letters in appendix 5.

Identifying Jobs and Pursuing Leads

Interviewing Effectively

Inside Chapter 5

Ideally, the interview is a two-way street: It is a comfortable conversation between two individuals with similar interests. Your social work training in interviewing skills will be a great advantage in achieving this effect. Just as being an effective client interviewer took preparation and practice, so will being an effective job interviewee.

Planning Your Agenda

Go to your interviews with a plan. Think about five things you want the interviewers to know about you and five things you want to know about them. Five is just a guideline; it could be four or eight—that is up to you. This outline will help you concentrate on your agenda and approach the interviewer as an equal.

What You Want the Employer to Know About You

Think carefully about the message you want to convey to the employer—make it a theme you continually present and support throughout the interview. Job hunters often focus on a theme that presents how they work or their work style, which of course is important. For example, an upper-level manager presented himself as a loyal, stable, straight shooter who kept management informed, thought in terms of the big picture, and liked to work on the cutting edge and face challenges, seeing problems as opportunities.

This style was manifested in the numerous accomplishments he wove into the interview and outlined in his résumé. Many social workers, however, simply focus on presenting a work style, making the false assumption that content—knowledge, skills, and accomplishments—will be evident on the résumé. Exhibit 5.1 shows some examples of types of jobs individuals may consider and the key content points that need to be stressed during the interviews.

One new graduate interviewed for a fellowship with an adolescent mental health program. The program entailed clinical work in an outpatient setting and a diagnostic clinic for developmental disabilities, as well as work at a Job Corps program. This applicant stressed the assessment and treatment planning skills she had developed in a community mental health practicum, experience with interventions used during a practicum at an adolescent shelter, knowledge of developmental disabilities gained as a part-time respite worker for families of children with autism, knowledge of adolescent issues, and leadership experience in student government.

Tailor your qualifications list to the specific employer. For example, if you are looking at entry-level positions as a policy analyst in a not-for-profit advocacy organization and in government, your list will be slightly different for each setting. In a not-for-profit policy office, you may be asked to quickly write several possible sound

Examples of Types of Jobs and Key Content Points

Geronotological Social Worker
- experience with many ethical dilemmas
- experience with clients who have Alzheimer's disease
- strong assessment skills
- understanding of the dual role of working with elders and families
- knowledge of Medicare and Medicaid

Policy Analyst
- concise, quick, clear writing
- experience writing fact sheets, option papers, and sound bytes
- understand the big picture
- broad knowledge of social issues and policies
- high threshold for frustration; have a long-term outlook
- astute learner; enjoy studying the opposition

Medical Social Work
- experience on neonatal and pediatric units
- emergency department experience
- discharge planning
- work with an interdisciplinary team
- like a fast-paced environment
- work with families in crisis

Clinical Social Work Supervisor
- licensed clinical social worker
- number of years of experience providing brief strategic and longer-term therapy
- provide in-service training on evidence-based practices
- supervise practicum students for [number] years

Day Treatment Social Worker
- culturally sensitive practice expertise
- individual and family therapy experience
- knowledge of development issues
- work with emotionally disturbed youths

bytes about a piece of legislation for a news conference. In the federal government, you will not write sound bytes, but you will need to be adept at teamwork. Again, your network of advisers and contacts can help you tailor your list.

The more you can anticipate the needs of particular employers, the better you can tailor your list. Listen to what those in the field say about their needs. For example, a director of social work services at a large university medical center looks for the following when selecting supervisors:

I look primarily at two criteria. The first is technical competence. Often this person will have patient responsibilities concurrent with supervisory responsibilities, so I look at the scope, complexity, and depth of past responsibilities. Has the person dealt with broad and diverse circumstances? Is he or she agile—does he or she respond well to spontaneous situations? If the person has not had direct patient responsibilities, I consider the complexity of the work history—experiences that required adaptability. I want to determine how quickly and effectively this person can become acclimated to a new setting and apply existing skills. This person must be less prone to making mistakes, for he or she will set the example. A sound thought process is a necessity—I must be able to depend on this person's ability to make accurate decisions. If the person has good clinical experience, the more likely he or she will be able to understand situations and make appropriate decisions.

The second standard is the ability to lead—to organize work and shepherd, encourage, and monitor staff. How much experience has the person had in leading people? What are the contexts and results? Was this experience in the same type of setting, with similar levels of staff, a similar number of subordinates, the same mix of part-time and full-time staff with similar shifts? All of these details tell me about the person's knowledge of the issues inherent in this position. What are this person's expectations— will he or she be able to meet those expectations here or be amenable to change? Is this person unflappable? Does he or she have the stamina to handle negative reactions to his or her own ideas? This person must be able to buy into a culture of excellence. Will he or she be part of the team pursuing that goal? Can he or she lead a mix of personalities in pursuit of that goal? Can the person accomplish this in a complex organization, a fluid environment of perpetual change, providing services that have significant consequences for clients and providers? Will this person be able to maneuver staff who have their own agendas to participate in a consensus process, deal with change, and as a team advance patient care?

What You Want to Know about the Employer and the Position

The second item on your agenda is determining whether the position and organization are a good match for you. What are you looking for in a position and organization? Think about a model organization in your field of interest, and then come up with a list of questions (see chapter 2 section entitled "Gather Information on Specific Organizations" and appendix 4). For more ideas, talk with people in your network who know your field and possibly the organization you are interviewing with. Read every page of the organization's Web site if it has one. Request a brochure on the program. If it is an organization that publishes reports, review them. (See appendix 7 for a sample list of information you might gather; see also chapter 6 for questions to consider in the section entitled "Making a Decision.")

In addition to reviewing materials and asking some questions during interviews, use your observational skills: look at facilities, personalities, energy levels, interactions, office arrangements, and location. How sensitive is the staff to the clients? Does the staff or social work department appear to be a cohesive group?

PREPARATION AND GOALS FOR THE INTERVIEW

You can expect a variety of questions during interviews—hypothetical questions; questions about work habits; questions about specific knowledge of issues, populations, policies, interventions, and evaluation; and questions about future goals, strengths and weaknesses, and so on. Suggestions for responding to questions are provided below. (See appendix 7 for additional questions social workers have encountered in interviews.)

Employers of social workers are similar to most other employers. They seek candidates with related experience, honesty and stability, maturity, commitment, skills and knowledge, direction, a high energy level, and familiarity with their organization's work. The following sections provide specific advice from employers.

Interpret Your Experience

"You need to convey a view of the world, in other words, go beyond describing the what, where, and when of your qualifications," recommends a clinical director of a youth service. Anyone can read your résumé for the where and when of your experience. Employers, however, are looking for you to interpret your experience, requiring you to think, summarize, and analyze your qualifications. Explain what you think, what you learned, and what you believe works and why.

"Take the pieces of what you have done and find the common thread that demonstrates you are analytical, can assimilate information, and so on," advises a vice president of a large funding agency.

A vice president of a community mental health agency suggests, "Think about what you have done that applies. If you have worked at the agency before, stress the fact that you know the agency and the population it serves. Many interviewers will describe the agency and the position early in the interview. Throughout the rest of the interview, relate your experience directly back to the information you were given."

Do not take for granted that the interviewers have thought carefully about how your background fits their needs, that they remember anything from your résumé, or that they have even read your cover letter and résumé.

Present a Clear Direction

As best you can, be clear with yourself about what you do and do not want in a job. One interviewer stresses that you "be honest about client populations with whom you do not want to work." This should be done in a professional way. If you learn in the interview that some clients in your caseload are known sex offenders and you do not want to work with this population, state that you do not think you could work effectively with that population. Your research on organizations should help you screen out those jobs that are not a good fit for you.

Demonstrate Your Motivation and Commitment

Explain what motivates you to pursue this work and how you have demonstrated your commitment. If you changed your career path, articulate your motivations for your new direction. How have you backed up your commitment to this work through jobs, professional activities, practicum, and volunteer work? This should include your academic work, not just your curriculum track, and the topics you chose for projects.

Convey Maturity and Sound Judgment Skills

At all times demonstrate that you can fill the role required of the position. This is especially important when you are attempting to move across functions—for example, from direct practice to supervision—or fields. Make it clear that you understand the ethical dilemmas, the evidence base for practice, the impact of funding sources and shifting policies on services, differences in philosophies, complexities of evaluation methods, and specific issues facing this particular field of social services.

In describing decisions you made in seeking funding, designing a treatment plan, dealing with a crisis situation, building an effective board, or whatever efforts your work demanded, you can present the employer with a picture of how you approach your work and the depth of your understanding of the employer's concerns.

"Appreciate what you do not know about practice, and at the same time show that you are confident. An unbeatable combination is someone who conveys confidence but knows that he or she has a lot to learn," counsels a clinical director.

Practice Interviews

Without careful forethought, it is difficult to be spontaneous, confident, and organized in your discussion. Here are some suggestions for practice.

- Prepare a two- or three-sentence statement about each item on your résumé
- Outline your related work or practicum experience, knowledge and skills gained, relevant coursework taken, and any leadership experience for each category of jobs you are considering (this will help you organize your thoughts and enable you to highlight specific qualifications).
- Review this outline often (if you did the exercises in chapter 1, refer to them).

One of the job candidates who was interviewing for a position working with families in crisis did not have family therapy experience, which was important to the job. However, she had worked with children whose parents were going through separation and divorce. She stressed her skills in helping families stabilize and make transitions. She successfully convinced the interviewers of her ability to handle crises and achieve resolution.

- Daydream your interviews. It's fun and great practice. If you were the employer, what would you ask?

- Practice interviews with friends or a colleague. Ask them to play different roles: unorganized interviewer, friendly interviewer, aloof interviewer, abrupt interviewer, unexpected caller. One social worker recommends taping your answers to questions.
- Think about what excites you about the area of social work you have chosen. Convey this enthusiasm through your attitude and responses to interview questions.
- Review notes from your previous interviews.
- Visualize a scene in which you introduce yourself, give a firm handshake, and when asked to take a seat, select an upright chair that puts you on the same level as the interviewer. View the end of the interview, as you remind the employer why you are the best candidate, inquire about the next step in the selection process and shake hands.

In the current job market you should look widely for opportunities, but do not interview just for practice. Interview only if you have a sincere interest in the job—do not waste your colleagues' time by interviewing for positions you know you do not want. Instead, thank that employer for the invitation and ask whether he or she has any suggestions for identifying an appropriate opportunity.

Difficult Questions
Common Questions

Several interview questions that are frequently asked often stump candidates. Most are dealt with in the following paragraphs. How much you say in response to the questions is up to you—the suggestions below are designed simply to get you in the habit of making well-thought-out, concise, targeted statements. Practicing responses and varying them to fit a variety of employers will help you develop a conversational interview style and avoid "canned" answers. None of the questions is as general as it may sound. All of them should be answered in terms of the position in question.

"What is your career goal?" Prepare a concise statement describing what type of work you would like to do. "My goal is to work with an employee assistance program where I can use my experience in mental health and chemical dependency treatment and have an opportunity to do some training and marketing. In the future I hope to manage an EAP."

"Tell me about yourself." Prepare a four- or five-sentence statement on your professional development to date. "As you know, I will complete the MSW program in December; my interest is domestic violence. I started the program with work experience in developmental disabilities and volunteer experience with a woman's shelter. My practicum entailed crisis intervention and counseling with women and program planning and administration for a shelter. I also assisted a faculty member who was studying policy issues and domestic violence. At this point I am looking for an opportunity to do direct practice, possibly combined with program planning."

"What are your skills?" Prepare a concise statement of your best skills that relate to the job. This should focus on social work skills, but you may include a sentence describing pertinent transferable skills and work habits. "I had wonderful practicum experiences that developed my confidence in my assessment skills, my ability to intervene in a crisis situation, my knowledge of discharge planning, and my ability to work effectively with the medical staff. I feel I am really ready to work in medical social work."

"What are your strengths?" Prepare two or three sentences about your strengths in terms of the job: experience, knowledge, and skills. Although you want to focus on your social work strengths, you can also weave life experience, previous career experience, and work habits into your statement. "I would say my strengths are in the management of mental health facilities, particularly in fiscal management and fundraising. I have considerable experience in clinical programs and staff development. And people have

complimented me on my ability to rebuild programs and staff morale."

"What are your weaknesses?" This is asked to ascertain your level of self-awareness, not to undermine you. Prepare two or three sentences about your weaknesses. The director of a community mental health center recommends focusing on a professional area of knowledge that you have not been able to concentrate on and wish to develop. Use positive language. Be sure that you follow through on your efforts to improve. If an employer hires you, they are likely to watch for results. "My work has been primarily in child welfare case management. Though I use my family therapy knowledge, I know I still have skills to develop in that area. I have attended several workshops and read books, and I hope to enroll in a certificate program next fall."

Hypothetical Questions

Expect employers to present hypothetical situations; your responses can reveal not only specific problem-solving skills, but also approaches to making decisions. In your answers, don't try to offer the solution; just describe your approach. The following examples provide the context for the questions that follow.

- *Supervisory position for an elder residential center.* "What if one of the people you supervise lied, mistreated a client, or breached confidentiality? What would you do? What if you saw a person who was supervised by someone else do the same thing? What would you do?"
- *Women's shelter.* "A woman comes in. What would you first say to her?" The response will reveal to the interviewer the candi date's philosophy. Does the candidate start by describing the rules of the shelter or by

telling the woman that what brought her here was not her fault?

- *Youth outreach program.* "A youth, whom you do not know, approaches you in a park and says that his parents locked him out of the house. What would you say? What issues would you be thinking about?"
- *Outreach program for families in crisis* (this question was posed to an African American candidate). "Someone with whom you have been working, a white woman, says, 'I don't think you can under stand what I am going through.' How would you respond?"
- *In-home therapy services.* "You are visiting a client family in their home when one person becomes very agitated. You are concerned about violence. What would you do?"

Improper Interview Questions*

"The aide prepared me. He said the senator really wants to get to know people before he hires them and that he might ask me personal questions. I knew that I would not get the job if I did not answer the questions."

Like this social worker seeking a legislative assistant position, you will want to be prepared for potentially illegal or inappropriate interview questions or both. Social workers have encountered them in large and small agencies when interviewing for direct practice positions, as well as in interviews with elected representatives for policy-related positions. It is important to educate yourself on these issues and have some ideas about how you will handle questions comfortably. At the same time, try not to let concerns over anticipated questions prevent you from focusing on the purpose of your interview.

---

*This section provides some general information and explores the subject of potentially illegal questions in social work–related settings, but it is not written as legal advice. Employment law is complex, dependent on federal court interpretation, and varies from state to state. For more specific or updated information, contact the federal Equal Employment Opportunity Commission (EEOC) office (see EEOC Web site at http://www.eeoc.gov), local state human relations offices, or a legal expert.

What Subjects Are Prohibited

Title VII of the Civil Rights Act of 1964 established that employers could not discriminate on the basis of race, color, religion, national origin, or sex in hiring or use discriminatory practices in hiring. The Age Discrimination in Employment Act of 1967 prohibited discrimination on the basis of age (over 40), and the Americans with Disabilities Act of 1990 further delineated physical and mental disabilities as issues of discrimination in hiring. The EEOC issued statements of "enforcement guidance" regarding discriminatory hiring practices including what questions it considered evidence of discrimination in the hiring process. EEOC regulations stated that questions employers use in the selection process should pertain to the requirements of the position and must be asked of all candidates. Case law has further defined legal issues around the hiring process. For further information on the subject, take a look at the EEOC Web site at http://www.eeoc.gov.

This section on improper interview questions attempts to give you some general information and explore the subject of improper questions in social-work-related settings.

Age

An employer may ask whether a candidate is over 18 years of age but should not ask other questions to identify a candidate's age, nor can the employer indicate a preference for an age group. Once an individual is hired, the employer can ask for age or date of birth when the employee is signing up for benefits.

Arrests

Generally, and for most positions, questions may not focus on an arrest record, but interviewers may inquire about convictions.

Citizenship

An employer should not ask whether you are a U.S. citizen. Once a position is offered, the employer must verify your personal identification and your right to work in the United States.

You can be asked whether your visa status prevents you from being lawfully employed.

Convictions

Questions about circumstances surrounding a conviction may be asked if they are asked of all candidates and if the information has a bearing on the job performance.

Disabilities

Questions regarding ability to perform essential functions of the job may be asked.

Education and Credentials

Questions about training and experience related to the position's requirements are fine. An employer may ask whether you have the certification or licensure necessary for the position or whether you intend to obtain certification or licensure.

Family

Employers may not ask questions regarding family planning, family size, children's ages, child care plans, or spouse's employment or salary. You can be asked about your ability to travel and to work the schedule required for the job; however, these questions must be asked of all candidates.

Health, Including Mental Health

Pre-employment questions regarding health status cannot be asked. Nor can employers ask whether you have received psychiatric care. However, you can be given a drug test. An exception is the military. Social workers seeking enlisted positions in the military must meet health requirements. A physical can be given after the person is provisionally hired.

Height and Weight

An employer cannot ask specifically about height or weight. There may be exceptions to this outside most social work positions. One exception would be the military. Social workers must meet health requirements in the military.

Marital Status

Nothing can be asked about marital status, including whether you are engaged.

Maiden Name

An employer cannot inquire about your maiden name.

National Origin

You can be asked questions regarding your facility with English or another language if required for the job. Questions regarding ancestry, birthplace, parents, or spouse are generally inappropriate. For instance, during an interview for a faculty position, a doctoral student whose résumé indicated that she had studied abroad was asked where her family was from. This was a potentially problematic question.

Organizations

Nothing can be asked about organizational affiliations that might indicate race, color, creed, sex, marital status, religion (see "Religion" below), or national origin. You can be asked about memberships in professional organizations, but questions about political leanings or your political party affiliations are improper for most jobs. However, positions that involve national security are exempt.

Pregnancy

You can be asked about how long you expect to stay in a position and whether you anticipate any absences. However, these questions must be asked of all candidates and may pose problems regarding motive.

Religion

Questions regarding religion cannot be asked, but an employer can ask whether you anticipate absences from work or about your ability to meet the work schedule. However, religiously based social services and other religion institutions are exempt from these restrictions under Title VII. They may ask you questions

related to religion and make a decision to hire based on your religious beliefs.

When Questions May Be a Problem

When are you networking, you may encounter questions about where you are from, your family, and your personal plans. You may or may not feel comfortable with these topics, but because they are not being raised during a job selection process, they are probably not subject to challenge in this context.

Questions about the subjects listed in the previous section pose a problem if they are used during the selection process. This applies to screening interviews in person or over the telephone, job applications, formal job interviews, and informal conversations while visiting employers for the purpose of being considered for a position (including conversations during meals and trips to the airport, for example).

Exceptions are affirmative action forms or equal employment opportunity questionnaires, which collect data on particular groups and enable employers to keep track of their progress in affirmative action recruiting. The forms might ask date of birth, martial status, number of dependent children, ethnicity, whether you have a disability, and whether you need accommodation if you have a disability. The personnel staff should handle these forms; the forms should not be distributed to those making the hiring decision. Sometimes the affirmative action form accompanies the application, in which case you may want to mail the form separately from the application.

Difficult Choices: Handling Questions
Decide Ahead of Time How You Want to Respond to Questionable or Inappropriate Inquiries

Some social workers decide that they are not interested in working for an organization that inquires into personal background. Others decide that the job opportunity is more important to them than the inappropriateness of the questions and choose to answer. Still others try to appreciate the concerns of employers and assure them that the requirements of the job will be met.

Be an Attentive Listener

It is easy to be caught off guard. A doctoral student who was applying for academic positions received a call at 7:30 AM. The dean of a school of social work was the person calling and he asked the student whether she had any children. The student, who was barely thinking at this hour, found herself answering the question before she was fully aware of what was happening.

Keep the Tone of the Interview Positive

Although you may be irritated by a question, want to ignore a question, or tell the interviewer what you really think about a question, consider the consequences carefully. You do not want to put the interviewer on the defensive or create a hostile atmosphere. Even if you decide that you have no interest in working for this organization, your work in the professional community or field may include interactions with the staff. Also, remember that many social services agencies do not have the benefit of a human resources specialist or training in interviewing techniques for their staffs. As a result, you may encounter an inexperienced interviewer who asks inappropriate or awkward questions.

Ask for clarification. "Can you tell me how this is important or related to the job?" or "May I ask how this might be helpful in selecting a candidate?" Here is an example of an inappropriate question and an appropriate response:

Let's do a genogram of your family.
You mean do I know how to use a genogram?

Respond to the Concern

You can identify the concern of the employer and respond by reframing the question. "I understand that I would be consulting with nursing homes throughout the state. The travel is not a concern for me; in fact, I think I would enjoy it." or "I am familiar with the ethical issues surrounding religion and the medical model such as . . . ."

Redirect the Interview

Your training in interviewing should aid you in facilitating the interview process. Use a transition in your response. End with a question for the interviewer, an illustration of your work, or comment on an accomplishment that refocuses him or her on the position and your qualifications; for instance, "I know how to use a genogram; let me tell you about a particular case for which I used a genogram."

Remember, You Have the Right Not to Respond to a Question

If you have attempted to clarify the question and addressed the concern but the interviewer persists with an inappropriate question, you can certainly choose not to respond. Just remember to keep your response professional, polite: "I would prefer not to respond to that particular question" or "That is not something I feel comfortable sharing." Then move on by redirecting the interview.

Responding to Particular Questions

The following paragraphs discuss some particular questions that social workers encounter during the hiring process. This discussion is meant to increase awareness but not to provide legal advice. As stated above, if you have questions, consult the EEOC, the appropriate state human relations office, or a legal expert.

Have You Been Through Your Own Therapy?

This question is commonly used in clinical social work settings. However, such questions may violate federal or state laws. Think carefully about how you respond to this question. If you choose to respond, keep your response simple;

do not state why you sought therapy. If you choose not to respond directly, you might indicate that you recognize your professional responsibility for your own issues and their possible impact on clients.

Can You Tell Me about Your Family?

When a group of family therapists was asked for their recommendations on handling this inquiry, they suggested the following: Consider treating it lightly and as well intentioned. Respond with "all is well," and redirect the discussion by focusing on your knowledge of families.

Are You Pro-Choice or Pro-Life?

If these questions are work related or the organization has a religious affiliation, interviewers may ask these questions and consider the responses in the hiring decision process. In addition, you can be asked whether you are willing to follow the agency's position on this subject.

Do You Belong to a (Church, Synagogue, Temple, or Other)?

Sectarian agencies can ask questions about religious affiliation and take this information into consideration when selecting candidates.

What You Can Do to Minimize Unwanted Questions

- Do not put personal information, such as marital status, number of children, height, weight, or health status, on your résumé or vita.
- Develop a rapport with the interviewer. If he or she trusts you and has a positive feeling about you, the need for personal information may not seem necessary. Leave no doubts that you are trustworthy, use good judgment, make an effort to engage others, know when to listen, have experience with ethical dilemmas, appreciate team efforts, and can take the lead when necessary.

- Anticipate issues. Before an interview, think about any items in the job description, your background, or on your résumé that might prompt an illegal, inappropriate, or awkward question.

For example, your name may be hyphenated, possibly indicating that you are married. Incorporate information throughout the interview that stresses your professionalism and addresses any concerns before the interviewer brings them up. This does not mean that you should reveal information or address unnecessary subjects, although you have the right to volunteer information an employer cannot ask questions about.

If the job requires you to be on call, for example, you might say, "I understand this position would require me to carry a beeper. That is not a concern for me; however, I would like to know more about how that works." If the job requires travel, you could say, "One of the reasons I am interested in this position is the travel" or "In my previous position I traveled; I am looking forward to doing that again."

If the position is in clinical social work, you could say, "I know that as a professional it is very important to be aware of one's own issues and how they can affect work with clients. I feel this is an ongoing process and I'll work hard to be aware of my own situation and its possible impact on my work."

Pitfalls

Be sure that the language you choose to describe your experience, accomplishments, and philosophy conveys the exact meaning and attitude you intend. In the interview situation, it is easy to use trite or vague phrases, over explain a situation, or try to impress the interviewer with a poorly thought-out response.

Keep Your Comments Positive, Serious, and Honest

Do not generalize about individuals, groups of

people, or institutions. For example, phrases such as "men are just horrible" and "corporations are the problem" do not indicate that you can be counted on to interact effectively with board members, elected representatives, funding organizations, members of the public, or clients.

As a general rule, do not joke with interviewers. Respond to questions seriously and sincerely. Although you may have a great sense of humor, be careful how you show it during interviews. If you are asked, "Why are you interested in our organization?" responding with "Your location is only an hour away from the ski slopes" probably will not the make the impression you desire.

Be honest. If you do not have an answer, do not bluff. You can say: "I don't know." "I don't think I have encountered that." "I have heard of that, but I am not familiar enough with the issues to respond at this time." "I have some familiarity with that. My understanding is [briefly outline a couple of issues or points]." "I have not worked with that issue directly, but this is how I would approach it."

Avoid Problematic Phrases

"I want to bring humanity to the field." "Mainstreaming is the way to go for all kids." "[Whatever approaches] are the only approaches." Be careful about speaking in generalities or making absolute statements. They can come across as naïve or narrow minded, and they do not reflect well on your education, analytical thinking, and judgment. Here are some examples.

- "Our children are our future." OK, but what do you want to do about it?
- "I am fluent in [whatever approach] treatment method." What does that mean? Does it mean that you have used the method with clients for many years and now train others in the approach? It is better to specify your degree of expertise.
- "I want to help people" or "I like people." These are vague phrases often used by

people with limited experience or by those who don't know how to articulate their direction.

- "At first I was gullible." Inexperienced social workers commonly have difficulty judging situations and a client's actions and verbal responses. Rather than using the term "gullible," which might leave a lasting impression, put your experience in context. "Like many new social workers, it took me a while to recognize when a client was being manipulative. I feel confident in my ability to recognize when this is happening now."
- "I don't know whether you know about this, but . . . ." Assume that your interviewer is up-to-date on policy controversies, current community issues, new programs, and treatment developments.
- "I plan to enter a doctoral program in a couple of years." This statement indicates your limited interest in the job at hand. Focus your discussion on the present. If your long-term goals do not serve the employer's interests, it is better not to mention them. You may unintentionally hit a raw nerve. One employer at a community mental health center said, "If [one more] person says, 'I want to start a private practice in a few years,' I'll throw up."

Focus on Professional Information

Do you reveal personal characteristics or experiences that explain your motivation for entering the field, your commitment to your work, or knowledge of a particular issue? It is best to separate your professional self from your personal self, particularly in job interviews.

Do not express your feelings about negative personal issues or professional experiences during an interview. These are red flags to employers, indicating that you are not ready to move forward, that your attitude will affect staff cohesion, or that you may not be approachable. If you need to describe a negative incident, do so objectively and indicate that you have looked back on the experience and have learned from it.

As one clinical director says, "I do not want to know what your personal issues are, but I do want to know your philosophy on how personal issues impact work as a clinician."

What Not to Ask

An employer occasionally gets the question, "What does this agency do?" or "What is this job again?" Think carefully about what you want to ask and how, or it could be a very brief interview.

Never ask interviewers personal questions such as, "How long have you been in your position?" "How did you get your job?" "Are you married?" or "Is that a picture of your family?"

Packaging

"Your appearance is a sign of respect for me, my agency, and the field," says one executive director of a shelter who has been surprised by interviewees wearing shorts, jeans, and sandals. Although social work staffs at many agencies may dress casually on the job, do not take that as a sign that you can present yourself casually at an interview. If you interview at a site where the staff is dressed casually, you might ask about the dress code and comment that you like the relaxed dress policy. Keep your appearance simple and appropriate for the job.

Women social workers in some settings wear slacks and a simple top on the job, particularly in settings working with children. However, if you are a woman interviewing for a position as a play therapist, for interviews wear a skirt and jacket, skirted suit, tailored pantsuit, or dress.

Tailor your appearance for the job. More than one employer of a program for adolescent boys has expressed concerns over female interviewees wearing short skirts, colorful makeup, and trendy hairstyles.

If the job involves contact with corporate clients and board members, demonstrate that you understand business culture, including attire.

Your clothing and accessories should project professionalism and not detract from the content of your presentation. Save the latest fashion fads for social and casual occasions; wear subtle, not flashy or too prominent, jewelry. Dress for an interview the way the executive director of an agency would dress for meetings with key staff from a funding organization.

The Interview Process

Organizations have their own interview processes. Some are simple, involving a single one-hour interview; others might request a second or third interview or another interview with a group or a different individual. Role playing, presentations, and writing exercises also may be used. The process will vary depending on the type and level of the opening and the employer's time frame for hiring.

Scheduling Interviews

Be prepared for an employer to call to schedule an interview. Keep a copy of your résumé, a list of the names and organizations you have contacted, a pad of paper, and several pens by your phone. This way you are always ready to identify a caller, take notes, and give a quick summary of your background.

Check the greeting on your message machine. A director of a women's shelter said the interview process began and ended with one candidate's message. When the director called to schedule an interview, she was greeted by a husky, sexy recorded message.

When you receive a call to schedule an interview, request details that will help you prepare. Get specifics on the interview process. Will this be a single interview, or a screening interview followed by a second interview? How long should you plan to be there? Will you be interviewing with several individuals or a group? Who will be the interviewers? If you do not already have information on the organization, request an annual report and a program brochure.

Interview Formats

Most hiring processes for line positions involve a single interview or a screening interview followed by a second interview. The higher the position, the more involved the interview process will be. You will meet with all the major constituents—for example, the search committee, board members, colleagues in other divisions, administrative staff, supervisors and line staff, clients, and volunteers.

First, Second, and Series Interviews

In most cases, the interviewer follows a specific format. The organization and position will be described, you will be asked questions related to the position, and you will have an opportunity to ask questions.

Screening interview. This is a brief interview to determine whether your background is in the ballpark for this position and your level of interest. The interviewer will spend time describing the job and ask basic questions about your experience. Limit your questions to determining whether you want to explore the opportunity further. Some screening interviews are done by telephone.

Second interview. If you are invited to a second interview, it means that what you offer generally fits the profile for the position and you made a reasonably good first impression. The second interview may be with the person making the decision or with a group; it will focus on how well you could perform the job and whether you would fit the organization. You should have an opportunity to see where you would be working, tour the facility, and meet coworkers.

Series interviews. You may have several interviews as part of the process. They could be with the director, other managers, the direct supervisor for the position, coworkers, board members, and volunteers. This is particularly true if you are interviewing for an administrative position.

All-day interviews. If you are traveling a long distance for an interview, you are likely to go through a series of interviews over a day or two.

This is especially true for management and executive positions. Even if you are applying for a line position, you can expect a series of interviews with the director, supervisors, and potential coworkers and with the human resources staff, if that is a separate entity in the organization. Interviews for fellowships often take the better part of a day. Interviews for tenure-track faculty and administrative positions often last more than one day.

If a schedule or itinerary is not provided ahead of time, ask for one with the names and titles of the people you will be seeing. Although you will find yourself repeating your story, have a strategy for addressing the individual interests of each party.

All-day interviews are tiring; pace the interview. You are "on" all day. The schedule may or may not allow you time to be alone. One doctoral student said her only time alone was in the restroom. Pace yourself. Chances are that your last interview will be with the executive director or dean or whoever makes the final decision.

Do not make assumptions about travel plans and reimbursement. Be clear from the beginning about what the employer will and will not pay for and who makes the travel arrangements. Except for high-level positions, social services organizations seldom cover travel expenses. Universities typically cover expenses for faculty and administration candidates. Keep a record of your expenses and get a receipt for everything.

Telephone Interviews

This is a screening interview that may be scheduled and under the guise of an introduction and friendly chat. It is a quick inexpensive way for an employer to shrink the pool of applicants. A director of a family program uses telephone interviews to identify those applicants who are really serious about providing intensive services in clients' homes. Because you cannot know which employers will use this technique, you need to be prepared at all times. If an employer calls you at an inopportune time, request an alternative time.

Regardless of whether the telephone interview is scheduled or a surprise, it presents a unique challenge to the interviewee: One cannot get visual cues from the interviewer. This is frustrating, especially if it is a conference call involving several staff members. A telephone interview requires intense listening. If there is more than one interviewer, write down each person's name and title, asking each to repeat that information if necessary, before you begin the interview. When someone asks a question, ask for that person's identity. This technique will help you begin to form a picture of each person and his or her particular interests. Pace yourself; you will probably find yourself responding to questions at a slower rate than you do in person. Take notes and ask for clarification when necessary. Try standing during this interview—it will give you a greater sense of command. To prepare for this type of interview, ask friends to play the role of the employer and practice interviews over the telephone. This is especially important for long-distance job hunters.

Panel Interviews

Although they are expedient for a staff, interviews with a group of staff members, board members, or other key people can be particularly demanding for the candidate. At least at first, you will not know whether the panel format was selected as a time saver or a test to see how well you can work with a group, among other reasons.

As people are introduced, write down their names and titles. If their roles in the agency are not clear to you, ask for clarification. This will help you tailor your responses. To help you keep names and functions straight and personalize the situation, address people by name at the beginning of a response. Obviously, you do not want to overuse this technique.

Some interviewers will play different roles, some friendly ("good cops" that put you at ease), some quiet and observant, and some challenging ("bad cops" who ask harder questions). As in individual interviews, you will want to use eye contact and develop a rapport with the panel.

Group Exercises

You might encounter a group exercise, involving several candidates, as part of the interview process. Its purpose is to observe how you and the other candidates work in a group: Do you take an active part, do you work toward consensus, do you work well in a team, do you take a leadership role? Usually the group is given a topic to discuss or a problem to solve within a set time limit.

For example, the selection process for a leadership-training program incorporated a group exercise. A group of five candidates were seated around a table and given the following scenario: "You are a group of local leaders in a city where a riot has erupted. Your task is to prepare a statement for a news conference that will take place in five minutes." Two members of the interview team observed the discussion.

Role Playing

It is common for direct services agencies to use role playing as part of the selection process. Staff members take the roles of clients and you take the role of the social worker for about 10 minutes. After the role play, there is a debriefing in which staff members ask you what you thought, why you chose to proceed as you did, and other questions specific to the situation. Sometimes they will give you feedback on your performance, but do not expect this. Beginning with the context followed by an individual role-playing scenario, here are two examples:

Youth outreach service

The employer has instructed you to de-escalate a situation, resolve the crisis, formulate a treatment plan, and come to a contract in the following scene enacted by staff: A mother and daughter come to the office to meet with you. Both start screaming at the top of their lungs without permission.

Family services

The staff plays members of a family whom you, the social worker from the family program, are visiting for the first time. You learn that the son has been involved in a burglary and is hanging around with a bad crowd, the father is gone most of the time working, and the mother is depressed and abusing alcohol. After 15 minutes of role playing the staff asks you the following question: What is your assessment of the situation? How would you work with each family member? What are the strengths of the family? What would you do during the next 45 minutes of the visit?

Presentations

Sometimes you are asked to give a presentation as part of the interview process. This is more likely to occur in interviews for positions involving training, teaching, educational programming, public speaking, or leadership. For example, people interviewing for tenure-track academic positions always give a colloquium, usually based on dissertation research. Presentations may be requested in settings other than higher education, however. A candidate for a position with an extension service in a rural area was asked to prepare a 10-minute presentation on how she would involve the community in developing a new program.

In most cases, you will prepare a presentation in advance. If possible, find out who will be your audience so that you can tailor your remarks; arrange to use visual aids such as PowerPoint, transparencies, or handouts; and practice your presentation with colleagues who can ask pertinent questions.

Sometimes the presentation will be in the form of an extemporaneous speech. Semifinalists for the federal Presidential Management Fellows Program give a five-minute speech. They are presented with a topic and given 25 minutes to prepare. The topic could be on any national issue—trade, environment, welfare, defense, health care, energy, or transportation, for example. To compete effectively in this situation, candidates must be well read. They certainly cannot be experts on every issue, but they should have some awareness of national issues. Of course, candidates also need to practice quickly outlining ideas and speaking for five minutes on a range of subjects.

Writing Exercises

In addition to asking candidates to furnish writing samples, an increasing number of employers are giving interviewees writing exercises during the interview process. This enables the employer to see how well candidates write without the benefit of time, or how well candidates think under pressure. You might, for example, be given three cases and instructed to write treatment goals for each.

Interviewers You May Encounter
Friendly

It is common in direct social services to find an interviewer who is very friendly, gives you encouraging feedback throughout the interview, and seems enthusiastic about you. Take this with a grain of salt; no matter how positive you feel during the interview, assume that all candidates are treated exactly the same. You want to be pleasant and build rapport, but do not step out of your professional role of candidate even if you know the interviewer.

Reserved

You may find yourself interviewing with a poker-faced, aloof, or abrupt interviewer. Do not expect someone to be a good listener, to reflect, or to encourage you in any way. Some interviewers collect information without showing the slightest reaction to it. They may appear objective or even disinterested. Do not let their demeanor rattle your confidence.

Unorganized

You may encounter an unorganized or uncomfortable interviewer. In this case, take the lead in bringing up topics you think are important.

Distracted

If the interviewer seems to be distracted or allows others to interrupt your appointment, take this opportunity to observe the work environment. More than one social worker interviewee has interrupted the interview and requested to reschedule the interview at a more suitable time.

Example of an Interview Experience at a Conference

This story describes the job interview and offers the experience of a new MSW graduate, referred to as "the social worker," seeking a position in employment, training, and micro enterprise development. She had two years of social services experience before graduate school and was searching for positions back in that general location in the United States. This interview, for a training position with a large multiservice organization, was arranged by phone in March and took place in late April at a conference that both parties happened to be attending. The position was with a self-employment program teaching skills, including marketing, pricing, advertising, operations, and finance.

The story, as interpreted by the candidate, illustrates both the advantages of meeting with agency staff at conferences and the hectic and unpredictable circumstances that candidates and employers encounter at conferences; it also shows that candidates must always be in the interviewee role or mindset, ready to respond at all times.

The interview was tentatively set for lunchtime on Thursday during the conference; the social worker would meet with the training coordinator, another supervisor, and the director. She was told that the interview would take place after the lunch and that the intense questioning during lunch really wasn't part of the interview, but the social worker knew that the interview really did start during lunch. She quickly discovered that she was meeting with three very different personalities; the director was quiet; the second supervisor was a strong, tough inter-

viewer; and the training coordinator was pleasant and encouraging without being overly promising. As it turned out, the planned formal interview after lunch did not take place, because the director had to leave for another meeting. Before parting they simply exchanged business cards, and the social worker met four or five more staff members who stopped by. The training coordinator said she would be in touch. At this point, the social worker thought she was home free.

The next day the social worker went to a conference session; unexpectedly, the director was on the panel. The social worker had learned the day before that the agency was starting a pilot project in a neighboring city, where she had worked before going to graduate school. During the conference session she realized that the agency's project could be more effective by working with the leadership of that community. At the session break, she went up to speak with the director; and as luck would have it, the pilot project director who the social worker had met the day before joined them. The social worker told them that she had a connection in [city] and thought she could help.

The directors both said, "Great." One director suggested that they meet after the session in the hotel lounge; the meeting turned out to be an impromptu interview, attended by the three people she had met with Thursday. "What was the most frustrating thing about your last position?" she was asked. She responded that the grassroots agency she worked with had a patchwork funding strategy, which was frustrating for her. The interviewer with the strong personality, who was the only one asking questions, said, "Can you handle another position like that? In this job you will not have an opportunity to do top-level administrative functions," to which the social worker replied, "Learning the training position will be my top priority. In three years, I want to be doing administration."

The social worker had not seen a job description or an annual report, so she requested them.

She got the sense that an annual report was something that was not usually shared beyond the administrative level. The interview was followed by lunch, during which the social worker gave the directors advice on their project. She spent the rest of the afternoon with them. Although everyone had been friendly and the organization's director had requested her list of references during the impromptu interview, the social worker was not sure at the end of the day whether she had the job.

On Saturday morning the social worker went to the conference's final session, which the agency staff had encouraged her to attend. The staff was presenting a session for supervisors of employment training programs. They included a list of eight criteria they used for selecting staff: independence, public speaking, good rapport with clients, understanding where clients are coming from, innovative thinking, knowledge of business skills, experience as an entrepreneur, and willingness to go the extra mile, such as when clients need an advocate in dealing with social services. The training coordinator said she would call the social worker a week after the conference. In the meantime, the training coordinator would be checking references.

The social worker hadn't expected this—in fact, she had not yet asked everyone on her list to be a reference, so she immediately called each person. Fortunately, all of her references thought well of her and responded positively to the surprise call. During the week after the conference, the social worker thought about the minimum salary she would accept if she got an offer and how she would negotiate on the basis of her experience and education.

The training coordinator called two days later than planned and offered the job at a salary higher than the social worker had expected. The social worker took detailed notes because she still did not have the job description (she got the description in the mail soon thereafter; requirements were a bachelor degree in business

plus five years of experience). She said she was interested and asked whether she could call with her answer the next day. After thinking about the offer and discussing it with a family member, she called to accept the offer as it stood.

The social worker thought that the key to landing the job was her understanding of clients' situations, realistic expectations of what clients can accomplish, and patience to work with clients. After accepting the position, she learned that the agency staff had not planned on hiring until June.

Before You Leave the Last Interview

When you are completing the last interview, find out when the organization expects to make a decision and who makes the hiring decision. Simply state your continued interest in the job and close the interview with a firm handshake.

Follow Up after the Interview

Write down everything you can remember from each interview as soon as possible. After a job interview, always send a typed thank-you letter as soon as possible. This letter summarizes your interest in the position and your qualifications. If you would like to emphasize or clarify any point from the interview, now is the time. In addition to thanking the interviewer, indicate your enthusiasm for the job and organization. It is also important to name any other interviewers or key individuals you met and express appreciation for their time.

If you would like to clarify any information about the position, call the employer after sending the thank-you letter. This type of call is appropriate and certainly indicates seriousness on your part.

If, after the interview, you are no longer interested in the position, state this in the thank-you letter. For additional information on interviews, read *The Smart Woman's Guide to Interviewing and Salary Negotiation* (King, 1997), *Every Employee's Guide to the Law* (Joel, 2001), and *Sweaty Palms* (Medley, 1993).

References

Joel, L. G. (2001). *Every employee's guide to the law.* New York: Pantheon Books.

King, J. A. (1997). *The smart woman's guide to interviewing and salary negotiation.* Franklin, NJ: Career Press.

Medley, J. A. (1993). *Sweaty palms: The neglected art of being interviewed.* Berkeley, CA: Ten Speed Press.

CHAPTER 5 QUICK TIPS

Interviews

- List five points you want an employer to know about you.
- List five or more questions you have about the organization and the job. Practice giving answers to common questions: What is your career goal? Tell me about yourself. What are your strengths? What are your weaknesses? Why should we hire you?
- Think about how you want to respond to inappropriate questions should they come up: Choose to respond to the overall concern, not the specific question; choose not to respond at all; or choose to respond to the question.
- Recap your qualifications in a typed thank-you letter.

CHAPTER SIX

Evaluating Job Offers

Getting an Official Offer

This is the moment you have been waiting for—they want you on their staff. You are excited and relieved, but there are many things to think about before making a commitment. For example, does the person offering you the position have the authority to do so? Is this opportunity consistent with what you know is available in the market? Do you need to negotiate the salary or starting date? Does this job fit your plans for the future? This chapter is designed to help you think through this process.

Congratulations, You Have an Offer (or at Least You Think You Do)

It is important to know whether you have an official offer. An official offer is made after the person with the authority to make a final hiring decision approves the selection. The offer includes the job title, salary, and starting date. If applicable, it should include the department and location.

Sometimes it is not entirely clear whether you have an offer. You may have a conditional or an unofficial offer. The employer might say you are a finalist for the position, or the interviewer might say simply, "We really want you." Although these are good signs, neither is an official offer requiring a decision to accept.

Conditional Offer

Were you told, "This is a conditional offer?" Is the offer contingent on positive outcomes of ref-erence checks, a police record check, information from the child or elder abuse registry, or a basic physical examination? Is it also contingent on a favorable review of your writing samples?

Unofficial Offer

Were you told, "This is an offer; the board just needs to approve it"? If yes, this gives you some extra time to weigh your options, but be aware that the person you talked to does not have the power at this point to make the offer; it could evaporate.

Finalist

In one hiring process two individuals were each told "You are the finalist; now all you have to do is meet with the division director at the umbrella agency." Each applicant had the understanding that she or he was being offered the job; that was not the case. Know who has the power to make the hiring decision and extend the job offer.

We Want You

Were you told, "You are the person we want"? If this was followed by "We are offering you the position of [job title] at a starting salary of [amount]," then congratulations you have an offer. If not, then ask whether they are offering you the position.

Marie and I responded to an advertisement just after Thanksgiving for family support specialist positions; we applied as a husband-and-wife team. Marie had been working for the state's family services department for 15 months and I with individuals with developmental disabilities. We applied together as we thought we had nothing to lose. Within the first week of applying we were called for an interview; at that point even if we did not get job offers we knew we could apply elsewhere. It was confidence building and allowed us to see just how marketable we could be with enough creativity. The first interview went well, and we were called in for a second interview. All had seemingly been going in our favor by Christmas, when we received a phone call from the program coordinator, who said, "I would like to talk to you [both] about placement in our agency." We interpreted this to mean that we were being offered jobs; however, by the middle of January we found that a decision had not been made. We learned to be careful about interpretations, but we remained hopeful because she [the program coordinator] still was interested in us. After three interviews, for which the agency paid our flight and lodging expenses, we were finally offered positions with the agency. In fact, although I was not hired for the initial position to work with a middle school, the agency felt so strongly about both of us that a position was created for me to work not with one area school but with each of the four area schools.

Interestingly, we had met with the executive director, program coordinator, program director of the adolescent treatment unit, the assistant principal, and the counselor of the middle school, on separate occasions, all before a decision was finally made. We never could say for sure whether we had the jobs, even with all the interviews and three expense-paid trips. In fact, following the third meeting, I was told that I had a 90 percent chance of having a job. The position had to be created and money for a salary had to be agreed on before the program coordinator could give a

definite yes. Quite an experience for us, but one that, fortunately, worked out.

The Offer

When you receive an offer, it is likely to be made over the telephone. The call should be followed by a letter or contract specifying the job title, unit or department, starting date, starting salary, location (if there is more than one), and moving or travel reimbursement terms, if relevant. If you negotiate any additional items successfully, you ought to receive a new letter or contract or contract addendum. Items you will want to see before accepting the offer include a job description and information detailing benefits.

Compensation and Benefits

Your compensation or salary may be stated in yearly, monthly, hourly, or, in the case of a project, a lump-sum payment. Be sure you understand the terms. Travel reimbursement, bonuses, and profit sharing (for-profit organizations only) also may be part of the compensation.

Benefits typically average between 25 percent and 30 percent of the total compensation package. Your benefits will consist of many, if not most, of the following:

- continuing education (memberships, conferences)
- dental insurance
- disability insurance
- family leave
- flexible ("cafeteria") benefits
- health insurance
- holidays
- liability/malpractice insurance
- life insurance
- long-term care insurance
- retirement
- sick leave
- social work professional liability insurance
- stock options
- supervision for social work licensure

- supplemental benefits
- tax benefits (social security, Medicare, unemployment)
- vacation leave
- workers compensation

Notes on Particular Benefits

The following are items to look for in the information given to you at the time of the offer. Ask questions if the written material is not clear. This information is an overview; particulars will vary across organizations.

Disability Insurance

Is there a waiting period for eligibility? Long-term disability insurance is as important than life insurance. If disability insurance is offered, seriously consider purchasing it. The premium is very reasonable—bills will continue to come in when you are disabled and not receiving your full salary.

Pretax Benefits

You may be able to designate some of your salary for either out-of-pocket health care or child care and pay those expenses with before-tax dollars. The money goes directly into an account for that specified purpose. If you choose to use this option, estimate realistically—by law, any funds left in the account at the end of the year are forfeited.

Health, Dental, and Long-Term Care Insurance

What are the premiums, deductibles, and copayments? If there is an employee premium, is it pretax or posttax? What is the out-of-pocket maximum? Are prescriptions, chiropractic services, and vision needs covered? To help you make comparisons, find out the community rates for health insurance. New federal law states that insurance companies may neither consider nor exclude from coverage pre-existing conditions. Just as in the interview phase, think carefully about person-al information you might disclose by asking particular questions. However, do obtain the information you need to make decisions.

Liability/Malpractice Insurance

Most employers purchase a blanket liability/malpractice insurance policy for the organization that covers the organization, if it is named in a lawsuit, and its employees, in which case an individual social worker is covered under the employer's malpractice/liability insurance policy. (See also "Social Work Professional Liability Insurance" below.) It is wise to inquire about liability coverage and to obtain or continue private coverage even if the employer provides it.

Life Insurance

Your employer may provide basic life insurance as part of your benefits. You may also be able to purchase conditional term insurance through the employer, which would cover burial costs and pay debts, such as home, automobile, and student loans, upon your death. Some people recommend that you do not buy whole life insurance because it is too expensive. Review this option with your personal financial adviser.

Social Work Professional Liability Insurance

Although not common, some employers pay the premium or reimburse employees who purchase a professional liability insurance policy from an independent firm such as the NASW Insurance Trust. Individuals should be encouraged to obtain a personal policy even if they have some coverage elsewhere. Although this may result in duplication of some coverage, the person who owns and pays for the policy has far better long-term control and coverage against a lawsuit. A personal policy is especially indicated if the social worker conducts any social work outside the employment environment, such as volunteer or private practice or teaching.

COBRA

The Comprehensive Omnibus Budget Reconciliation Act, or COBRA, is stipulated by federal law for organizations of 20 or more employees and enables you to continue your health care insurance at your own expense for a limited time after you or your dependents are no longer eligible for health care coverage under your employer's plan. COBRA is important for bridging health insurance between jobs.

Retirement

The most common retirement benefits are defined-benefit plans and 401(k) and 403(b) defined-contribution plans. If the employer offers a retirement benefit, find out when you can become eligible for the plan and whether it is a defined-benefit plan or a defined-contribution plan. Under the defined-benefit plan, the employee is paid a set amount by the employer upon retirement. There are five major types of defined-contribution plans:

1. *Money purchase plan.* The employer makes a contribution, based on a percentage of your salary, to an account in your name.
2. *401(k) and 403(b).* Both you and the employer make contributions to an account. If you choose not to sign up for this benefit at the outset of employment, ask whether you can do so in the future (this option may come up once or twice a year).
3. *Profit sharing.* At the end of the year, the employer makes a contribution, based on a percentage of the company's profits, to an account in your name.
4. *Employee stock purchase plan.* For-profit companies may offer a stock purchase plan as their retirement benefit. This means that you have the opportunity to buy stock in the company. The cost is deducted from your paycheck, and the company covers any brokerage fees.
5. *Employee stock option plan.* The employer purchases shares of its own stock and puts

them in an account in your name. This is sometimes considered a defined-benefit pension plan.

Tax Benefits

The employer pays federal and state unemployment taxes and workers compensation. These costs are not deducted from your paycheck. However, 7.65 percent of your salary is deducted from your paycheck under Federal Insurance Contribution Act (FICA) regulations for social security (6.2 percent) and Medicare (1.45 percent). Note that the salary cap on social security is indexed annually, which affects the amount deducted.

Supplemental Plans

The employer may offer supplemental plans such as life insurance through payroll deductions.

Making a Decision

To make a wise choice, you'll need to look carefully at your original goals and the information you have about the market. Ask yourself a few more questions.

Questions Related to Job Fit

- Is this job directly related to what you want to do now?
- Is this opportunity in line with what you learned in researching the market?
- What are the positive and negative aspects of this job?
- Will you be giving up anything by taking this position? (This is an especially important question when you are comparing two offers.)
- Can you work with the supervisor, coworkers, subordinates, volunteers, and board members?
- Can you support the mission of the organization?
- How well do the philosophy and values of the organization match yours?

- Does this job offer enough challenge? In other words, can you do this job without thinking, will it challenge you, or is it out of the range of your current skills? Is there a good balance between the two extremes?
- What can you learn from your superiors in this job?
- How well does this job fit the dream job you originally outlined?
- Is there an orientation? Is it "Here are the policy manuals and go to it," or is there a detailed orientation?

Questions Related to Career Goals
- Is this a good stepping stone for future jobs?
- Will you be using the skills that you want to develop?
- What type of supervision will you receive?
- Will the job meet your needs for licensure or certification?
- Will future employers regard the experience you gain on the job as valuable to their organizations?
- How well does this job prepare you for what you want to do next?

Questions about the Compensation Package
- Is this a salaried, hourly, contractual, or per diem position?
- Is the pay in the appropriate range?
- Does the employer require that you directly earn through billable hours a percentage of your salary? How do you do this? What is the penalty for not meeting that target? How often does the percentage goal change and at what rate?
- Do you pay for the supervision required for licensure? Will a qualified staff member, other than your direct supervisor, be able to provide supervision? Did you meet her or him?
- Will you be traveling for the job? What is the reimbursement rate?

- What opportunities are there for continuing education? Does the employer pay for enough continuing education hours to meet licensure requirements? Do you get time off to attend seminars?
- How flexible do you need to be with your time? Many, if not most, social work jobs require hours beyond a 37- to 40-hour workweek. Is there a policy on compensatory time?
- Must you meet a required number of billable hours each week? How many? What happens if you do not meet that minimum?
- Does the agency prohibit staff from doing outside contract work or consulting or holding a second job?

Questions about the Hiring Process
- Were you given a tour of the facility? Did you see where you would be working?
- Did you meet your direct supervisor, coworkers, and other pertinent people?
- Did you see a job description? (Sometimes organizations do not have job descriptions.)
- Did the staff take time to consider whether you were the right candidate? Did they interview other candidates? If your answers are no and it seems that the decision to hire you was made too quickly, consider whether you are looking at a red flag. Why are they so enthusiastic and hasty?
- Is the job too good to be true? Is the salary unusually high for your experience and this type of position, organization, and geographical area? Why? What can your network advisers tell you?
- Is there a probation period, and how long is it?

An Early Offer
Like the person described in the chapter on researching the market, you may get an offer early in the job-search process. If so, you may have some anxiety about your decision to accept

or decline the offer. Often, an early offer is an unusual opportunity; it may be extremely attractive monetarily, a chance to do something out of the ordinary, or a chance to get you into a field you hadn't considered before. In any case, you will need to weigh your options carefully.

If the offer is a solid stepping-stone to your future and you feel positive about the job and organization, take advantage of the opportunity. This is a particularly important decision if you are geographically restricted.

For alumni or new graduates with previous experience who are seeking a promotion, changing functions, or even changing fields, knowledge of the market and a clear sense of direction are critical to decision making.

Waiting for a Second Offer

A challenge in the job-search process is timing a decision on your offers. When the offer is made, ask when the employer needs a decision.

If you have another interview scheduled or are waiting to hear about another offer, see if you can negotiate a decision date for the offer you have. Respect the needs of the employer as well as your own; he or she may not be able to extend the deadline. Be certain to explain to the employer that you want to make the best decision for you and the organization. Being able to consider the other option will help you do that.

Of course, you may have to make a decision on the offer without a second offer to consider. This is when your knowledge of the job market is particularly critical. Is the market so tight that you ought to secure this opportunity? Or does your research and overall feedback from contacts and employers indicate that the market is good, and you have a chance at other opportunities? And how long can you wait for another opportunity to come along?

Sometimes employers want a decision the same day they extend an offer. It may be that their first-choice candidate accepted the job two weeks ago and changed his or her mind just a few days before the training program began. On the other hand, it could be a red flag indicating that the organization does not plan ahead. Regardless, ask for an extension, if only for 24 hours.

In December, a social worker interviewed with two hospitals for comparable jobs. She would have enjoyed either position. The first hospital director called to say that she would be away for a few weeks and would make a decision when she returned. She also requested that the candidate call her if she got a second offer. The second hospital director did not indicate when she would make a decision. After the holidays, the social worker, having not heard from either employer, decided to send a copy of a paper she had written to the first hospital director—they had discussed the project during the interview, and the social worker thought it would demonstrate her continued interest in the job. A couple of days later, she received a temporary job offer from a third hospital. The social worker called the first hospital director to say that she had a second offer but was still interested in the job.

Perhaps because she was pressed for time, the director was not very talkative on the telephone. The social worker, who wanted to give the third hospital a decision soon but remained more interested in the pending opportunities, sought advice from a contact. Consequently, she took the following steps: She called the third hospital and asked whether they could wait until Friday for an answer; they understood the circumstances and said yes. Next, she called the second hospital director, told her of the offer and deadline, and asked when the director might make a decision. The director said that she would call back with an answer but could not be more specific. The social worker then sent a fax to the first hospital director, indicating her continued interest and the deadline for the decision on the temporary job. The first hospital director called the social worker that evening to invite her in for a second interview. They met.

The director said that she was her first-choice candidate if a current staff member did not accept the position. Late Friday morning, the director of the first hospital called to offer the job. The social worker accepted, called the third hospital to decline the temporary job, and later that day received an offer from the second hospital.

Unfortunately, the timing of job offers does not always work so well. In another instance, a social worker received an offer for a job she would be satisfied with. The agency wanted a decision the next day. The social worker made a request for more time to decide, but it was not granted. In the time that she had, she called the second organization with which she had interviewed and whose job was more interesting to her. The person she spoke with told her that the person who would be making the decision was out of town and that he did not know how likely it was that an offer would be extended. Although the person she talked to in the office tried to be of assistance, nothing could be done before the social worker had to make a decision on the first agency's offer. She decided to take the position—she knew from her research and job-search experience that the market was tight. Later she learned that the second agency had planned on offering her a job.

Negotiation

If you decide that you want the job but you want to negotiate the terms, this is the time to do it—before you accept the job. Although it is best to negotiate before accepting the job, it is not unheard of for social workers to successfully increase their salaries after beginning work, for example, a home health social work director who made a point of raising the issue every six months, or a master's degree holder who after a week on the job with supervisory responsibilities decided that she was underpaid. It is especially important for women to negotiate an offer; women in social work continue to lag behind their male counterparts (Linsley, 2003).

What to Negotiate

You may want to discuss salary, benefits, job duties, job title, resources to do the job, moving expenses, time off for your wedding or the family reunion that was planned a year ago, or a starting date. For example, you may be able to negotiate a starting date so that you can take a break between jobs or begin on a part-time basis before graduation.

Information to Gather

Before you discuss salary or the compensation package of salary and benefits, you need to answer several questions and consider special cases:

- How much do you want the position? Do you anticipate another offer soon? Is the market strong enough that you could decline this position?
- Based on your research (see chapter 2), what salary do you want and think is appropriate for the position and title?
- What is the salary range for this position?
- What salary would you accept? Based on your budget, what is your minimum?
- What specific assets (value) do you bring that would justify a higher figure?
- Is this a permanent position, a consulting position, or a temporary, for example, grant, position?
- When are raises given and on what basis? Are they based on performance and contributions? What has been the average annual salary increase in the past two years? How does that compare with national and local trends?
- Is there a bonus plan (primarily offered by for-profit organizations but occasionally seen in nonprofit groups) or profit sharing (for-profit organizations)?
- Does the package include benefits? If yes, how do they compare to benefits for your present position or for other positions you considered? How much will be taken out of your paycheck for benefits? If the

compensation package does not include benefits, you will want a salary that is at least 25 percent higher than a comparable position that includes benefits.

- If you are applying for a faculty position, you might have questions about summer salary and faculty housing.
- Who is the appropriate person at the organization regarding decisions on the compensation package?
- Make a list of priorities for items you want to negotiate (see exhibit 6.1).

Other Considerations
Contract Positions

If you take a contract job and you do not make enough to pay taxes, you must prepay social security quarterly in a lump sum. Also check on social work professional liability coverage, because you probably are not covered as a contract worker.

PRN Positions

If you are a PRN (pro re nata or, whenever necessary) employee, you work on an as-needed basis. You are not likely to have benefits, but your social security and other taxes are withheld. Be certain that you do not take all of this for granted—check it out.

Process

The following is a suggested process for coming to an agreement on a position offer. Your training in communications skills in social work, particularly your listening skills, will be to your advantage.

- Express your appreciation for the offer and indicate your interest in the position. This could include specific aspects.
- Go over your questions regarding the job description, benefits, etc. If possible, conclude this conversation by thanking the employer and stating when you will call back. Now is the time to review this new information. Then make a second call

to review and negotiate the offer if possible in person.
- Again, affirm your interest. Then state what you would like included or changed in the offer, for example, "I would like to discuss the starting date and salary."
- Reaffirm interest in a package that will work for both you and the employer.

If you are interested in negotiating the salary, do the following:

- Ask, "How did you determine this offer?" "What factors did you take into consideration?"
- Confirm or ask what the salary range is for the position.
- Confirm or ask what is the midpoint for the position.
- State a salary range (such as in the mid-forties). Your target figure should be the midpoint and your minimum figure should be the bottom of the range.
- State why you are seeking a salary in this range (See "Factors to Consider When Negotiating" below). Keep your argument simple; three reasons are sufficient. You do not want to give a laundry list even though all factors might apply.
- Do not expect a decision on the spot. Do arrange when and with whom you will follow up.
- Restate your interest in reaching an acceptable agreement and your continued interest in the position.
- If you are fully or partially successful in negotiating your offer, request the new offer in writing.
- Follow up with a letter(s) to confirm your acceptance and appreciation with those involved in the negotiation process and other key individuals.

Not everyone goes through all these steps. Each of the following approaches has been used by social workers:

- Tell the employer what you are looking for, such as a specific salary figure, and state your reasons.
- When negotiating a salary, give the employer a figure that is higher than you are willing to accept.
- If you have another formal offer that you will accept if this negotiation is not successful, tell the employer with whom you are negotiating that you have another offer and what the salary is. The employer may match or exceed that offer. Do not bluff.
- For example, a new MSW graduate decided to negotiate a salary for a position she had been offered in fundraising for a large development organization. She had completed a practicum in this organization and had at least one additional opportunity with a similar organization.

In preparation for this meeting, I put all my thoughts down on paper. Before I started negotiating, I told him that I appreciated the offer. I added that I would take the job, but I wanted to know I had made all the effort I could to negotiate a higher salary. He seemed to appreciate my honesty and initiative. I negotiated for an increase by referring him to my experience in the office and community and pointed out that he did not have to spend money to "bring me out" for an interview, a cost which this organization, which recruited nationally, would normally incur. He agreed with my negotiating points and asked me how much additional salary I would like. Now, here is where I was a little taken aback, because I had not predetermined an amount. My offer from the similar organization was $1,500 more for a higher level position, but it was for a job I did not want as much. I asked for $1,000. He increased the base salary by $500.

An MSW graduate seeking a policy position in a very small and difficult market decided to consider other locations. Her spouse had a teaching commitment for another semester, but was willing to move after the term. She quickly found a position that matched her interests:

The offer was okay for the geographic location, cost of living, and my level of experience. However, accepting the offer meant additional expenses for moving, setting up a second residence, and traveling to see my spouse. After consulting with others, I told the director that my decision on the job did not depend on salary, but I would greatly appreciate it if she met me halfway between the salary range (she had stated a range giving the high number first and then the low number, which was the original salary offered). The difference between the offer and the high figure was $3,500). The director quickly got my point and agreed to increase the starting salary by $1,700.

After searching for six months and turning down several positions, an MSW graduate seeking a supervisory position finally found the position she wanted and decided to negotiate the salary and some benefits:

They had given me the salary range for the position and I knew quite a lot about comparable positions with other organizations. I wanted the top of the range and beyond. This was a significant position with a lot of responsibility, not just for a population of clients, but for a program as well, and required significant work on a computer. I outlined my value to the organization— capability in both clinical treatment and program development, and training skills. I sent them a written counteroffer that included the salary figure I was looking for, plus flex time to work from home certain days, a laptop computer, and a cell phone. The organization was ready to make this arrangement; they agreed with my request.

Many in the field lament that social workers undersell themselves, taking their skills and experience for granted and settling for less money than they are worth. Even if you do not intend to negotiate an offer, read about negotiation. Your understanding will increase your confidence, particularly in making decisions about offers. If you plan to negotiate, be sure that you adapt what you read to your circumstances and the market. One social worker found that reading about negotiation gave her a framework to consider, but that elements of it did not fit her field of social work. (For more details on negotiation, read the books listed at the end of appendix 3.)

Deciding among Offers: Some Examples

I turned down the program director position for one agency—low pay, no benefits, and an executive director with whom I would have had great difficulty working. I also turned down the position of executive director of the assistance program, a homeless shelter under the umbrella of another agency. This job probably would have been extremely stressful, partly because of the nature of the agency's work, but also because its board, although supportive of the agency's work, is not sufficiently involved to provide a good working relationship with the executive director. It also needs a lot of work on diversifying its funding base—it has solid revenue from government, but cash-flow challenges. It would have been a very lonely job—lots of responsibilities and stress, but with no built-in support for the executive director.

The job I accepted is in the family division at an agency. It has the decidedly unglamorous title of project coordinator, but is designed to serve as a leadership position to help expand the division. I have several major assignments: (1) provide leadership in getting the division's center accredited, (2) develop and implement a marketing plan for the center, and (3) help in development of management systems to integrate an early childhood program grant with the existing regular research project. Other possible smaller projects include diversity work for the division and help in the area of job placement and retention for division clients.

The plus side of this job is that I know and like this agency, they know and like me, and the job content is work that will be important to them and fulfilling to me. The minus side is that the project work will be completed in about 18 months, so I will have to find another position afterward. But the agency really wanted me—including the executive director and the human resources director—so I'm willing to deal with that situation.

A new MSW graduate had two interviews. One was for a youth development position in a small community for a university extension service; she received an offer after the interview. The second was for a position as an entry-level public policy specialist with a multiservice agency for people with disabilities. The second agency said it would try to let her know the outcome before the next week, when she had to make a decision on the first offer. This is how she compared the positions, anticipating a second offer:

The job description for the extension position sounds interesting, the benefits and salary are good, there's a lot of flexibility and autonomy in the position; the drawback is location. My fear is that I may not be in an ideal part of the state to network and eventually to move into policy, which is what I ultimately want to do.

The job description for the second job also sounds like I'd have a lot of the tasks and responsibilities that interest me. I could obviously gain the public policy skills in this job. The drawback is that it is not directly related to children and families. It came out in the interview that I would not be doing any child-specific policy work. The issues they deal with are accessibility, telecommunications, transportation, appropriations for independent-living centers, and so on. The salary would not be as high as that for the first offer.

A third possibility is to not take either job and keep looking, but this may be based on the false notion that there is a "perfect" job.

She did receive the second offer and took it. Although the population of the first job met her interests, she concluded that she had a better chance of working in the child and family policy by getting policy experience, even though it was on behalf of a different population. Furthermore, during discussions with the employer about her acceptance of the position she was able to negotiate for the opportunity to develop some policy initiatives for children with disabilities.

Accepting or Declining the Offer

Give yourself at least 24 hours to think about a job offer. If you are having difficulty making a decision, consider calling one of your advisers. Then accept an offer as soon as you make your decision. A telephone call followed by a letter is appropriate. Confirm the following in your letter and keep a copy of it:

- position title
- specific department in which this position is located (if applicable)
- one sentence stating the responsibilities
- salary
- starting date
- special items (moving expenses, for example).

After you accept an offer, you should receive a letter or contract from the employer that states the title, salary, and starting date for the position. Read it carefully; make sure it is what you agreed to orally. Keep the formal letter of offer or a copy of the contract. It is not recommended that you start a position without a formal written offer and job description. Both you and the employer could encounter a surprise in this process, as the following example shows:

A school district made an offer over the phone to a social worker who was looking for her second career position.

She accepted it and requested the offer in writing. A week and a half later, she received a contract showing a lower salary than what was stated over the phone. The social worker called the employer, who said that he lowered the salary after reviewing her transcripts. The employer assumed that the 60 credits for the master's degree were in addition to credits at the bachelor degree level. However, the social worker had received advanced-standing credit in her master's program for some of her BSW course work. According to the district's salary schedule, which sets salary steps by credits and not by degrees, the credits could not be applied to both degrees.

The change in salary was a disappointment, but the social worker accepted the position because it met her goal to work for the district.

If you decide to decline the offer, then let the employer know as soon as possible by telephone and follow-up with a letter of thanks. These courtesies leave the door open for future communication.

After Accepting the Offer

Stay in touch with the supervisor between the time you accept the offer and your starting date. This is particularly important if you are relocating. Keep the employer informed about how to reach you, particularly during your move.

You may be asked to take care of personnel paperwork, get a physical, meet with the staff, attend a particular function, or participate in a training session before your starting date, without pay. This is not uncommon.

Changes in the Job

For most people, the process of starting a new position goes smoothly. They find their perceptions and sources of information were accurate, the job descriptions they were given match what they are doing, and the organizations anticipated their arrival.

However, unforeseen events not under the control of the employer sometimes occur: A new grant comes through or is unexpectedly not renewed, a staff member leaves suddenly or becomes seriously ill, upper-level management decides to cut all department budgets and eliminates positions, or a natural disaster hits. Such events can quickly affect positions at all levels. You might discover that your new job will be at a different location or that, instead of working with adults, you will work primarily with children. You may look at such a change as an opportunity. Alternatively, you could decide to leave, if you feel the change takes you too far afield from your goals or you do not like the way the organization handled the situation.

References

Linsley, J. (2003). Social work salaries: keeping up with the times? *The New Social Worker, 10,* 7-8.

CHAPTER 6 QUICK TIPS

Evaluating Offers

- Make sure that you have an official offer that does not need to be approved by anyone else.
- If the organization has not given you information on benefits in addition to the salary figure, request it and ask for clarification if you need it.
- Spend at least 24 hours considering whether the offer fits your career, salary, and benefits needs. If you need more time, request it—especially if you are waiting to hear about a second offer—but be reasonable.
- Contact other organizations with which you have interviewed or applied to inform them that you have an offer; and inquire about their timetables for making a decision. Try to determine whether you are among their top candidates, and remind them of your interest in and qualifications for the job.
- If you choose to negotiate for salary or benefits, carefully outline the reasons the organization should compensate you differently for your services. In the case of salary, state a range starting at your minimum acceptable figure if the employer will negotiate at all. Expect to state your reasons and attempt to reach an agreement at the midpoint of the range.
- As soon as you have made a decision (either yes or no), speak to the employer and follow up with a letter.

CHAPTER SEVEN

Career Management and Professional Development

Inside Chapter 7

Career Management
Professional Development

"People do not plan careers—they happen." This is the observation of one social worker whose career has consisted of many positions, including a transition into the managed care industry. You might agree with this statement, but if you ask people how they heard about each job they had and what enabled them to make each move, you will hear about actions each person took that triggered changes or created circumstances that eventually made that strand of career opportunities happen.

That focus on personal actions that galvanize careers has never been more important than today. The volatile employment patterns of the for-profit sector continue to affect social work, even more powerfully than did the political changes of the early 1980s. There are no guarantees of permanent employment in any economic sector today (Bridges, 1994; Hakim, 1994; Rifkin, 1995). However, there are actions you can take and habits you can develop that will increase your confidence and options.

"Career resilience" (Waterman, Waterman, & Collard, 1994) and "career self-reliance" (Collard, Epperheimer, & Saign, 1996) became slogans in the business environment of the 1990s, when employers could no longer guarantee jobs, much less manage careers for employees, as some corporations once did. Although social workers typically have not received career management assistance from organizations, they enjoyed relative stability in employment in social services in the 1990s. However, the cost-cutting, outcomes-driven business environment is increasingly adapted to traditional social work employment settings and is exacerbated by the current state budget crises. Social workers, even in the most stable of settings, are not protected by niches or profession-specific work carved out over the past century. Social workers now have to define what they do and demonstrate their cost-effectiveness.

"Social workers must be able to demonstrate competencies rather than advocate only for discipline protection. The fact that one is a social worker does not guarantee that one can achieve the outcomes that a given employer is seeking," says Vivian Jackson, cochair, Council on Social Work Education (CSWE) Commission on Social Work Practice (personal communication, January 30, 2003). Discussion in social work education about competencies—what graduates should know and be able to perform—has been extensive. Like social workers at all levels and in all types of work, you must be able to define what you can do, verify how effective your work is, and articulate your contributions to the organization, regardless of whether you are in or are competing for a job titled "social worker." Assume that you will be competing with people from other disciplines for every opportunity you seek and that management, with rare exceptions, will not fully understand what social work has to offer.

Career Management

To manage a career today, you need to think proactively, experiment, and pursue specific interests. This is not a clear-cut strategic planning process but a journey, as Stumpf (1989) and others described career management. The following approaches will help you address your social work career management needs:

- stay current on trends
- improve your performance
- increase your visibility and reputation
- build and use your contact network
- advocate for political and professional change
- research your options
- experiment with ideas and expand goals
- update your self-assessment and résumé or vita
- increase your qualifications through professional development.

In each section that follows you will find questions and suggestions to consider as you think about strengthening and managing your career. Interviews with social workers in various fields and functions generated several of these ideas.

Trends

Your career opportunities and daily work activities will continue to be influenced by several of the following trends.

- *Economics.* In recent years reductions in public and private funding have increased expectations for managing health and mental health care costs. Accountability for results will continue the increased expectations for basing practice on the best evidence and documenting all service outcomes. This climate has spurred competition for funding resources, increased fundraising, fee for service revenue, and pushed the need for entrepreneurship in social services and health care. Limited funding also has prompted privatization, partnership, acquisition, collaboration, reorganization, teamwork, merging, downsizing, and declassification among public and private entities, and it has created a trend toward temporary employment.

- *Technology.* Your work will depend more and more on your ability to manage information through technology, whether you are following cases, providing treatment, manipulating budgets, analyzing records, researching program options, or evaluating policies and programs.

- *Demographics.* The increasing average age and cultural diversity of the U.S. population is changing policies, services delivery, and funding not only for elders but also for other populations.

- *Policy.* Changes in social policies and continued efforts to balance budgets, among other national and state issues, also are affecting services, practice, and funding.

- *Regulation and financing.* Changes in regulations are pushing for treatment data standardization, greater controls on records, higher levels of accountability, and more flexibility in managing funds across public programs. The increases in licensure, certification, privatization, and declassification of jobs in the public sector are giving more options to some social workers and limiting them for others. State-regulated credentials have emerged in several fields of practice, such as marriage and family therapy, thereby increasing the competition for jobs and, in some cases, restricting the scope of work previously done by social workers.

- *Globalization.* As in all industries and professions, communication, cooperation, and competition across cultures are growing. Although the U.S. not-for-profit sector has not felt the impact of globalization to the same degree as the for-profit sector, exchanges around intervention technologies and, ultimately, competition for funding resources are increasing.

• *Knowledge.* The growth in information, particularly that which results from research, will continue to affect the field. Social work's own research arena is beginning to build and guide practice. New thinking on effective delivery of services is resulting in "co-occurring treatment" for mental health and substance abuse patients as well as cross training for professionals. Managed care is suggesting a "co-location," which places mental health professionals in the same location with primary care health care services for easier access.

Keeping up with internal organizational changes; shifts at the local, regional, and national levels; developments in credentials; and advances in technology can be overwhelming. Professional associations (for example, NASW, CSWE, International Federation of Social Workers) and advocacy or trade associations (Child Welfare League of America and Alliance for Children and Families among others) with strong advocacy, legislative, or credentialing committees can help you keep track of the progress on various issues through action alerts, news summaries, and reports. Following Web sites and reading key publications can help you stay abreast of situations. For example, for people following the field of domestic relations, LaDeana Gamble (manager, Family Mediation Center, Las Vegas) recommends the *Family Court Review—An Interdisciplinary Journal, Journal of Family Issues*, and reviews done by the Association of Family and Conciliation Courts on research in the child custody arena (personal communication, January 21, 2003). The Internet and listservs are excellent sources for clarifying and expanding your knowledge of issues (some Internet sites are listed in appendix 8).

Ask yourself these questions and follow this advice:
• How are you keeping up with changes in funding, policies, and services?
• How are public and private funding patterns changing?

• What will be the focus tomorrow in social and economic policy and social services?
• What opportunities do these changes present?

Try to anticipate the outcomes of new or anticipated legislation. Make it your business to know how the objectives of your organization are being adapted to the current environment. Legal credentials, state licenses and certificates, and employer or third-party preferred professional credentials could restrict mobility among fields of practice and work settings. Who is your source for information on these issues?

Performance

Peak performance adds leverage to any career move you make. If you are performing well in your current professional work, chances are your accomplishments and contributions are being noted by others. In addition, your confidence is probably high and your messages are crisp. This is when special projects and invitations to participate in particular groups are likely to be offered to you, or you begin to see a solution to a problem or a new way to approach your work, for example. Think about past opportunities you discovered or received unsolicited.

Were you at peak performance? What is your performance level now? If you are at peak performance, are you thinking about how your reputation might enable you to make a change? Or is your performance preventing you from making a career move? Do others see you as an effective problem solver, a team player with a positive attitude, a strong advocate, an independent staff member, a leader, a staff member with good judgment, or as someone who looks for opportunities tied to change? Is your work based on evidence as well as practice wisdom? What would references say about your performance? Do you need to improve your performance before you apply for new positions?

For example, on the basis of her performance, a social worker with an MSW degree who was employed by a county foster care unit was offered the position of supervisor of a newly created mini-unit designed to improve the supervisor-to-staff ratio. She had excelled in managing a caseload of foster care, adoption, independent living, and adolescent foster care services. Her work had included supervising one social worker with a BSW.

Visibility and Reputation

Although a contact network is important to your day-to-day work and job-search efforts, the visibility of your work is even more powerful. A contact may be able to introduce you to someone, but a colleague who has seen your performance or products can recommend you highly. It is the person whose work is seen by audiences outside his or her organization who receives unsolicited opportunities.

Ask yourself these questions: Who sees your work? Are your job tasks, community efforts, or professional activities visible to other social workers, community leaders, politicians, and people from other disciplines? Have you sought out opportunities for projects, writing, presenting, and leadership, which let others see you perform? Does your work distinguish you from others, particularly those from other disciplines? If you are looking for a job, consider positions that give you opportunities to work with professionals and volunteers from outside your organization, positions that give you visibility. If you are reentering the field, what volunteer work will offer visibility?

For example, one social worker who was a labor representative and lobbyist for a union used his community-organizing skills to tackle social issues at the state and national levels; he ran for the state legislature and narrowly lost. In his campaign he brought new social issues of pay equity, family leave, and health care access to the political debate. After the election he continued his work on these key issues. His visibility enabled him to win a legislative seat in the next state election.

Contact Network

"Who you know"—whoever that is—cannot guarantee you a job, but your network of contacts can provide a critical communication conduit. A well-developed contact network increases the chances that you will find out not only about jobs but also about changes in organizations, trends, policies, funding, and leadership. Contacts, especially distant contacts, can be particularly useful in identifying jobs and other professional opportunities those in your more immediate network are not likely to hear about (Granovetter, 1995). The research of your network and the care you give it (currency) will influence the types of information you receive. A social worker whose job required participation in the local chamber of commerce had a broader understanding of the community and its opportunities. Laura Groshong, chair of government relations, Clinical Social Work Federation, recommends that private practitioners maintain three networks: a referral network, a clinical colleague network to deal with isolation, and a network through a different social work role, such as advocacy (personal communication, January 21, 2003).

Ask yourself how well you have maintained your contact network. For example, do you know the local leaders in your field of practice? Do you know those at the state, regional, national, or international level? Are you involved in a professional, advocacy, or community organization that enables you to be part of the discussions of issues and puts you in contact with others in your field? Do you have contact with political leaders or professionals in other disciplines who are working on issues critical in your field of practice? If you use a referral network on the job, is it as up to date as you would like it to be? Do you need to get involved to reconnect? What steps can you take to establish your presence?

For example, a social worker had networked to find work at the federal level. Her work as a child protective services supervisor entailed contact with a coworker who had recently moved from the county child welfare system to the federal government. The social worker heard about an opening for a child welfare policy specialist from the coworker. She applied and received an offer.

Advocacy

You have seen how public policies and regulations affect every aspect of social work. They affect the policies of private, not-for-profit organizations and corporations such as insurance companies, health corporations, and banks, as well as the regulations of credentialing bodies that concern your clients, your work, and even your future. If you are not already involved in advocacy, look into the efforts of professional societies, such as NASW, the Clinical Social Work Federation, Inc., chapters, and the American Society on Aging; advocacy and trade associations, such as the National Assembly of Health and Human Service Organizations and Child Welfare League of America; advocacy or consumer groups specific to your local community, such as units or committees associated with United Way, Junior League, or Urban League; and state licensing boards. (See appendixes 1 and 8.)

How can you advocate for clients and legislation and policies that affect practice and vendorship? John Morris, MSW, professor in the Department of Neuropsychiatry and Behavioral Science at the University of South Carolina and former director of mental health for that state, cautions: "Your career is at high risk if you are simply doing your assigned duties every day; in an increasingly competitive work environment, professionals need to be active in professional organizations that further the broad goals of the field" (personal communication, January 17, 2003).

Options

Options for your next career move and later moves can be grouped into actions that enhance your current position, opportunities in your organization, social work opportunities in other organizations, and opportunities to make contributions in other fields. These categories can give you a starting point for exploring alternatives.

Enhancing Your Current Position

Are there aspects of your job that you can do differently? Could you delegate more work? Could you rotate responsibilities with another staff member? Could you take on a special project? Is there a program for cross training at your organization, or can you create one?

Opportunities in Your Organization

For what other positions in your agency do you qualify or could qualify for in the future? What changes are anticipated in your organization, and what needs or opportunities might those changes create (Bridges, 1994)? Does your organization need expertise on a new issue, or computerization, evaluation, or fundraising skills that you could develop? How have others with or formerly with the organization enhanced their jobs, received promotions, or moved to new agencies?

Perhaps others on staff also are ready for a change. Listen to the needs expressed by staff, and consider their skills and the expanding needs of your employer. Could you propose a new staffing configuration to management? Use the skills listed in appendix 10 to help you detail job tasks in a proposal. If you work in a large bureaucracy, consider moving into central administration.

Social Work Opportunities in Other Organizations

If your position and organization do not offer attractive career growth options, what else is available in the community? Do you want to make a lateral move, look for a promotion, or find temporary work? Do you want to work for an organization that serves many social services where you will get a broad look at operations and models? Refer to the following resources, especially to sort out your options for moves across social work fields.

- Use appendix 4 and *What Social Workers Do* by Margaret Gibelman (2005) for additional ideas on your options in social work.
- Read appendix 10 if you need help deciding on a new functional area.
- Use chapter 2 as a guide for researching options in your market.
- Use the exercises in chapter 1 and the lists in appendix 10 to assess your background.
- If you are a member of NASW or other associations, ask the staff, leaders, and members whether they know of others who have switched fields. Ask for information interviews with those who have made transitions.
- Use the alumni online directory of your undergraduate or graduate school or ask for names of alumni working in the fields that interest you; contact them and seek their advice on transferring your present social work skills to their specific fields.

A social worker who had several years of experience in services for people with mental retardation, foster care, and family preservation wanted to make a move to macro level social work at the national level after adjunct teaching and part-time consultation for a couple of years while raising children. The move was proving difficult, so she took a lateral position and continued to teach part time. A colleague who was working for a national association encouraged her to continue applying for national arena jobs—the social worker had been the number two candidate for nine national-arena jobs over the years she had been looking. Then another part-time instructor told her about a part-time temporary job at a national organization. She got the temporary job, proved herself, and when her supervisor left, the organization promoted her to that full-time slot. Her later projects and publications established her reputation and resulted in invitations from outside organizations to sit on commissions.

Opportunities to Make Contributions in Other Fields

If you went through the exercises in chapter 1, you may have found that you would like to try switching fields in social services or moving outside the traditional realm of social work. Here are some resources for exploring options.

- Use the sections in chapter 1 on educating yourself on new areas and moving across fields and functions to look at the process of making a move.
- If you are having difficulty identifying options, start with an issue area that you now address and brainstorm all the roles, disciplines, types of organizations (not-for-profit, for profit, public), fields, and services that research or study, organize, problem solve, serve, finance, regulate, coordinate with, and in any other way interact with or affect that issue. Think beyond the settings and roles in appendixes. 1 and 10, which focus on more traditional social work. Who else has to deal with this issue, use this skill, and so on? Who else works on these issues? How are they funded? Who does something related? How much do you know about the other field or industry?
- You could do the same exercise with a population, a field of practice, a skill, a technology, a job function, a subject matter, or any other knowledge or skill asset you have. As described in chapter 1, using part of a present knowledge or skill base increases your chances of finding a realistic option. Perhaps you have years of experience managing social services agencies and see yourself as a manager who could lead other types of not-for-profit organizations, using those broad knowl edge and multiple skills sets that all not-for-profit organizations need. Or perhaps you have identified new settings where you could use your knowledge and experience with diversity issues or with older adults.

Make a list of needs associated with that same issue, population, or whatever category you are using; make another list of trends that are affecting or may affect that category. Study the lists. What questions do these lists suggest about how problems are being tackled and by whom? Use networking and information interviewing to find answers to these questions. From this process you may be able to identify some problems that your knowledge and skills can help solve. Consider these questions if you arc just beginning to think about options for work:

Are you ready to leave a social work focus, a social services focus, a not-for-profit or public setting culture, a functional role? Would you or could you accept a contract or temporary job or a constellation of part-time, contract, and temporary jobs? One social work administrator recommends that you stay open to new opportunities and develop a training or consulting business on the side. Can you see yourself working in other settings described in appendix 4? Have you developed a new interest that you would like to explore? Are you happy with your current work but need to design a backup plan for your peace of mind?

As you think about recent changes in social policy, trends in services delivery, and alternatives for future legislation and funding, think also about what opportunities those changes might bring about. What do you have to offer in those arenas? Perhaps there is someone in your organization, community, or specialty with whom you would like to work or study.

Social workers have transferred their skills to city economic development departments, small business councils, banks, foundations, university research projects, university student services, human resources consulting firms, political offices, training and development departments, corporate account management, corporate employee relations, and city management. Here are stories of those who are making a variety of contributions.

A project manager for an association outgrew his position. From time to time he had assisted staff members of an information technology consulting firm by offering contact names in various states, and he had talked to them about automation of systems and seen them give demonstrations at conferences. When the firm began to expand its business with state governments, he received a call. The firm expressed interest in hiring him specifically for the contacts he had in state governments and his understanding of their information management needs.

An MSW graduate with a clinical focus and a wide range of interests wanted to find a temporary position while her spouse completed his degree. An undergraduate classmate who was working for a business consulting firm doing workshops for client companies saw a potential fit between the MSW skills and the workshops. The consulting firm, which was hiring temporary staff to be on workshop teams, offered the position, which was a great fit. The MSW began exploring a career in business consulting, attending recruiting seminars by the consulting firms at her new alma mater. It took a great deal of persistence, but after several months of pursuing one company, she was hired for a team consulting on organization performance issues.

A private practitioner with extensive experience in mental health and substance abuse treatment including development of services in a prison and psychiatric hospital environments, and creation of an employee assistance company, read an article in a local NASW newsletter. The article described the job of a social worker with a public defender program. The private practitioner followed up, was invited to a conference, and in a short time was working on a murder case. Today he has a full-time mitigation practice of capital murder and felony trials. In addition to consulting with the attorney, conducting extensive interviews, and writing a detailed psychosocial history, he identifies witnesses, participates in selecting experts, and assists the families with resources.

A new MSW graduate, who was a former elementary school teacher, had returned to her home community in the southwest to find a job. During an evening out with friends, she ran into an old college classmate who asked about her search. As a result, he recommended that she talk with his employer, an information technology consulting company. She followed up and was hired to manage a federal government contract for an asset management system on an American Indian reservation. Her ability to effectively manage people and projects, graduate coursework in management and her field education experience developing a database for a large United Way, and demeanor convinced the company to hire her. Within five years she was managing a team of 150 people.

As a school social worker, one MSW graduate had the opportunity to work in a district where school reform and innovative thinking were encouraged. In addition to her social work duties, she created and moved school and community projects and reforms. After two years she realized how much she enjoyed the conception and fruition of new ideas, working collaboratively, and relationship building. She interviewed and was hired by a state advocacy group for children as a program associate to help grow a public awareness campaign. Her job was to establish relationships with community leaders, social services providers, and parents by providing training, quality parenting materials, and technical assistance. The success of this project led to expanding a statewide network of partner organizations to advocate for children's issues among legislators.

An MSW graduate with an interdisciplinary undergraduate degree in philosophy, medical ethics, and psychology worked for several years in state bureaucracies, a university, research foundations, and a community-based not-for-profit organization doing program evaluations, outcome studies, and policy analyses. While directing research and evaluation projects on maternal and child health, she earned a doctoral degree in social welfare. During this time she began a small consulting practice, which grew into a full-fledged consulting firm in research and evaluation in many areas of the health and human services fields. She specializes in qualitative methods, focus group research, and consultation and technical assistance to organizations locally, statewide, and nationally.

An MSW graduate worked as a policy officer doing advocacy on economic development and housing for a community reinvestment intermediary for several years. Later, she worked on regulatory compliance of banks as the community-based lending manager for a local government. After moving to the west coast, she used her network to find consulting opportunities, including writing a grant to run an individual development account program. When the grant ended, she did some temporary work for a vice president of an international appliance company. He hired her as the marketing relations manager to run that department including government affairs. Shortly after, the federal government began offering tax incentives for energy efficient appliances. Her communications and advocacy skills plus knowledge of government regulations transferred well to this marketing environment.

A clinical social worker with more than 15 years of experience had to rethink her options when managed care dramatically changed her role. While between positions, she saw a documentary on the civil rights movement, which led to a trip to Mississippi to learn more about the experience of ordinary people. The social worker, who at one time had been an interviewer of holocaust survivors for an oral history project, began to think about recording these stories. She began to explore possibilities—funding, film making experts, subject experts, and so forth. The resulting film won an award, encouraging the once clinical social worker to pursue related projects. She credits her transition to social work communication skills, that is, to build trusting environments to develop relationships.

A crisis service hired their graduating MSW intern to start a for-profit division, an employee assistance program. While in the position, she developed rapport with agency board members. As a result, a board member recruited her as a human resources generalist providing performance management and other services for employees in multiple cities. Later, she worked in the benefits and compensation office as well as in acquisitions and divestiture work. Her broad experience in human resources enabled her to locate a position with a new company whose culture better fit her values. Based on her early human resources experience in field services, she became director of human resources for the sales division. Her ability to organize groups of people to produce results, plus her skills in group dynamics and active listening, enabled her to make all these transitions.

After working in a Head Start program and in foster care services, and while working in victim services for a hospital, a psychology major with a bachelor's degree pursued her MSW. When she graduated, she became the director of the hospital's rape crisis services. Later she moved to a family service agency to run a prevention program for at-risk youth that was tied to a public school. When a large family and children's agency in a large city began developing partnerships with newly created community schools, she was hired to manage the agency component. She and the principal are partners in what is now the flagship community school among several schools partnering with the agency. She oversees an after-school teen program and a program to get parents involved in the school as well as aspects of the agency's health and mental health services.

Experiments and Goals

Stumpf (1989) found that for successful, experienced managers, the career management process is largely one of repeated discovery and diagnostics around the following questions: (1) What do I want to do? (2) What do they (significant others) want? (3) What (skills) can I do?

You may want to work toward a long-range goal, or others may be encouraging you to seek advanced positions. If this is the case consider how much you know about reaching the goal you have. For example, Elizabeth Cole explains that there are two routes you can take to move from direct practice to the central office in public child welfare: (1) either you become noticed for your management skills or (2) you are recognized for substantive expertise in a program or service, such as adoption. These routes represent a career split. The first is based on strong management problem-solving skills. You must be mobile to pursue this path, and at higher levels your job tenure will be subject to political changes. The second is based on consultative skills and expertise in particular topics and, perhaps, recognition at the national level (personal communication with E. S. Cole, former president, Elizabeth S. Cole & Assoc., New Hope, PA, January 30, 2003).

Have you sought advice on the basic and intermediate achievements that can prepare you for those additional steps? Have you identified opportunities to learn from working with leaders and management staff? In the course of seeking advice, is there potential for a mentor relationship?

To discover opportunities and assess their fit, you can also experiment. This approach is cleverly illustrated in Dale Dauten's (1996) book *The Max Strategy*: "Achievers don't know where they are headed—they just figure they'll play around and see what happens" (p. 24). Such experimentation not only rejuvenates careers by expanding personal interests and confidence, but also encourages thinking outside the professional box, which experienced social workers strongly recommend, thereby enabling you to adapt to the changing environment.

Many books on career management stress the importance of setting goals. Crafting plans and timetables result in valuable strategy maps for some people, but not for all—some people feel overwhelmed and boxed in by goals and action plans whose lifespan can be short lived in this economy. Some social workers find it helpful to identify particular interests or a general direction and use short-term goals to build the skills, knowledge, and experience they will need to take a next step. Others like structure and the process of thinking something through before initiating change, but they may be unable to move beyond this point. Use such approaches to outline and support your experiments in your career management journey rather than to detail elaborate schemes for final aspirations. For example, you might

- try out a leadership or advocacy role through professional activities
- get experience in a new area through volunteer work, a special project on the job, a part-time job, coursework or training program, or self-directed study—this will broaden your base and perhaps become a stepping-stone in a new direction
- gain supervision experience by supervising practicum students
- work with your boss to take on additional responsibilities
- brainstorm a list of all the things, personal and professional, you might like to do some day or just think are interesting
- think about ways to incorporate some of these experiences into your present activities—would any of these items serve as a diversion while you try to renew interest in your job or make a transition? Think about what you would like to state on your résumé in six months.

Also, ask yourself what work settings value the knowledge and skills developed in another environment. For example, people who work for the federal government often move to consulting firms that have contracts with federal agencies, and social workers with state and local experience "outside the beltway" are recruited by advocacy organizations that want to bring those perspectives to the national level. Could you experiment with an opportunity in another sector and pick up a different knowledge or skill set, with the goal of taking those assets back to your core field? Note that such transitions, although they may be only temporary, often require that you step outside the boundaries of traditional social work values or put commitments to causes and populations aside until you develop new skills to take back.

On the other hand, social workers have always experimented with service delivery options that meet their values. J. Robin Robb, PhD, past vice president for professional development and private practitioner, Clinical Social Work Federation, Inc., Chester Springs, PA, reported that some private practitioners are not pursuing third-party reimbursement: "They are keeping overhead low in order to offer low fees. Some are forming networks with others committed to social work values, marketing services together, offering confidential services to low- and middle-income clients" (personal communication, February 6, 2003). Other social workers are developing products for managed care companies, taking the lead in creating public–private partnerships and community-based collaborative services, training people with low incomes to start businesses, and setting up services in physician practices.

Self-Assessment

At least once a year, go through the exercises in chapter 1. You will have new accomplishments, skills, knowledge, and possibly new interests. Record them and update your résumé or vita. You may also have a new perspective on your values and needs. Through this process you may find yourself renewing your commitment to social work values. You may find yourself questioning your direction, however, in turn motivating you to explore other options. One person working in mental health at the state level recommends that you routinely do a self-assessment, thoroughly know your own values, and carefully think about your overall goal or mission. As a result, you may reevaluate your personal criteria for work—for example, autonomy may have become more important to you than money or just the opposite. One social worker suggests that you ask whether you are satisfied with the salary and influence. Perhaps you have decided that moving up the management ladder is no longer important or that the new philosophy of your organization is unworkable. For example, consider this scenario:

> *A social worker who had been working in the chemical dependency unit of a multiservice children's center decided to leaved her position, in part because she questioned the center's treatment philosophy of sending some kids to psychiatric facilities for institutionalization when she felt it was not necessary. She began seeking a new position, which she found in the newspaper. On the basis of her experience with adolescents and chemical dependency, she was hired as a psychiatric reviewer for an insurance company.*

Qualifications and Retooling through Professional Development

"The question is, do you have the competencies, knowledge, and attitude to accomplish the objective?" offers Steve Fishbein, Office of Human Resource & Rehabilitation Development, New Jersey Division of Mental Health Services, Trenton (personal communication, January 22, 2003). This question is at the heart of any potential employer's inquiry or that of colleagues who might consider you for leadership positions in professional or community groups. It also is a query for yourself as you test new career directions. Your qualifications for work opportunities typically include an academic degree, specialized training, licensure and certifications, work and community experience, and skills and knowledge acquired through self-directed study. What will it take for you to upgrade your qualifications and pursue your interests or meet market needs in the environments to come?

If you have not analyzed what you need to compete for the opportunities you desire, see the sections on options in this chapter and on out-lining your qualifications in chapter 1. Answer these questions as well:

- Do you need another certificate to qualify for work in a new interest area?
- Have your professional interests expanded to include research and a doctoral degree?
- Will you need specific training or education for your new role in, for example, supervision, budgeting, or management?
- Would a specialized training program give you a stepping-stone into a new field?
- Would taking a leadership role in advocacy or a professional association enable you to make a move from, say, program management to policy analysis?
- Do you need a coach with expertise in financial management or another skill or knowledge area to improve your skills?

Here is one person's experience:

> *I hired an "executive coach." After interviewing several professionals who did coaching and consulting, I chose the one I felt could best meet my needs—someone to whom I could turn for help in leadership skills. We talked through how to implement my vision, how to work with inherited middle management staff, how to deal with change (that which was being imposed by changes in the organization and that which I wanted to institute), and how to work with my superiors. She supported me but also challenged my leadership style. I was able to be completely honest with her so that I could truly be coached. She was a clinical social worker who had practiced for several years prior to getting her PhD in organizational development and then had her own consulting company. We worked together in two different time periods—about 4 years in all.*

A small leadership or study group is another excellent professional development tool. One CEO who belongs to a group of 12 to 15 not-for-profit and for-profit executives finds that this tool, because it is ongoing, really makes a difference in follow through. "We hold each other accountable. If someone is putting off dealing with an organizational dilemma, we put them on the spot." Although an intensive management training program can be valuable, the application of the training takes ongoing support, which a leadership group provides.

You might also look at the trends discussed earlier in this chapter. How are these affecting your field? What others would you add to the list? Consider selecting one or more areas as the center of your professional development activities this year. Here are some questions to think about:

- Could you take courses on advanced or basic computer packages, including spreadsheets and databases; the Internet and Web page design; fundraising; languages; cultural differences; or small business development or entrepreneurship?
- Is there a continuing education program available on documenting outcomes, evaluating services, or using technology to manage information?
- Can you join a committee of a professional society or trade association that concentrates on technology in human services, issues in aging, practice, and cultural diversity, policy development, or managed care? Request membership information, a publications list, and a sample newsletter from an association in a field that is new for you; consider joining. Use your contact network to identify newsletters, journals, magazines, books, listservs and news groups on the Internet, and possibly video and CD-ROM material. You probably already participate in one work team or collaborative group.
- Can you develop expertise in making such groups succeed? If work abroad interests you and you have the resources, consider a long-term volunteer commitment overseas.

J. Robin Robb (PhD, past vice president for professional development and private practitioner, Clinical Social Work Federation, Inc., Chester Springs, PA, personal communication, February 6, 2003) offers this advice for clinicians: "One will constantly need to retool through continuing education, structured peer supervision groups, informal mentors, mentor programs offered through professional associations, group mentoring, consultation, and purchased supervision."

Marie Sanchez, executive director, National Latino Behavioral Health Association, recommends: "There is a great need for social workers and other clinicians to be trained to work effectively with culturally diverse populations, particularly non-English-proficient and limited-English-proficient populations. Social workers going out into the field should pay attention to demographic trends and cultural backgrounds of clients in areas being considered for employment. Is there a match between the needs of potential clients and their professional skills? What communication skills do they have? How knowledgeable are they about the client's culture, beliefs, values? Do their personal views conflict with the needs of their clients? Are they willing to work at developing or improving their culturally competent practice skills if they are needed?" (personal communication, February 13, 2003).

Reed Henderson, president and CEO, Family Lifeline, Richmond, VA, observes this about qualifications for not-for-profit managers: "Boards are looking for executives who have the rare ability to couple traditional social service values with an entrepreneurial approach and leadership style. If you can demonstrate this hybrid combination of traditional values and entrepreneurial leadership, you can compete against business and other disciplines for executive positions. Focus on developing entrepreneurial thinking and experience (risk taking, strategic planning, fee-for-service revenue generation) that positions not-for-profit organizations for long-term growth" (personal communication, January 24, 2003).

No matter what field-specific qualifications you develop, the following skills, common to all fields, are worth enhancing throughout your career:

- Your writing skills—quick, concise, and in the appropriate format—are your core skill set. They reveal your subject knowledge and your ability to think critically and to organize your thoughts. Improving your writing skills will positively affect all other aspects of your qualifications, regardless of your social work field or function.
- Your ability to articulate your competencies, and in many instances what the discipline of social work is, will directly affect your career path. Believe in yourself as the product, and practice marketing yourself.
- Your ability to assert your argument professionally—particularly with the use of documented outcomes, including data—is critical to your ability to compete in all arenas.
- Your attitude toward change—your ability to welcome and adapt to major change—will be an ongoing factor in your future.

Four Social Workers' Career Development
The career paths described in the following show how people found new opportunities—or new opportunities found them—and explain the keys to the progression of their careers. None of these people mapped a series of moves in advance. All performed their roles well and made decisions about options, experiments, and interim jobs as they came along.

Social Worker with BS and MSW Degrees
A social worker with a bachelor of science degree and an MSW earned part time while working has held seven positions. Upon graduation from college, he found a position as a juvenile probation officer through the newspaper. Next, he was promoted to domestic relations counselor after hearing about the job from other staff members and seeing the inter-

nal posting; he got the job on the basis of his performance on the first job. Through his work at the court, staff of a private agency became familiar with his work and approached him about a position running a group home, which he took. His contact network expanded, and staff of a residential center approached him about a job as a house manager. He held this position as he began working on his master's degree. Performance on the job resulted in one promotion and then a second promotion to the new position of program director, which the agency had created as a result of ideas he suggested to the executive director. In his most recent position as an independent contractor, he is associated with a group practice that provides services for his previous employer. He had a conversation to discuss mutual interests with the practice group; they liked his work and his values.

Social Worker with BA, MSW, and DSW Degrees
A social worker with a bachelor of arts, an MSW, and a DSW has held 13 positions over a 22-year career. Fresh out of college and with a suggestion from a faculty member, she landed a foundation fellowship that placed her in the mayor's office working on aging issues. She decided to go to graduate school and researched agencies to determine whether any paid for graduate school; she found one and successfully applied.

After graduate school, on a tip from a friend, she moved to a department of education as an adult education and family life teacher. A professor from graduate school told her about the next position she held, associate project director for research and education in geriatrics. While serving on the board of a hospital's women's auxiliary, she identified a project that interested the auxiliary; the auxiliary gave initial funding for the project; and the social worker wrote grants for outside funding. This three-quarters-time position enabled her to work on her doctorate.

Through a contact made at the hospital project, she learned of a position as director of a geriatric adult health education center. She had developed an acquaintanceship with the former director of the center, who told her about a special assistant position in a state health department; this position provided her with a dissertation topic. Someone who knew her work in an earlier position had become the CEO of a hospital; that CEO asked her to take a position as vice president of human resources and program development, a job that gave her high visibility and allowed her to participate in the chamber of commerce. That exposure expanded her contact network.

When colleagues learned that she was interested in career moves, they passed on information about a geriatrics project and program directorships, which she filled in succession. By this time she had developed a reputation in the long-term care field through her positions, board work, publications, and awards. One day, while waiting to have a manicure, she entered into a conversation with someone who turned out to be the manager of health care services for a consulting group. They discovered that, although they had not previously met, they knew of each other. The manager said that he had considered offering her a position before but had assumed that she would not make a move into the private sector. They spoke further. The CEO of the consulting group also knew of her work; he was on the board of a hospital she had worked with earlier.

After this initial move into the for-profit sector, she continued as a health care consultant when the initial company merged with another consulting group. Later, when a client company began growing and decided to hire its own health care staff, she was offered the position of vice president of state accounts. The CEO of the company was someone whom she had known for several years—she liked his values and signed on with the company.

Social Worker with BA and MSW Degrees

A social worker with a bachelor of arts degree and an MSW degree has held nine positions since completing his undergraduate work. On graduation from college, he went to stay with a friend in a Pacific Rim metropolis where English is widely spoken; he landed a job with a large group–work organization. After a year, he returned to the West Coast and located a job with a similar organization through a newspaper ad. A year or so later, he enrolled in an MSW program. Between his two years of graduate school he took a summer job as program director for an employment program in an Asian community; he had seen a notice for the position posted at his practicum site. His final MSW field practicum turned into a full-time job in the same Asian neighborhood after graduation.

In less than a year, he was ready to move to another city. He found the next two jobs he held through notices posted at his agency (in one instance, friends had brought the job to his attention). While waiting to hear about an offer in his target city, he took a temporary training and supervision job with youths. The offer to work on a federal grant in the new location did come through, thanks to his community experience abroad, his summer experience supervising youth programs, and his voluntary leadership role in the Asian community. Part of his job entailed anticipating the needs and interests—specifically, the issues of resettlement, adjustment, and welfare for refugees—of the federal officials that he would host on their routine visits to the community mental health care project. Two years later, when he was interested in a new challenge, he sent one official a letter indicating his interests. The official, who happened to have a job opening, encouraged him to apply and eventually hired him. The key to this transition was his knowledge of federal government needs for information and his analytical skills.

After moving to Washington, DC, and spending about five years examining budgets for several programs, including Medicaid, he wanted to further develop his career. He again looked to the private sector. One day he happened to see a former colleague, who was now working for a consulting firm. He sent her a letter and then called to get her advice on making a transition from the public to the private sector. She not only gave him advice, she arranged an interview with the firm. He was particularly interested in this firm when he learned that it had an office in his home state, where he eventually wanted to return. For its part, the firm was anticipating a change in health care policy and was thus quite interested in the knowledge the applicant could bring to the job. The personal connection with someone who knew the applicant's work, coupled with his federal experience and a successful interview, resulted in an offer for the position of senior associate.

Although it was exciting to work for a company that was continually developing business ahead of trends, the heavy travel schedule was hard on his family. Eventually, he transferred to the office in his home state to consult with health and insurance providers, and he began to look for a position that would be a better lifestyle fit. That search took him back to the local government through an ad in a government job bulletin. Earlier, when he had run the federal grant program, he had become familiar with the inner workings of the local government. When he interviewed for this new position, he therefore focused on how he would address the critical issues of concern to the administration—funding, political sentiments, and privatization. He believes this was the key to securing a position as a staff officer managing several projects and services in a system that usually promoted from within.

Social Worker with BA and MSW Degrees
With assistance from a friend who was a hospital administrator, this social worker participated in a management training program in the business office of a hospital before going to college. When he completed his bachelor's degree, he left the hospital to attend an MSW program full-time. After he had finished his graduate education, he returned to the hospital to complete the process for state licensure. While working as a medical social worker, he began moonlighting with a home health agency to which he sent business (patients). He had good relationships with the social work and nursing staffs at the agency. His interest in management prompted the social work manager of the agency to recommend him for her position when she was preparing to leave. Based on the relationship he had built with the agency over time and the interview, management hired him.

About two years later, he was ready for a new challenge and applied for a job listed in the newspaper as a hospital social work director. The chief operating officer (COO) liked him—there seemed to be a personality match—and the hospital was looking for someone who respected and could be respected by the nursing staff. He got the job, won the respect of the nurses, strengthened social work's role in a new organizational matrix, and began talking with the COO about new ideas. After a year he was given more departments, including utilization review—he knew the big picture and the utilization review process and its part in the mission of the hospital, and he could entrust the operation to the nurse supervisor. The key to his increasing responsibilities was his cost-conscious approach—others respected him as a health care manager. He continued to pursue his entrepreneurial interests by setting up a continuum-of-care program that included outpatient case management to reduce recidivism, obtaining grants for projects, and recruiting physicians for programs he designed. When the hospital went through a major reorganization, he acquired additional departments and now focuses on business development, contracting, marketing, and fund development.

Professional Development

Professional development can occur through unstructured self-directed study or work with a mentor or coach, or it can take place through structured mechanisms, such as professional certifications, professional affiliations, training programs, fellowships, and academic programs. State regulations, although not created for professional development, do entail meeting standards and increasing one's qualifications, so they are included in this section.

State Regulations: Licensure and Certifications

All states regulate the practice of some types of social work or positions social workers might hold. State legislatures pass laws to regulate practice. The resulting regulations or rules are designed to protect the state's citizens by ensuring a minimum standard for clinical or direct services. State statutes affect requirements for social work practice in several fields:

- state licensure or certification for social workers
- certification for school social workers
- licensure for marriage and family therapists
- certification and licensure for substance abuse counselors.

Some states are also beginning to regulate social workers in the domestic violence arena and those providers addressing gambling addiction, and there is some discussion of licensing for the fields of employee assistance and managed care as well. Stay informed about anticipated or potential changes in state licensure and certifications through the professional societies in your state, which follow licensure and certification issues. NASW state chapters, which usually follow legislation affecting a range of practice areas, can help you locate a contact.

Various state departments and regulatory boards administer state regulations for licensure and certification for fields of social work practice. They are not housed in a central office in each state. The descriptions below will give you some direction.

Because most states license social workers rather than certify them, the term "license" is used throughout the remainder of this section. Acronyms such as LCSW are used to describe the type or level of licensure a social worker has earned. LCSW refers to "licensed clinical social worker," LBSW refers to "licensed baccalaureate social worker," CSW refers to "certified social worker," and LSW refers to "licensed social worker." Other titles, which vary from state to state, are used as well.

Who Needs to Be a Licensed Social Worker?

Social work licensure has long been associated with mental health services, particularly those offered by private practitioners, and many states have passed legislation in recent years regulating three or four levels of social workers, covering a much broader array of service areas. Now, however, social services agencies usually must have licensed staff to be reimbursed by funding organizations or contractors of social services agencies—insurance and managed care companies and government. As Medicaid and managed care increasingly join together, so social workers providing services outside mental health increasingly need to be licensed. Licensure has been added to the academic degree as a measure of minimum competence.

Licensure rules and their effect vary across states. Social workers must therefore understand the specific requirements of their states. Some general guidelines on who should be licensed follow:

- Social workers intending a career as a solo or group private practitioner must be licensed.
- In general, social workers in or planning a career in clinical or direct services in organizational settings must be licensed.

- Social workers pursuing a career in program planning or management of social services should be licensed. North Carolina, although an exception, has a license termed "certified social work manager."
- If you are pursuing a career in such areas as policy, community organizing, social development, and fundraising, you probably do not need to be licensed. States do not regulate practice in these fields, nor do funding organizations require particular credentials. However, read the section on long-term considerations before you decide not to pursue a license. In some states and the District of Columbia, any one calling himself or herself a social worker or practicing as a social worker must be licensed.

Long-Term Considerations

If you anticipate moving to another state, you will want to look at licensing requirements in that state, or at least be aware of how regulations differ among states. According to the Association of Social Work Boards (ASWB), some contiguous states have reciprocal agreements, but most states do not have reciprocity—that is, a second state will not automatically recognize your license and grant you an equivalent license. You may need to take a different exam, do additional coursework, earn approved continuing education credits, or complete additional supervised hours (personal communication with D. DeAngelis, executive director, ASWB, Culpeper, VA, January 8, 2004. If the new state requires the same exam level, the new state will accept your score on an examination taken in another state.

If you are considering "stepping out" of social work to pursue other interests, seriously consider getting and maintaining your license. People do return to the field. A license could mean the difference between a position comparable to the one you left and an entry-level job when you reenter the field.

It is not uncommon for those working in a macro area of practice to change to a direct practice or program development area as professional interests or personal circumstances change. For this reason it is highly recommended that you obtain and maintain your license. For example, one person who had both direct practice and policy experience worked for several years as a legislative aide. When it seemed that she and her spouse might move overseas, she thought about working in employee assistance services for an American corporation with overseas operations, but licensure was required. In this case, the license could have been from any state.

Like other aspects of the profession, licensure continues to evolve. ASWB recommends that you be prepared to meet new criteria not only if you are moving across jurisdictions, but also if you stay in the same location. The trend is to verify continued competence by requiring documentation of continuing education for recertification (personal communication with D. DeAngelis, January 8, 20004).

Obtaining Information

Each state has a governing board that determines and reviews licensure regulations, reviews applications, and issues licenses. You should have your own copy of the licensure regulations in your state. Web sites and telephone numbers are available from ASWB; call 1-800-225-6880 or visit their Web site at http://www.aswb.org.

ASWB offers the following publications: *Social Work Laws and Regulations: A State Comparison Guide* briefly notes state licensure requirements in a chart format and also outlines continuing education requirements for each state. *The ASWB Candidate Handbook* outlines the content of each exam and details how and where to take the exams. Each state gives this free publication to social workers who inquire about licensure. ASWB study guides are available for each of the four exam levels. In addition to sample questions, they offer references for further reading and advice on taking the exams.

Requirements

Although requirements for licensure vary among states, most include a social work degree from a school accredited by CSWE, often a set number of hours of supervised experience and a written examination. In California, two exams are required. Many states have several levels of licensure.

All state licensing boards except California, which has its own exam, contract with ASWB to administer examinations. ASWB offers four types of examinations: bachelor's, master's, advanced generalist, and clinical. The type of exam taken depends on the regulations of a particular state and the level of licensure a social worker is pursuing. The *ASWB Candidate Handbook* is usually included in the packet you receive from the state. ASWB exams are computerized tests, and results are prompt.

Note that the *ASWB Candidate Handbook* usually includes an insert with details on taking the exam. It does not tell you what exam you need to take or whether you need to take one, however—you must read your state's licensing rules to determine whether the exam is applicable. Details on the exam registration process are on the ASWB site.

Exam Study Guides

You can order a study guide from ASWB by completing the form in the *Candidate Handbook*, going online, or by calling.

Private groups offer study courses, which are often advertised in *NASW News*. Be advised that courses vary in quality and may not be necessary because the tests are practice based.

Structure of the Exams

Each state, depending on the type of licensure it requires, determines which ASWB exams match its level of licensure. The exams are based on a job analysis and a lengthy test development procedure. The Web site details topics and percentage weights for each exam. The major topics are as follows:

- *Bachelor examination*—Human development and behavior in the environment; issues of diversity; assessment in social work practice; direct and indirect practice; communication; professional relationships; professional values and ethics; supervision in social work; practice evaluation and the utilization of research; service delivery; and social work administration.

- *Master's examination*—Human development and behavior in the environment; diversity and social/economic justice; assessment, diagnosis, and intervention planning; direct and indirect practice; communication; professional relationships; professional values and ethics; administration; supervision; policy; practice evaluation and utilization of research; and service delivery.

- *Advanced generalist examination*—Human development and behavior in the environment; issues of diversity; assessment, diagnosis, and intervention planning; direct and indirect practice; communication; relationship issues; professional values and ethics; supervision and professional development; practice evaluation and the utilization of research; service delivery; and administration.

- *Clinical examination*—Human development and behavior; issues of diversity; diagnosis and assessment; psychotherapy and clinical practice; communications; the therapeutic relationship; professional values and ethics, clinical supervision consultation, and staff development; practice evaluation and the utilization of research; services delivery; and clinical practice and management in the organizational setting.

Certification for School Social Workers

More than half of the states require certification of school social workers through the state department of education. Some states require an

MSW and other states require a BSW. If you intend to be a school social worker, you must obtain your target state's certification requirements from the department of education. Like social work licensure and other certification, specific coursework and an exam may be necessary. If you think you may want to work in another state, check with the state department on certification for reciprocity information. You can link to each state department of education Web site from http://www.sswaa.org/links/state-doe.html on the School Social Work Association of America Web site.

Marriage and Family Therapy Licensure

You can find contact information for the state boards regulating marriage and family therapy at the Web site for the American Association for Marriage and Family Therapy (see appendix 1).

Substance Abuse Certification and Licensure

Most states have a certification or licensure process, but certification is not mandatory in all states. The credential is often referred to as "certified drug and alcohol counselor" or some variant thereof. The trend is toward a more demanding level of competency to include co-occurring disorders and pharmacotherapies. The small number of states that offer licensure have a wide range of requirements—for example, not all require degrees, but most require an exam. Unlike social work, some states have multiple credentialing boards for substance abuse counselors. For the address of your state contact check with http://www.naadac.org.

Domestic Violence Worker Certification

According to the National Coalition Against Domestic Violence (NCADV), there is a trend in some states to certify domestic violence workers. This trend puts the focus on services delivery rather than on social change, a concern for NCADV. (See appendix 1 for address and telephone number.)

Gambling Certification

There are a few states that certify gambling counselors. Connecticut, Louisiana, Massachusetts, Missouri, Nebraska, and Oregon have state regulations. Links to contact information in these states can be found at the Web site of the Association of Problem Gambling Service Administrators (http://www.apgsa.org).

Licensure for Long-Term Care Administrators

Nursing home administrators are licensed in all states. Regulations vary. All states require the National Association of Board Examiners for Long Term Care Administrators (NAB) nursing home administrator exam. The education requirements for nursing home administrators range from a high school education to a baccalaureate degree. Most states also require completion of an administrator-in-training or intern program specified by the state, which can range from two months to two years. Some states also require a state-specific examination. You will find links to state licensing boards at http://www.nabweb.org or contact NAB at 1444 I Street, NW, #700, Washington, DC 20005-2210; 202-712-9040, or e-mail: nab@bostromdc.com.

Residential Care and Assisted-Living Administrators

A few states now license residential care and assisted living administrators. Three states that license residential care–assisted living administrators currently use NAB's residential care–assisted living administrator exam. For residential care–assisted living administrators, regulations are very minimal in most states. However, NAB has recommended licensure requirements for candidates. You will find links to state licensing boards at http://www.nabweb.org or contact NAB at 1444 I Street, NW, #700, Washington, DC, 20005-2210; 202-712-9040, or e-mail: nab@ bostromdc.com.

Qualified Mental Retardation Professional

The Medicare and Medicaid services regulations require that Medicaid intermediate-care facilities for people with mental retardation have qualified mental retardation professionals on staff; these may include social workers. To qualify, you must have at least a bachelor's degree and one year of experience working with people with mental retardation or other developmental disabilities (personal communication with Dianne Tackett, Mental Health Manager, Missouri Division of Mental Retardation and Developmental Disabilities, Jefferson City, January 21, 2003). For details, contact the nearest regional Centers for Medicare and Medicaid Services office; check the list at http://cms.hhs.gov/careers/worklite/locations.asp or your public library for telephone numbers.

Professional Certifications

State laws set minimum competence levels, whereas professional credentials set standards for practice (personal communication with D. DeAngelis, executive director, ASWB, Washington, DC, January 8, 2004). Professional credentials are not the same as licensure. States pass laws regulating social work practice through licensing (although the term "certification" is used in some state regulations). Other credentials are professional certifications. These are not required by law, yet "private practitioners who lack professional certification find it more difficult to get third-party reimbursement and referrals from other professionals" (Barker, 1995, p.1907). If you are thinking about adding a professional credential, look carefully at the vendorship law in your state, if it has one. Reimbursement for services may depend on your professional credentials, not just on your state license (personal communication with J. Robin Robb, PhD, past vice president for professional development and private practitioner, Clinical Social Work Federation, Inc., Chester Springs, PA, February 6, 2003).

Professional credentials and certifications are usually offered by professional associations. Some common credentials and certifications are described briefly in the sections that follow.

Academy of Certified Social Workers Credential

This credential offered by NASW, is often referred to as simply "ACSW." To become a member of the academy, you must have a graduate degree from a CSWE-accredited school, be a member of NASW, complete two years or 3,000 hours of supervised and paid postmaster's social work experience in an agency or organized setting, and provide three professional references.

Diplomate in Clinical Social Work

The DCSW is NASW's highest clinical credential. It requires an MSW from an accredited graduate school; five years or 7,500 hours of postgraduate direct clinical practice with two years under the direct supervision of a clinical social worker in an agency setting; clinical state licensure or certification; documentation of two years of practice in the past 10 years; a colleague reference; successful completion of an advanced or clinical examination; and be a member of NASW. Each candidate must affirm adherence to the *NASW Code of Ethics*, Standards for the Practice of Clinical Social Work, and Continuing Education Standards. As a DCSW, you are listed in the *NASW Register of Clinical Social Workers*, a referral guide for those searching for a social work clinician, which is available in print copy, CD-ROM, and online.

Qualified Clinical Social Worker

NASW offers the QCSW to clinical social workers with an MSW from an accredited graduate program; who is a member of NASW and who has two years or 3,000 hours of postgraduate, supervised clinical experience in an agency or organized setting, and state licensure or certification based on an examination requiring an MSW or PhD/DSW and/or

ACSW certification. As a QCSW, you are listed in the *NASW Register of Clinical Social Workers*. (For a description of other NASW certifications, see appendix 12.)

Certified School Social Work Specialist

NASW offers the SSWS credential. It requires NASW membership; an MSW from a CSWE-accredited school; two years of postgraduate, supervised school social work experience; and a reference from an MSW colleague.

Board Certified Diplomate

The American Board of Examiners in Clinical Social Work (ABE) offers the BCD. This is an advanced certification for clinical social workers. It requires a master's degree with specialized clinical coursework from a CSWE-accredited school; five years and 7,500 hours of clinical practice (including 3,000 hours under supervision); the highest level of state licensure or certification; and completion of the BCD examination process, with requirements for currency of practice, maintenance of license, and continuing education. ABE publishes in CD-Rom format a directory and has an online database of those who hold the BCD, which it markets to the health care industry. For more information, contact ABE (see appendix 1 for Web site, mail, and e-mail addresses and telephone number).

Certified Case Manager

The Commission for Case Manager Certification offers the CCM. Among the requirements are a license or certification to practice in one's field independent of supervision, verified employment experience, an examination, and recertification every five years. For more information, contact Commission for Case Manager Certification, 1835 Rohlwing Road, Suite D, Rolling Meadows, IL 60008; 847-818-0292; info@ ccmcertification.org; http://www.ccm certification.org.

Certified Employee Assistance Professional

The Employee Assistance Professionals Association offers this certification for employee assistance professionals. Among the requirements are experience and an exam. Contact the association for details (see appendix 1 for contact information).

Certified Fundraising Executive and Advanced Certified Fundraising Executive

The Association of Fund Raising Professionals offers a certification program for fundraising professionals with a minimum of five years' experience. Contact the association for more information (see appendix 1 for contact information).

Substance Abuse Credentials

NAADC and other groups offer professional certifications, which in some states meet regulations for state certification. National certification is available through NAADC, the Association for Addiction Professionals. NAADC offers the Master Addiction Counselor (MAC) for master's-prepared counselors and NCAC II for bachelor-level counselors. For details see the NAADC Web site at http://www.naadac.org.

Compulsive Gambling Credentials

Three organizations offer credentials for those serving individuals with gambling issues. The American Academy of Health Care Providers in the Addictive Disorders also offers the Gambling Specialist Certification, which has education, licensing, training, experience, supervision, and examination requirements. See http://www.americanacademy.org or contact them at 314 West Superior Street, Suite 702, Duluth, MN 55802; 218-727-3940, info@americanacademy.org. The National Council on Problem Gambling administers the National Certified Gambling Counselor (NCGC) credential. Both levels of the NCGC credential have training, experience, supervision, and examination requirements. For details go to http://www. ncpgambling.org. The American Compulsive Gambling Counselor Certification Board offers a professional certification, which requires an exam, curriculum, field training, experience, and sometimes an interview. The contact information is 3635 Quakerbridge Road, Suite 7, Hamilton, NJ 08619; 609-588-9338.

Long-Term Care Credentials

The American College of Health Care Administrators offers professional certification for licensed nursing home subacute care and assisted living administrators. Contact them at 300 N. Lee St., Suite 301, Alexandria, VA 22314. 703-739-7900; Web site at http://www.achca.org.

Health Care Management Credentials

The American College of Healthcare Administration offers several levels of membership and credentialing, including board certification in health care management. The address is One North Franklin St., Suite 1700, Chicago, IL 60606-3421; 312-424-2800, fax: 312-424-0023.

Professional Affiliations

Membership at particular levels of some professional associations is itself often considered a credential. Requirements to qualify for such membership are extensive. The standards are similar to those for licensing and professional credentials.

Additional Credentials

You may come across other desired credentials that are not licenses, certificates, or memberships. For example, if you meet the requirements to become an approved American Association for Marriage and Family Therapy (AAMFT) supervisor, then you may find social workers and others seeking you out as they work on their supervised practice requirements toward AAMFT membership.

Special Opportunities: Fellowships, Internships, and Training Programs

Fellowships, internships, and training programs are sponsored by academic institutions, professional associations, public and private organizations, and foundations. These internships and postdegree training opportunities are excellent vehicles for enhancing your qualifications, expanding your professional network, and building a résumé or vita. Many of these programs serve as springboards for career growth, and competition for these opportunities is often stiff. If you are a student, ask your field education office whether a program could meet your practicum requirements. A list of these opportunities is in appendix 9.

Before applying for these programs, ask for names of current program participants and consult with them on the quality of the experience and strategies for making a successful application. Always address the interest of the program in every aspect of your application, and ask several people with knowledge of the subject to critique your essays. Your writing should be concise, analytical, and focused on results. Sponsors are not looking for essays that merely describe well-known problems and offer nothing but rhetoric.

Although you can apply for many programs like those in appendix 9, other programs require that someone nominate you. Examples are the Annie E. Casey Foundation Children and Family Fellowship, which develops leaders in child welfare, and ASHOKA, which develops social entrepreneurship worldwide. Still other training programs are specific to organizations and their affiliates. In the world of community development, organizations and intermediaries contract with the Development Training Institute to provide specific training for leaders in community development in the United States.

Academic Degrees

As you explore options, you may find that you want to pursue a graduate degree at the master's or doctoral level to bolster your qualifications for social work practice, to move into research and teaching, or to complement your social work education with training in another field. Graduate education is a serious time and dollar commitment that will have a great effect on the remainder of your career. Below are brief overviews of social work education at the master's and doctoral levels and a few thoughts on seeking degrees in other disciplines; also appendix 11 offers suggestions for considering advanced education.

Master's Degree Programs in Social Work

The master's degree is considered the terminal practice degree in social work. Programs at the master's level are organized by methods or fields of practice. CSWE lists those methods as direct practice, community organization and planning, administration or management, and generic. Fields are categorized as aging or gerontological social work; alcohol, drug, and substance abuse; child welfare, community planning; corrections and criminal justice; family services; group services; health; mental health or community mental health; mental retardation; occupational or industrial social work; public assistance and public welfare; rehabilitation; and school social work. Many programs offer combinations of methods and fields of practice (Lennon, 2004). You can obtain a list of master's degree programs from CSWE (see appendix 1).

Doctoral Degree Programs in Social Work

If you are interested in advancing the field of social work through research, education, leadership, and policy development, doctoral education may be your next step. All doctoral programs require coursework, a comprehensive or qualifying exam, and a dissertation. Most doctoral programs focus on research and teaching on social work practice. A few programs provide advanced training in practice skills; degrees from these programs are sometimes called "advanced practice doctorates." Regardless of the focus, all programs prepare students to do research on

practice. Note that some universities offer the PhD (Doctor of Philosophy) and others the DSW (Doctor of Social Work). For a list of doctoral programs, visit the Group for the Advancement of Doctoral Education's Web site at http://www.socwk.utah.edu/gade/index.html.

Considering Degrees in Other Disciplines

As work environments become increasingly interdisciplinary, social workers are often asked to fill multiple functions. Consequently, you may want to build on your social work education by earning a degree in another field. One social worker employed by a large fundraising organization considered pursuing a master's degree in business administration to complement her work in financial planning with major donors. For those pursuing upper management positions, it is quite common to add a business degree. Another social worker with a concurrent degree in law is seeking a doctorate in geography; she plans to advocate for people with low incomes who face environmental problems in their communities. Another social worker chose a law degree to complement her background in family therapy; she now works in estate planning. If you are considering an additional degree, research the job and academic program markets carefully.

The following passage is about a master's-prepared social worker who broadened her background with a second master's degree, always called herself a social worker, and pursued international interests.

A bilingual MSW graduate with several years of practice experience in pediatrics decided that she wanted to expand her knowledge of health care policy. While still working as a perinatal social worker, she earned her master's degree in public health. At the completion of her program, someone she knew through earlier consulting work asked her to apply for a position as public health social work consultant with the state health department. She was offered the job in part because she also had the public health degree. In this position she provided consultation and technical assistance for child and maternal health programs, reviewed grant proposals, negotiated and monitored contracts and budgets, and analyzed proposed state legislation. She also had the opportunity to conduct a study and oversee a large statewide program.

Several years later, she received a call from a social worker who led a federally funded program at a major teaching hospital and was now retiring. The social worker encouraged her to apply for the position, which she did. Shortly afterward, she was hired. Reputation was the key. Through her work and professional activities, she was known to federal funders and had developed a network statewide and across the country in the field of maternal and child health.

A couple of years later, through her leadership in a multidisciplinary professional society, she became a contact for a Central American country seeking funding in the United States. A private not-for-profit agency included her name in a grant proposal, which lead the U.S. government to arrange for her to provide training in the not-for-profit agency's country. That work led to consultation and teaching opportunities throughout Central America and later to a temporary position with an organization in the original country.

In the meantime, she had remained in contact with the dean of her master's program, who gave her name to the faculty of another school of social work that was creating an institute on children and families at risk. The director of the institute recruited her to head international projects and hired her for her knowledge of Latin America and program development. When the funding for the institute ended, she returned to consulting work in the United States and Latin America.

While visiting a chapter office of a national health care organization to gather information for a parent education group she was forming, she met the chapter president. Because she was then actively looking for employment, she always carried her résumé to give to people she met. In a conversation conducted in Spanish, she gave a résumé to the president and told him about her background. He invited her to an event, at which he introduced her to a vice president of a public relations firm. The firm had just established a Latin American office and, although there were no current job openings, the vice president asked that she stay in touch.

In the meantime, the public health social worker, as she called herself, had decided to move back to Latin America. She was so busy making plans that she did not return a couple of calls form the vice president at the public relations firm until shortly before moving. When they did talk, it was about a potential job opportunity; nothing was firm, however, and the social worker moved abroad as planned. Soon thereafter, she received a call informing her that the public relations firm had made a proposal to a client company, and if she was interested the firm would book her on a flight to join the meeting. She followed through and in less than two weeks was hired. As before, she continued to call herself a social worker in her new capacity as program developer for health and social development projects in the United States and Latin America.

References

Barker, R. M. (1995). Private practice. In R. L. Edwards (Ed.-in-Chief), *Encyclopedia of social work* (19th ed., Vol. 3, pp. 1905–1910). Washington, DC: NASW Press.

Bridges, W. (1994). *Job shift.* Reading, MA: Addison-Wesley.

Collard, B., Epperheimer, J. W., & Saign, D. (1996). *Career resilience in a changing workplace.* Paper adapted from Information Series 366, ERIC Clearinghouse on Adult, Career, and Vocational Education, Center on Education and Training for Employment, College of Education, Ohio State University, Columbus.

Dauten, D. (1996). *The max strategy.* New York: William Morrow.

Gibelman, M. (2004). *What social workers do* (2nd ed.). Washington, DC: NASW Press.

Granovetter, M. S. (1995). *Getting a job: A study of contract and careers* (2nd ed.). Chicago: University of Chicago Press.

Hakim, C. (1994). *We are all self-employed: The new social contract for working in a changed world.* San Francisco: Berrett-Koehler.

Lennon, T. M. (2004). *Statistics on social work education in the United States: 2001.* Alexandria, VA: Council on Social Work Education.

Middleman, R. R. (1998). *A study guide for ACSW certification* (4th ed. rev.). Washington, DC: NASW Press.

Rifkin, J. (1995). *The end of work: The decline of the global labor force and the dawn of the post-market era.* New York: G. P. Putnam's Sons.

Stumpf, S. A. (1989). Towards a heuristic model of career management. *International Journal of Career Management,* 1, 11–20.

Waterman, R. H., Jr., Waterman, J. A., & Collard, B. A. (1994, July–August). Toward a career-resilient workforce. *Harvard Business Review,* 87 95.

Professional Associations

Appendix 1 is an alphabetical list of professional associations and professional societies, all of which individuals can join. Some of these groups offer membership to agencies or programs as well. These associations often lobby on behalf of their individual or institutional members. Other membership services may include training, consulting, research, program development, publications, and personnel services. Remember that their purpose is not to provide career and job-hunting services, although some of their services may be beneficial to those seeking positions and career development. Most important, associations and societies offer the opportunity to network and work with others interested in the same issues. For national networks of organizations, see also appendix 8.

AMERICAN ASSOCIATION FOR MARRIAGE
AND FAMILY THERAPY (AAMFT)
112 South Alfred Street
Alexandria, VA 22314-3061
703-838-9808
Fax: 703-838-9805
Web site: http://www.aamft.org

AAMFT offers Job Connection, a service for members and employers, on its Web site. Members can post resumes and search a job database. The Web site also offers information on salaries, licensure, and practice issues.

AMERICAN ASSOCIATION ON MENTAL
RETARDATION (AAMR)
444 North Capital Street, NW
Suite 846
Washington, DC 20001-1512
800-424-3688
202-387-1968
Fax: 202-387-2193
E-mail: aamr@access.digex.net
Web site: http://www.aamr.org

Membership is offered to individuals. The AAMR Web site offers job-posting and resume-posting services. The annual conference, held in May, features a job bank.

AMERICAN BOARD OF EXAMINERS IN
CLINICAL SOCIAL WORK (ABE)
27 Congress Street
Suite 211
Salem, MA 01970

800-694-5285
Fax: 978-740-5395
E-mail: abe@abecsw.org
Web site: http://www.abecsw.org

ABE offers an advanced certification, the board-certified diplomat (BCD), for clinical social workers. Career-related resources include a directory and online database for those who hold the BCD. The Web site offers job search, company profiles, and career articles. Registered members may post their resumes and apply online for jobs.

AMERICAN PLANNING ASSOCIATION
1776 Massachusetts Avenue, NW
Washington, DC 20036
202-872-0611
Fax: 202-872-0643
E-mail: CareerInfo@planning.org
Web site: http://www.planning.org

Individual memberships available for professional and student levels. Career-related resources include an online job database, internship information, and salary survey. The association offers a certification for planners as well.

AMERICAN PUBLIC HEALTH ASSOCIATION
(APHA)
800 I Street, NW
Washington, DC 20001
202-777-2742
Fax: 202-777-2500
E-mail: comments@msmail.apha.org
Web site: http://www.apha.org

Membership is at the individual, student, and organizational levels. The annual conference, held in October or November, features a job placement service; positions for social workers are included. Job seekers may also search APHA's online database and post their resumes.

AMERICAN PUBLIC HUMAN SERVICES ASSOCIATION (APHSA)
810 First Street, NE
Suite 500
Washington, DC 20002-4267
202-682-0100
Fax: 202-289-6555
Web site: http://www.aphsa.org

Membership is at the individual and organizational levels; specialized meetings are held throughout the year. APHSA publishes *Public Human Services Directory*, which is a nationwide list of public social services agencies at all levels. Key contacts are listed in over 75 program areas. An online job bank is currently available with future plans for a searchable database for members.

AMERICAN SOCIETY ON AGING
833 Market Street
Suite 511
San Francisco, CA 94103-1824
415-974-9600
Fax: 415-975-0300
E-mail: info@asaging.org
Web site: http://www.asaging.org

Membership is at the individual and organizational levels. The association offers job and career resources on the Internet, including job postings, sections on continuing education, and Web seminars.

THE ARC (A NATIONAL ORGANIZATION ON MENTAL RETARDATION)
1010 Wayne Avenue
Suite 650
Silver Spring, MD 20910
301-565-3842
Fax: 301-565-3843
Web site: http://www.thearc.org

Membership is offered at the individual level; the annual meeting is held in November. The Web site offers links and contact information for local chapters.

ASSOCIATION FOR THE ADVANCEMENT OF BEHAVIOR THERAPY (AABT)
305 Seventh Avenue
Suite 1601
New York, NY 10001-6008
212-647-1890
Fax: 212-647-1865
Web site: http://www.aabt.org

A special student membership rate is available. The annual convention is held in November, at which job placement services are offered. Job openings are listed in AABT's newsletter.

ASSOCIATION FOR THE ADVANCEMENT OF SOCIAL WORK WITH GROUPS (AASWG)
c/o University of Akron
Akron, OH 44325-8050
800-807-0793
Fax: 330-072-5739
Web site: http://www.aaswg.org

Membership is at the individual level; conferences are held annually in October. AASWG offers opportunities for networking and continuing education. The association also has a listserv; refer to the Web site for subscription information.

ASSOCIATION FOR EXPERIENTIAL EDUCATION (AEE)
2305 Canyon Boulevard
Suite 100
Boulder, CO 80302
303-440-8844
Fax: 303-440-9581
Web site: http://www.aee.org

Membership is at individual and organizational levels; the annual conference is held in November. The association has an online job clearinghouse as well as links to other experiential education job resources. There are multiple professional groups organized through AEE.

ASSOCIATION OF FAMILY AND CONCILIATION COURTS (AFCC)
6515 Grand Teton Plaza
Suite 210
Madison, WI 53719-1048
608-664-3750
Fax: 608-664-3751
E-mail: afcc@afcnet.org
Web site: http://www.afccnet.org

Membership is at the individual and organizational levels; student rates are also available. The annual conference is held in May. Members may purchase AFCC's annual directory of members. The association also offers various professional development training.

ASSOCIATION FOR ONCOLOGY
SOCIAL WORK (AOSW)
1211 Locust Street
Philadelphia, PA 19107
215-599-6093
Web site: http:://www.aosw.org

Membership is at the individual level; there is a special student rate. The annual conference is typically held in April. Job announcements are posted on the AOSW's listserv.

CHRISTIAN COMMUNITY DEVELOPMENT
ASSOCIATION (CCDA)
3827 W. Ogden Avenue
Chicago, IL 60623
773-762-0994
Fax: 773-762-5772
E-mail: Cheryl@ccda.org
Web site: http:://www.ccda.org

CCDA offers organizational, individual, and student memberships; the annual conference is held in November. Members may access a membership directory. Career-related resources include online job postings, which describe administrative and community outreach positions in Christian organizations located throughout the United States.

CLINICAL SOCIAL WORK
FEDERATION, INC.
P.O. Box 3740
Arlington, VA 22203
703-522-3866
Fax: 703-522-9441
Web site: http://www.webcom.com/~nfscsw

Membership in this organization, which offers opportunities for networking and continuing education, is through state chapters. National meetings are held, but not annually.

COMMUNITY DEVELOPMENT SOCIETY
17 S. High Street
Suite 200
Columbus, OH 43215
614-221-1900
Fax: 614-221-1989
E-mail: CDS@assnoffices.com
Web site: http://www.comm-dev.org

Membership is at the individual level; student rates are available. The annual conference is held during the summer months. The society publishes *Vanguard*, a quarterly newsletter; some job openings are listed therein. Resume posting is available online, as well as links to other job sites.

COUNCIL OF NEPHROLOGY
SOCIAL WORK
National Kidney Foundation
30 East 33rd Street
New York, NY 10016
800-622-9010
Fax: 212-689-9261
E-mail: info@kidney.org
Web site:
http://www.kidney.org/professionals/CNSW

Membership is at the individual level; there is a reduced student rate. The annual meeting is held in April; there are also local meetings held throughout the year.

COUNCIL ON SOCIAL WORK EDUCATION
(CSWE)
1725 Duke Street
Suite 500
Alexandria, VA 22314
703-683-8080
Fax: 703-683-8099
E-mail: info@cswe.org
Web site: http://www.cswe.org

Individual membership is at the national level. An annual program meeting is held each year in March. Career-related resources include a teachers' registry and information service, which publishes Vacancy Announcements three times each year. If you are looking for a faculty position, you can register with the service, which sends candidate profiles to schools of social work. The Web site also posts listings of jobs in social work education.

EMPLOYEE ASSISTANCE
PROFESSIONALS ASSOCIATION (EAPA)
2101 Wilson Boulevard
Suite 500
Arlington, VA 22201-3062
703-387-1000
Fax: 703-522-4585
E-mail: eapamain@aol.com
Web site: http://www.eap-association.org

Membership is at individual, student, and organizational levels; the annual conference is held in October or November. EAPA offers an online job posting site, a resume databank for members, and a job-listing board at conferences. Individuals interested in the field of employee assistance are encouraged to network at local chapter meetings. A certification program is available.

GERONTOLOGICAL SOCIETY OF AMERICA
1030 15th Street, NW
Suite 250
Washington, DC 20005
202-842-1275
Fax: 202-842-1150
E-mail: geron@geron.org
Web site: http://www.geron.org

Membership is at the individual level; the annual conference is held in November, at which the society sometimes sponsors a job fair. The Web site posts job openings and provides multiple links to other gerontology job sites.

INTERNATIONAL FEDERATION OF
SOCIAL WORKERS (IFSW)
Postfach 6875
Schwarztorstrasse 20
CH-3001 Berne
Switzerland
(41) 31 382 6015
Web site: http://www.ifsw.org

Membership is available to individuals and organizations. Global and regional meetings are held in alternate years. The IFSW roster of member associations worldwide is available on the Web site. The Web site also posts worldwide job openings and links to other international job sites.

The Association for Addiction Professionals
NAADAC
901 North Washington Street
Suite 600
Arlington, VA 22314
800-548-0497
Fax: 703-741-7698
Web site: http://www.naadac.org

A reduced student membership rate is available. The annual convention is held in September at which employment agencies have informational booths. Job openings are listed on the NAADAC Web site.

NATIONAL ACADEMY OF CERTIFIED
CARE MANAGERS (NACCM)
P.O. Box 669
244 Upton Road
Colchester, CT 06415
800-962-2260
E-mail: naccm@snet.net
Web site: http://www.naccm.net

NACCM provides a credential for care management professionals, including master's and bachelor level social workers.

NATIONAL ASSOCIATION OF BLACK
SOCIAL WORKERS (NABSW)
1220 11th Street, NW
Washington, DC 20001
202-589-1850
Fax: 202-589-1853
Web site: http://www.nabsw.org

Individual membership in NABSW, open to those of African descent, is at the national and state chapter levels.

NATIONAL ASSOCIATION OF PERINATAL
SOCIAL WORKERS (NAPSW)
Address and phone number is specific to the current officers (see Web site)
Web site: http://www.napsw.org

Address varies according to the addresses of officers; refer to the Web site for current listing. Membership is open to students and other individuals. NAPSW, which holds its annual meeting in May, offers opportunities for networking.

NATIONAL ASSOCIATION OF REGIONAL
COUNCILS (NARC)
1700 K Street, NW
Suite 1300
Washington, DC 20006
202-457-0710
Fax: 202-296-9352
Web site: http://www.narc.org

Membership is at the organizational and individual
level; conferences are held several times throughout
the year. NARC publishes a member directory, and
job announcements are listed in its newsletter and
on the Web site.

NATIONAL ASSOCIATION OF
SENTENCING ADVOCATES
514 10th Street, NW
Suite 1000
Washington, DC 20004
202-628-0871
Fax: 202-628-1091
E-mail: ghebron@sentencingproject.org
Web site: http://www.sentencingproject.org

Membership is at both the professional and associate level. The annual conference is held in early
spring. Job postings are listed on the Web site as
well as links to other useful sites related to the field
of sentencing advocacy.

NATIONAL ASSOCIATION OF
SOCIAL WORKERS (NASW)
750 First Street, NE
Suite 700
Washington, DC 20002-4241
800-638-8799
Fax: 202-336-8340
Web site: http://www.socialworkers.org

Individual membership is at the national and state
chapter levels; a student membership is available.
Members may use Job Link to post and send
resumes, receive e-mail alerts of job openings, and
search nationwide job listings. Many state chapters
also offer career-related resources, including newsletters with job listings and position-wanted ads.

NATIONAL COALITION AGAINST
DOMESTIC VIOLENCE (NCADV)
P.O. Box 18749
Denver, CO 80218
303-839-1852
Fax: 303-831-9251
Web site: http://www.ncadv.org

Membership is at the individual and organizational
levels; a reduced student rate is available. The coalition publishes the *National Directory of Domestic
Violence Programs*. The NCADV Web site also l
ists nationwide domestic violence organizations
and programs.

NATIONAL COALITION FOR THE
HOMELESS (NCH)
1012 14th Street, NW
Suite 600
Washington, DC 20005-3471
202-737-6444
Fax: 202-737-6445
E-mail: info@nationalhomeless.org
Web site: http://www.nationalhomeless.org

Individual and student memberships are available.
The NCH Web site offers access to nationwide listings of homeless and housing advocacy coalitions as
well as national and international housing organizations. Job openings are posted online.

NATIONAL CONFERENCE OF
STATE LEGISLATURES (NCSL)
1560 Broadway
Suite 700
Denver, CO 80202
303-830-2200
Fax: 303-863-8003
Web site: http://www.ncsl.org

Memberships are available to state lawmakers and
legislative staffers; the annual conference is held in
July. Job openings in state legislatures are listed at
the NCSL Web site. An online directory of state
legislatures and legislative staff is also available.

NATIONAL COUNCIL ON THE
AGING (NCOA)
409 Third Street, SW
Suite 200
Washington, DC 20024
202-479-1200
Fax: 202-479-0735
E-mail: info@ncoa.org
Web site: http://www.ncoa.org

Individual memberships available at the professional
and student levels; organizational memberships
available. NCOA's annual conference is held in the
spring.

NATIONAL COURT APPOINTED SPECIAL
ADVOCATES ASSOCIATION
100 West Harrison Street
North Tower, Suite 500
Seattle, WA 98119-4123
800-628-3233
Fax: 206-270-0078
Web site: http://www.nationalcasa.org

Membership is at the program and individual
levels; the annual conference is held in April or
May. The Web site has a directory of programs
nationwide.

NATIONAL HOSPICE AND PALLIATIVE
CARE ORGANIZATION (NHPCO)
1700 Diagonal Road
Suite 625
Arlington, VA 22314
703-837-1500
Fax: 703-837-1233
E-mail: info@nhpco.org
Web site: http://www.nhpco.org

Membership is at the individual and organizational
levels; the annual conference is held in the spring.
The NHPCO Web site offers online classifieds as
well as a resume-posting option.

NATIONAL LOW INCOME HOUSING
COALITION (NLIHC)
1012 14th Street, NW
Suite 610
Washington, DC 20005
202-662-1530
Fax: 202-393-1973
E-mail: info@nlihc.org
Web site: http://www.nlihc.org

Membership is at individual and organizational levels; NLIHC's annual conference is held in April.
The Web site has links to state coalition partners,
as well as job listings.

NATIONAL MENTAL HEALTH
ASSOCIATION (NMHA)
2001 N. Beauregard Street
12th Floor
Alexandria, VA 22311
703-684-7722
Fax: 703-684-5968
Web site: http://www.nmha.org

Membership is at the individual level; individuals
may join at the national or state level. The annual
meeting is held in May or June. The NMHA Web
site has links to state affiliates.

NATIONAL NETWORK FOR SOCIAL
WORK MANAGERS (NNSWM)
P.O. Box 11391
Columbia, SC 29211
803-933-9911
Fax: 803-771-1595
Web site: http://www.uncg.edu/swk/nnswm/htm

Individual membership is at the professional and
student levels. The NNSWM promotes networking
among members and provides a membership directory. Certification as a social work manager is available, as well as online job ads and online listings of
organizational members.

NATIONAL ORGANIZATION OF FORENSIC
CLINICAL SOCIAL WORK (NOFSW)
5784 E. Silo Ridge Drive
Ann Arbor, MI 48108
E-mail: nofswoffice@aol.com.
Web site: http://www.nofsw.org

Membership is at the individual level; members are
classified into a membership category based on
their credentials. The organization publishes a
newsletter, provides training, and holds a conference in May. Certification as a Diplomate in
Forensic Social Work is available to full NOFSW
members who meet specified requirements.

NATIONAL SOCIETY OF FUND RAISING
EXECUTIVES (NSFRE)
1101 King Street
Suite 700
Alexandria, VA 22314
703-684-0410
Fax: 703-684-0540
Web site: http://www.nsfre.org

Membership is offered at the individual level; a
new professional membership rate is also available.
The annual meeting is held in March. Training and
certification programs are also available. The
NSFRE Web site offers job search, resume posting,
and e-mail notification of new job openings.

NORTH AMERICAN ASSOCIATION OF
CHRISTIANS IN SOCIAL WORK (NAACSW)
P.O. Box 7090
St. Davids, PA 19087-7090
610-687-5777
Web site: http://www.nacsw.org

Membership in NAACSW is for individuals and
organizations. Annual conferences are held at
which some employers have booths. Some jobs are
posted in the newsletter. An online membership
directory and resume posting is available.

POVERTY AND RACE RESEARCH ACTION
COUNCIL (PRRAC)
3000 Connecticut Avenue, NW
Suite 200
Washington, DC 20008
202-387-9887
Fax: 202-387-0764
E-mail: info@prrac.org
Web site: http://www.prrac.org

PRRAC is a network of researchers and activists; it
does not have a membership structure. The Web
site lists job openings and fellowship opportunities.
The council also prints job and fellowship opportunities in its newsletter *Poverty and Race*.

SCHOOL SOCIAL WORK ASSOCIATION OF
AMERICA (SSWAA)
PO Box 2072
Northlake, IL 60164
847-289-4527
E-mail: info@sswaa.org
Web site: http://www.sswaa.org

Membership is at the individual level; SSWAA's
annual conference is held in the spring. The association connects people who are interested in school
social work with information on contacts; it also
provides telephone numbers for state departments
of education. Links to job openings are also on the
Web site.

SOCIETY FOR SOCIAL WORK LEADERSHIP
IN HEALTH CARE (SSWLHC)
1211 Locust Street
Philadelphia, PA 19107
866-237-9542
Fax: 215-545-8107
Web site: http://www.sswlhc.org

Membership is at the individual level; a discounted
student rate is available. The annual meeting is
held in the spring. The SSWLHC Web site offers
contact information for local chapters. Members
may also access a membership directory online.

SOCIETY FOR SOCIAL WORK RESEARCH
11811 Cedar Valley Cove
Austin, TX 78753-2207
Web site: http://www.sswr.org

Membership is for individuals interested in
research; the annual conference is held in January.
The organization offers the Teachers and Employers
Registry (TER) listing openings for tenure track
faculty and other academic, senior level research
positions, and administrative positions. TER, only
available at the annual conference, includes abbre-
viated curriculum vitae of job seekers.

TASH: AN ADVOCACY ORGANIZATION
FOR INDIVIDUALS WITH DISABILITIES
29 W. Susquehanna Avenue
Suite 210
Baltimore, MD 21204
410-828-8274
Web site: http://www.tash.org

Membership is at the individual and organizational
level; the annual conference is held in December.
The Web site offers job listings as well as contact
information for local chapters. The TASH newsletter, *TASH Connections*, also lists position openings.

Work Preferences

The following questions regard work preferences. For each question, think of specific examples from your recent experience that support each choice and underline your preference in each item or write a response to the side; then select the five most important items. Think about these preferences in terms of how you would naturally operate in an ideal social work role, not in terms of current market opportunities. If you try to fit your choices to market trends or constraints alone, you will probably make poor work choices or inadequate work matches. Once you have thought about your preferences, then you can go back over your choices to see whether they also reflect your other needs.

Keep in mind that these questions are meant to provoke reactions, trigger ideas, and clarify preferences. The extremes depicted are not meant to assign negative views to any settings but are written to create exaggerated contrasts. There are no right, wrong, or clear answers to these questions. Students and social workers with limited experience may find it difficult to respond to these questions. However, the items may be helpful to keep in mind when exploring career options. In that case, answer those that you can and skip the others.

- How important are the aesthetics of the work environment for you?
- Do you prefer the challenges of a competitive or political work environment?
- Do you prefer organizations with clear lines of authority, strict procedures and clearances, specific job descriptions, and defined career paths or a less-structured, fluid, quick response, experimental organization?
- Do you prefer to work for well-known institutions or organizations?
- Do you prefer or aspire to have authority, power, or influence, or are these unimportant?
- Do you aspire or prefer to be a leader?
- Do you want to advance to supervisory or management functions?
- Do you want to found a social services or advocacy organization?
- Do you want to influence the big picture?
- Do you want to own an organization, consulting group, or private practice?
- Do you prefer to work autonomously or with a team?
- Do you prefer close supervision?
- Do you prefer designing and creating solutions or implementing plans and maintaining efforts?
- Are you interested in or willing to work in communities that are not considered safe?
- Are you interested in work that develops specific skill sets related to a long-term goal or work that is interesting and meets your lifestyle needs at this time?
- Do you prefer a regular menu of work activities, constant new challenges, or a mix of both?
- Do you prefer an organization or field offering job security or opportunities that might be temporary?
- Do you prefer an adequate income and work that you enjoy or excellent income and work you can tolerate?

- Do you prefer to take risks and experiment or to follow well-established models, procedures, or operations?
- Do you prefer to be involved in cutting edge interventions, programs, or policy developments?
- Do you want to work on the leading edge or the cutting edge?
- Do you prefer routine and regular hours or a flexible schedule?
- Is there a theme or commitment that describes your life's work?
- Do you want to make a specific contribution to society? Do you prefer work that uses your specialized knowledge or focuses on your commitment to an issue?
- Do you prefer to work in a relaxed, informal environment, or in a structured, formal one?
- Do you prefer full-time work or the flexibility of a combination of contract, part-time, and temporary work?
- How important is it to work with a staff that is as strongly committed to services and advocacy as you are?
- Do you prefer a work culture that encourages staff interaction and socializing, or one that encourages independence or perhaps competition?
- Do you prefer to be near extended family and friends rather than moving for the best opportunities in your field of social work?
- Which takes priority, personal life or work life?
- Do you prefer to work with organizations that follow a particular philosophy or model?
- Are you looking for a steady pace in your work?
- Do you like to be "on the go," switching from one activity or location to another throughout the day, or to be stationary with a consistent set of activities?
- Do you prefer to work with established organizations or with young, grassroots initiatives?
- Would you like to work in a particular geographic environment?
- Do you prefer an internal focus of creating, analyzing, and conveying ideas, information, knowledge, and problem solutions or an external focus on activities that connect the organization to outside groups and institutions?
- Do you prefer an environment with constant deadlines and short learning curves or ongoing assignments requiring few radical changes in your knowledge base?
- Do you prefer to be a provider, gatekeeper, or designer of services?
- Do you prefer to set your own schedule and not be bound by specific sick leave or vacation requirements, or have a position that fits your professional interests?
- Do you want to work in a specific culture or a multicultural setting?

Directories and Career Information Publications

Community Services Directories for Specific Cities
If you are looking for a job in a particular community, use the local community services directory. Publisher information for major cities is listed below. Libraries usually carry the local directory.

Atlanta: *The Help Book*
Publisher: United Way of Metropolitan Atlanta, 404-614-1000, annual. An online searchable version is also available at http://www.unitedwayatl.org.

Baltimore: *Agency Services Directory and Contributor's Guide*
Publisher: United Way of Central Maryland, 410-547-8000, annual. Online at http://www.uwcm.org.

Boston: *Human Service Referral Directory of Massachusetts*
Publisher: George D. Hall, annual.

Chicago: *Human Services Directory of Metropolitan Chicago*
Publisher: United Way/Crusade of Mercy, 312-876-1808, biannual.

Cincinnati: *Directory of Community Services*
Publisher: United Way, Community Chest Information, Information and Referral Center, and United Way Helpline, 513-762-7100, annual.

Columbus, OH: *First Link*
Publisher: First Link, 614-221-6766, annual.

Dallas: *Source Book 2002*
Publisher: Community Council of Greater Dallas, 214-871-5065, annual. Online at http://sss.ccgd.org/pubs.htm.

Houston: *Community Resources & Services Directory*
Publisher: United Way of the Texas Gulf Coast, 713-685-2300, triennial.

Indianapolis: *Family of Agencies Directory* 2002–2003
Publisher: United Way of Central Indiana, 317-923-1466, biannual.

Los Angeles: *United Way Service Directory*
Publisher: United Way of Greater Los Angeles, 213-630-2100, annual. An online version is also available at http://www.unitedwayla.org.

Miami: *Helpages*
Publisher: Switchboard of Miami, 305-358-1640, annual. Online at http://www.switchboardmiami.org/helpages.htm.

Minneapolis: *United Way's First Call for Help*
Directory of Community Services
Publisher: United Way, 612-340-7400, biannual. Online at http://www.unitedwaytwincities.org/impact/agencies.cfm.

New York: *Cares Directory*
Publisher: United Way of New York City, 212-251-2500. Online at http://www.unitedwaynyc.org.

Phoenix: *Directory of Human Services & Self-Help Groups for Maricopa County*
Publisher: Community Information and Referral, 602-263-8856, annual.

Portland, OR: *Directory of Human Services of Multnomah County*
Publisher: Guideline, 503-226-3099, annual. Online at http://www.co.multnomah.or.us.

San Diego: *Directions*
Publisher: United Way Information and Referral Division, 619-767-5315, annual. Online at http://www.informsandiego.com/index.asp.

Seattle: *Where to Turn Plus*
Publisher: Where to Turn, Crisis Clinic, 206-461-3210, annual. Online at http//www.crisisclinic.org.

St. Louis: *Community Service Directory*
Publisher: United Way of Greater St. Louis, 314-421-0700. Online searchable database available at http://www.stl.unitedway.org.

Washington, DC: *Agency Directory*
Publisher: United Way of the National Capital Area, 202-488-2070. Downloadable version available at http://www.unitedwaynca.org.

National Directories of Organizations By Subject Category

Directories of organizations across the country and throughout the world can be found in print and, increasingly, online. Printed directories are published by associations, government departments, and publishing companies. Many are costly. When you are talking with your contacts, ask whether you can look at any pertinent directories in their offices. For directories or lists of local organizations in a particular field, check with state government offices and local association chapters, collaboration groups, or task forces.

Children and Youth Services

Directory for Exceptional Children: A Listing of Educational and Training Facilities, 2001–2002
P. Sargent (ed.). Boston: Porter Sargent.

Directory of Member Agencies
Washington, DC: Child Welfare League of America. Available online at http://www.cwla.org.

Directory of Public Elementary and Secondary Education Agencies
Washington, DC: U.S. Department of Education, Office of Educational Research and Improvement, annual. Also, a search for public school districts is available at http://nces.ed.gov/ccd/districtsearch; and the National Association of Independent Schools at http://www.nais.org/schools/schools.cfm.

Head Start Yellow Pages
Alexandria, VA: National Head Start Association, annual.

National Directory of Children, Youth and Families Services, 2000–2001
Englewood, CO: Marion L. Peterson.

Resource Guide to Careers in Child and Family Policy
R. Gordon & P. Chase-Lansdale. Chicago: The Irving B. Harris Graduate School of Public Policy Studies & the Chapin Hall Center for Children, University of Chicago, 1995.

Community Development, Government, and Public Policy

The Community Action Directory
Washington, DC: National Association of Community Action Agencies, annual.
Government Job Finder, 1997–2000
Daniel Lauber. River Forest, IL: Planning/Communications, 1997.

A Guide to Careers in Community Development
Paul C. Brophy & Alice Shabecoff. Washington DC: Island Press, 2001.

Public Human Services Directory
Washington, DC: American Public Human Services Association, annual.

Public Interest Profiles
Washington, DC: Congressional Quarterly, 2001–2002.

Ten Steps to a Federal Job: Navigating the Federal Job System, Writing Federal Resumes, KSAs and Cover Letters with a Mission
Kathryn Kraemer Troutman. Baltimore: Resume Place, 2002.

United States Government Manual
Washington, DC: Office of the Federal Register and National Archives and Records Administration, annual.

Criminal Justice and Victim Services
Directory of Juvenile and Adult Correctional Departments, Institutions, Agencies, and Paroling Authorities Lanham, MD: American Correctional Association, 1996.

Membership Directory
Reno, NV: National Council of Juvenile and Family Court Judges, annual.

Disabilities
The Complete Directory for People with Disabilities Lakesville, CT: Grey House, 2002.

Domestic Relations and Domestic Violence
National Directory of Domestic Violence Programs: A Guide to Community Shelter, Safe Home and Service Programs, 1999–2000
Denver: National Coalition Against Domestic Violence, 1999.

Family and Multiple Services
Directory of Alliance Member Organizations
Milwaukee: Alliance for Children and Families,
annual.

Directory of Jewish Family and Children's Agencies
East Brunswick, NJ: Association of Jewish Family
and Children's Agencies. Available online at
http://www.ajfca.org.

National Directory of Nonprofit Organizations
Rockville, MD: Taft Group, 2000.

National Directory of Private Social Agencies
San Diego: Croner Publications, 2002.

Gerontology and Health Care
AAHSA Directory of Members
Washington, DC: American Association of Homes
and Services for the Aging, annual.

Directory of Investor-Owned Hospitals,
Hospital Management Companies and Health Systems,
Residential Treatment Facilities and Centers,
Key Management Personnel
Little Rock, AK: Federation of American Health
Systems, annual.

The Directory of Nursing Homes
Phoenix, AZ: Onyx Press, annual.

The Directory of Retirement Facilities
Phoenix, AZ: Onyx Press, annual.

Eldercare Directory
Washington, DC: National Association of Area
Agencies on Aging, annual.

Encyclopedia of Medical Organizations and Agencies:
A Subject Guide to Organizations, Foundations,
Federal and State Government Agencies, Research
Centers, and Medical and Allied Health Schools
L. Pearce & J. Zielinski. Farmington Hills, MI: Gale
Group, 2001.

The Guide to the Managed Care Industry
Baltimore: Health Care Investment Analysts, annual.

Hospital Blue Book
Atlanta: Billian, annual.

The Hospital Phone Book
Richmond, VA: Douglas Publications, 2002.
Medical and Health Information Directory: A Guide

to Organizations, Agencies, Institutions, Programs,
Publications, Services and Other Resources Concerned
with Clinical Medicine, Basic Biomedical Sciences
and the Technological and Socioeconomic Aspects of
Health Care
Detroit: Gale Research, annual.

The National Directory of Adult Day Care Centers
Manasquan, NJ: Health Resources Publishing,
2002.

National Directory for Eldercare
Washington, DC: National Association of Area
Agencies on Aging, 2002.

National Directory of HMOs
Washington, DC: Group Health Association of
America, annual.

International Work
Alternatives to the Peace Corps: A Directory of
Third World and U.S. Volunteer Opportunities
J. Powell. Oakland, CA: Food First Books, 2000.

Careers in International Affairs
Maria Pinto Carland & Michael Trucano (eds.).
Washington, DC: Georgetown University Press,
1997.

Encyclopedia of Associations and International
Organizations
Detroit: Gale Research, annual.

How to Live Your Dream of Volunteering Overseas
J. Collins, S. Dezerega, & Z. Heckscher. New York:
Penguin Books, 2002.

InterAction Membership Profile
Washington, DC: InterAction, annual.

International Jobs: Where They Are and How to
Get Them
Eric Kocher. Reading, MA: Perseus Books, 1999.

Mental Health, Employee Assistance, and

Chemical Dependency
Membership Directory
Rockville, MD: National Council for Community
Behavioral Healthcare, annual.

*National Directory of Drug and Alcohol Abuse
Treatment Programs*
Rockville, MD: U.S. Department of Health and
Human Services, Substance Abuse and Mental
Health Administration, annual.

*Open Minds Yearbook of Managed Behavioral Health
Market in the United States*
Gettysburg, PA: Open Minds, 2000.

**Research Centers, Consulting Services, and
Foundations**
The Foundation Directory
New York: Foundation Center, annual.

Research Centers Directory: A Guide to About 13,000

*University-Related and Other NonProfit Research
Organizations*
Alan Hedblad. Detroit: Gale Research, 2002.

Social Work Education and Graduate Studies
*Directory of Colleges and Universities with Accredited
Social Work Degree Programs: Baccalaureate and
Master's Programs*
Washington, DC: Council on Social Work
Education, annual.

*The Social Work Graduate School Applicant's
Handbook*
Jesus Reyes. Harrisburg, PA: White Hat
Communications, 2002.

*Statistics on Social Work Education in the United
States*
Alexandria, VA: Council on Social Work Education,
annual.

Career Planning and Professional Development

---

101 Salary Secrets: How to Negotiate Like a Pro
Daniel Porot & Frances Bolles Haynes. Berkeley,
CA: Ten Speed Press, 2000.

The Academic Job Search Handbook
Mary Morris Heiberger & Julia Miller Vick.
Philadelphia: University of Pennsylvania Press, 2001.

*Career Change: Everything You Need to Know to Meet
New Challenges and Take Control of Your Career*
David P. Helfand. Lincolnwood, IL: VGM Career
Horizons, 1999.

*Careerpreneurs: Lessons from Leading Women
Entrepreneurs on Building a Career Without
Boundaries*
Dorothy P. Moore. Palo Alto, CA: Davies-Black
Publishers, 2000.

Careers in Management Consulting
Joseph Dehni (ed.). Boston: HSB Press, 1999.

Careers in the Nonprofit Sector
Stephanie Lowell. Boston: HBS Press, 2000.

Careers in Social Work
Leon H. Ginsberg. Boston: Allyn & Bacon, 2001.

*Changing Hats: From Social Work Practice to
Administration*
Felice Davidson Perlmutter. Silver Spring, MD:
NASW Press, 1990.

*The Curriculum Vitae Handbook: How to Present and
Promote Your Academic Career*
Rebecca Anthony & Gerald Roe. San Francisco:
Rudi Publications, 1998.

*Days in the Lives of Social Workers: 50 Professionals
Tell "Real-Life" Stories from Social Work Practice
(2nd ed.)*
Linda May Grobman (ed.). Harrisburg, PA: White
Hat Communications, 1999.

*Every Employee's Guide to the Law: What You Need
to Know about Your Rights in the Workplace and
What to Do If They Are Violated*
L. G. Joel. New York: Pantheon Books, 2001.

*Fired, Downsized, or Laid Off: What Your Employer
Doesn't Want You to Know about How to Fight Back*
Alan L. Sklover. New York: Henry Holt &
Company, 2000.

From Making a Profit to Making a Difference
Richard King. River Forest, IL:
Planning/Communications, 2000.

*Get Paid What You Are Worth: The Expert
Negotiator's Guide to Salary and Compensation*
Robin L. Pinkley & Gregory B. Northcraft. New
York: St. Martin's Press, 2000.

Getting to Yes
Roger Fisher, William Ury, & Bruce Patton.
London: Arrow Business Books, 1997.

Graduate School Funding Handbook
April Vahle Hamel, Mary Morris Heiberger, & John
Miller Vick. Philadelphia: University of Pennsylvania
Press, 2002.

The Guide to Internet Job Searching
Margaret Dikel & Francis Roehm. Lincolnwood, IL:
VGM Career Books, 2002.

Job Savvy: How to be Successful at Work
LaVerne Ludden. Indianapolis, IN: Jist Publishing,
2003.

Job Shift
William Bridges. Reading, MA: Perseus Books,
1999.

Losing Your Job—Reclaiming Your Soul
Mary Lynn Pulley. San Francisco: Jossey-Bass, 1997.

*Making a Living While Making a Difference:
The Expanded Guide to Creating Careers with
a Conscience*
Melissa Everett. Philadelphia: Chipping Norton,
2000.

*Negotiating Your Salary: How to Make $1,000
a Minute*
Jack Chapman. Berkeley, CA: Ten Speed Press,
2000.

*The New Social Worker: The Magazine for Social
Work Students and Recent Graduates*
Harrisburg, PA: White Hat Communications, serial.

The Non-Profit Handbook
Gary Grobman. Harrisburg, PA: White Hat
Communications, 1999.

Non-Profits and Education Job Finder
Daniel Lauber. River Forest, IL:
Planning/Communications, 1997.

The Perfect Cover Letter
Richard H. Beatty. New York: John Wiley & Sons,
1997.

Power Tools for Women
Joni Daniels. New York: 3 Rivers Press, 2002.

The Practical Dreamer's Handbook
Paul Edwards & Sarah Edwards. New York: Putnam
Publishing Group, 2001.

*The Smart Woman's Guide to Interviewing and Salary
Negotiation*
Julie Adair King. Philadelphia: Chelsea House,
1997.

*Social Work Laws and Board Regulations: A
Comparison Study*
Culpeper, VA: American Association of State Social
Work Boards, serial.

*Social Work in Private Practice: Principles, Issues and
Dilemmas*
Robert L. Barker. Silver Spring, MD: NASW Press,
1992.

Sweaty Palms: The Neglected Art of Being Interviewed
H. Anthony Medley. Berkeley, CA: Ten Speed Press,
1993.

*We Are All Self-Employed: The New Social Contract
for Working in a Changed World*
Cliff Hakim. San Francisco: Berrett-Koehler, 1994.

*What Color is Your Parachute? A Practical Guide for
Job-Hunters and Career-Changers*
Richard Nelson Bolles. Berkeley, CA: Ten Speed
Press, 2004.

What Social Workers Do
Margaret Gibelman. Washington, DC: NASW Press,
2004.

Who We Are: A Second Look
M. Gibelman & P. H. Schervish. Washington, DC:
NASW Press, 2000.

*Win Win Career Negotiations: All You Need to Know
about Negotiating Your Employment Agreement*
Peter Goodman. Washington, DC: Gut Instinct
Press, 2001.

*Zen and the Art of Making a Living: A Practical
Guide to Career Design*
Laurence G. Boldt. London: Arkana, 2000.

Information Specific to Fields

Appendix 4 is a reference for those looking for positions in
- aging, health care, and disabilities
- children, family, and school services
- domestic relations, domestic violence, justice services, and victim services
- macro level social work
- mental health, substance abuse, and employee assistance

Aging, Health Care, and Disabilities

Work Settings
adult day care and respite programs
area agencies on aging
assisted-living centers
chemical dependency or substance abuse
    treatment programs
community health clinics
courts
dialysis centers
education programs
family planning or reproductive health services
family services
family support programs (case management
    services and respite care)
geriatric case management agencies and
    practices
government divisions or departments on aging
guardianship programs
health maintenance organizations (HMOs)
home health services
hospice programs
hospitals or medical centers
housing (apartments, assisted living, public
housing, retirement centers or campuses)
long-term care facilities
managed care firms
multiservice agencies for HIV/AIDS, head
    injuries, and breast cancer
national health organizations (for example,
    American Cancer Society)

physician offices
public health facilities
public and private schools
recreational programs
rehabilitation centers
residential programs
senior centers and nutrition programs
sheltered workshops
skilled nursing centers
small group homes
supported employment programs
veterans' medical centers
vocational programs
wellness programs
work/life programs

Job Titles
activity coordinator
advocate
care manager, case manager
clinical social worker
community advocate
community integration specialist
coordinator of community services
coordinator of family and infant
development program
coordinator of geriatric services
director for adult day care
director of geriatric partial hospitalization
    program
eldercare unit director and case manager
emergency unit social worker

executive director

geriatric care manager or social worker

geropsychiatric social worker

HIV prevention specialist

home care social worker

hospice social worker

human services counselor or specialist

job placement counselor

long-term care administrator

long-term care ombudsman

manager of group home

medical social work department director, coordinator, or manager

medical social worker

older adult specialist

oncology social worker

pediatric medical social worker

program analyst

program manager or director

rehabilitation specialist

resident manager or residential services coordinator

social work or social services manager supervisor

supported living coordinator

Information to Gather

- How does the community care for its dying people? What hospital and independent hospice programs exist? Do the managed care organizations have their own hospice programs or do they contract for those services?

- What public, non-profit, and for-profit organizations provide services (for example, wellness or health promotion programs; primary, acute, trauma, or pediatric care; skilled nursing; residential programs; assisted living; nursing home care; home health; day care for older adults; geropsychiatric services; dialysis; hospice; and rehabilitation)?

- Who is driving policy change in the state? Is it the budget office of the governor or the division of aging experts?

- Is there a long-term care planning commission or similar group with a mandate from the state legislature? How strong is it? What organizations are advocating for change?

- What organizations provide guardianship or geriatric case management services? Do banks or funeral homes in the area use social workers?

- How do the roles of social workers vary across nursing homes? Are they focused on psychosocial aspects or on a combination of admissions, discharge planning, and marketing?

- What do the guidelines of funding sources say about the number of allowed social work home visits? Is this number comparable to other regions? Is it changing?

- What do the state regulations require regarding social workers in hospitals? Do they require MSWs in all units or in specific units (for example, psychiatric, oncology, rehabilitation, dialysis, or burn units)?

- Which hospitals are open to or are pursuing new programs or services involving social workers—for example, social workers working in primary care physicians' offices, in outpatient services, in preventive services, or in disease management programs?

- Medical social work departments in hospitals are dismantled and recreated as hospitals cut costs or determine other staffs cannot perform the roles. Where do social workers fit into the organizational charts of the local hospitals?

- What is the relationship between the state's department on aging and the area agencies on aging? Is the focus in this community on institutional care or on alternative care for older adults, or both?

- How are home health services funded—through managed care or a prepayment system, for example?

- Which hospitals have formed networks and which have recently merged?

Where are those hospital groups in the process of streamlining their operations and eliminating duplication?

- Does the state organize disability services by county or region?
- Is there a single advocacy association for all types of disabilities in the community or does each type have its own organization?
- Which organizations have particular programs for children, adults, and older adults with developmental disabilities?
- Are there residential programs, sheltered workshops, vocational programs, supported employment programs, small group homes, home care, family support programs (including case management services and respite care), or guardianship programs for people with disabilities?
- How is education provided to people with developmental disabilities?
- Is there an individual services coordination system?
- Which organizations are developing alternative care programs? What is being done for those individuals who are not currently capable of independent living? Does the state provide a continuum of services?
- Has the state been operating under a waiver for Medicaid? How has the state changed eligibility and services?
- Where are developmental disabilities services located in the state government structure? Are they part of the mental health department or social services department? How does the location affect philosophy, programs, and funding?
- How does the state law define develop mental disabilities—that is, which disabilities are covered by state programs?
- What is the funding configuration (Medicaid, state funds, and private funds) for services? How dependent is the state on federal funding? What is the potential for fiscal growth in programs?

Children, Family, and School Services

Work Settings

adoption services
alternative school
chemical dependency treatment center
  for children
child day care center
child protection service or child welfare
children or adolescents residential treatment
  center
children's hospital or children's psychiatric
  hospital
court-appointed advocates program
family preservation or families first program
family services
foster care services
gang prevention programs
juvenile or family court
mental health services for children and families
multiservice clubs or agencies for youth
public school systems or private schools
services for children with autism, etc.
teen pregnancy services
youth or children's shelter

Job Titles

adolescent therapist for alternative school
adoption social worker
assessment specialist for residential center
assistant superintendent of treatment
behavior management specialist
case manager for residential treatment center
child care director
clinical social worker, supervisor, or
  clinical manager
coordinator of outreach programs
counselor
developmental therapist
director of child abuse program
drug and alcohol counselor
educational support counselor
executive director
family advocate
family clinician or therapist

family preservation worker
family services worker
family support coordinator
family unit manager
field executive
foster care or adoption recruiter
foster care coordinator
home–school liaison
home visitor for new parent support program
intervention counselor or specialist
management analysis specialist for
   child support enforcement
Medicaid director
parent educator
prevention specialist
program administrator
program assistant for mentor program
program director
residential services program director
school social worker
social services worker
student assistance specialist
support manager for family services program
teen parent group educator
therapeutic foster care home coordinator
therapist or case manager
therapist for juvenile sex offender
   treatment program
truancy case manager
youth division administrator

Information to Gather

- What is the value base? Social work values are not universally held by social services organizations. Communities differ in practice and politics. For example, in child welfare, is a family-focused, community-based approach used or is it a law enforcement model?
- If collaboration is taking place, is it at regular meetings among many parties or a multidisciplinary group that has a mission statement; shares resources, funding, and power; struggles with issues; and is culturally responsive?

- What public, not-for-profit, and for-profit organizations are providing social services for children, youths, and their families? Where are the services delivered or based: onsite at schools, linked to schools, or in community agencies?
- What types of relationships does the public system have with private agencies: Does the state provide direct services or does it buy services? How do policies translate into programs and contracts with nonprofit organizations?
- How are terms defined in the state: collaboration, wraparound services, integrated services delivery, family support, strengths-based practice, partnering with the community family-based services, and family-centered practice? What "buzz" phrases are being used in that state?
- Is there a commitment to family-centered practice? How is this approach being integrated into services, funded, and staffed? Are there training funds for it? Is it being integrated into child welfare services only or across the board in state services (legal, mental health, juvenile justice, aging, or community)?
- Are services run through a state system or a county system? That is, are decisions made at a state, county, or regional level? What effect does this decision level have on quality assurance standards?
- Are the family services agencies serving primarily individual clients and families through clinical services or do they also have community interventions in place?
- Are social workers employed by the schools or by outside agencies providing services onsite or in the community, for example, family resource centers or mental health agencies?
- Where are social workers involved in schools: truancy programs, guidance offices, or reading and math tutoring programs? What roles or titles do social

workers have: counselors, school social workers, intervention specialists, student assistance specialists, family resource coordinators, or home and school visitors? How do funding differences among school districts affect school social work services?

- Are there schools that specialize in education for particular populations?
- What is the role of social workers in schools? Are they concerned primarily with basic needs of students and their families, or are they members of interdisciplinary teams focused on academic and behavior issues or are they in a transdisciplinary role with an emphasis on cross training for meeting high volume needs? Has the role changed recently? Is it expected to change?
- What percentage of services is Medicaid driven? Are services under managed care? If yes, is managed care part of mental health services and family services? If not, when is that anticipated?
- What has been the impact of declassification on hiring in the public sector? What is the background of the beginning-level worker? How much experience do senior staffs have?
- How do other public services interact with public child welfare? What is the quality of relations? Is it difficult to get children into the public mental health system? Is it a detention-only service? Does it have an advocacy role?
- What are the programs that schools have, are discussing, or should have (for example, school-to-work initiatives, conflict resolution, character education, parent involvement or education, early prevention, and drug prevention or intervention programs)?
- Is there a current or recent court order in effect and, if so, how is it affecting hiring, caseloads, salaries, and career paths?
- How are services funded? Are they funded primarily through public dollars? What is

the mix of funding dollars and how does it affect public and private services?
- Has the state legislature guaranteed mental health or managed care mental health services for children?
- What has been the state's investment in social services? How is the state dealing with cutbacks?

Domestic Relations, Domestic Violence, Criminal Justice, and Victim Services

Work Settings
advocacy and protective services
child advocacy centers
court-appointed special advocate programs
domestic relations divisions of courts
domestic violence prevention programs
domestic violence programs or shelters
family courts
family violence councils
guardian ad litem programs
juvenile courts
legal aid or legal services
police departments
prisons
probation/parole
public defender offices
restorative justice programs
sex offender treatment programs
victim services councils

Job Titles
alternative sentencing specialist
case manager
children's program coordinator
crime victim advocate or educator
custody evaluators
deputy juvenile officer
detention youth leader
director of client services
director of court services
director of a domestic violence program

evaluators—domestic relations
facilitator of a guardian program
family specialist
family therapist
foster care social worker
juvenile justice youth officer
mediator for domestic relations
mitigation specialist
parent educator
parenting specialist, domestic relations
parole officer
probation officer
sex crimes case manager
social worker
social worker for domestic relations
training specialist
victim or witness coordinator
victims advocate
volunteer coordinator

Information to Gather

- Where in the court system are family cases heard?
- Is there a family court system? What types of cases does it hear: divorce, paternity, adult abuse (domestic and elder), domestic violence, juvenile delinquency, criminal cases? Does it hear both civil and criminal cases?
- What programs are in place: restorative justice, family group conferencing, victim impact programs, or victim offender dialogue?
- How do judges get on the family court? Are they appointed or do they volunteer? How many have law and social work degrees?
- How are the citizen advisory boards structured? How hard is it to get on a board?
- In this state or community, which organizations emphasize services for battered women and children and which organizations emphasize social change targeted at domestic violence?

- Are there residential and nonresidential services for battered women and children: volunteer crisis lines, shelters, multiple services, and advocacy programs?
- What family and domestic relations court services are provided in this state or county? Do they provide education programs for parents; mediation, arbitration, custody evaluations, assessments, and home studies; therapeutic mediation; supervised visitations?
- What services are provided outside the court?
- What victim services or advocacy organizations exist? Are they part of the circuit attorney's office or are they independent organizations? Do they work with civil and criminal aspects?
- Does the court encourage mediation? Do they have court-affiliated mediators?
- If the state is regulating domestic violence workers, what impact is that regulation having on the scope of services and advocacy for domestic violence programs?
- How has the increased federal funding for domestic violence changed services? What is the mix of funding for these services?
- Is there a coordinated community response around domestic violence? Is there a task force addressing this?

Macro Level Social Work

Community development includes the areas of housing, homelessness, employment, neighborhood stabilization, and economic development. It is closely linked with macro functions including advocacy, consulting, organizing, policy, research, political involvement and program planning. A valuable resource for those in community development is *A Guide to Careers in Community Development*, Paul C. Brophy & Alice Shabecoff, 2001.

Work Settings

citizen groups
community action agencies
community centers
community development corporations
community reinvestment programs
employment projects
faith-based organizations
family services agencies
foundations
fundraising organizations
government departments: housing,
    economic development, labor
homeless shelters
housing corporations
individual development account programs
job training programs
micro enterprise projects
neighborhood centers
regional planning offices
research centers
settlement houses
think tanks
university extension services
university research or project offices

Job Titles

budget analyst
county program director, university
    extension services
director, church division human development
program
director of development
director of youth and community services
economic development director
employment specialist
executive director for community
    gardening group
executive director, foundation
executive director, neighborhood association
family literacy program coordinator
functional analyst, human services department
    intervention specialist
manager for disaster services
neighborhood coordinator

neighborhood planning and enforcement
    specialist
placement specialist for job program
policy analyst
program analyst
program director for foundation
program director for neighborhood services
program evaluation administrator
project coordinator
project director, research project for
    refugee program
public policy specialist
regional developer of community services
research administrator
research analyst
resident assistant for shelter
senior program officer for foundation
social science analyst
special events coordinator
survey researcher
union organizer
welfare director

Information to Gather

- What organizations are studying and influ-
  encing policy, conducting research, or
  providing consulting and training at an
  international, national, or state level in
  your interest area? What are their positions
  on issues?
- What public, not-for-profit, and for-profit
  organizations are providing multiple
  services to neighborhoods and at-risk
  populations? These might be settlement
  houses, neighborhood centers, or community centers.
- What organizations are the key players
  in housing, economic development,
  crime prevention, neighborhood
  planning, employment, services for
  homeless people, advocacy, disaster, and
  emergency services?
- What roles are local and state governments playing in the social and economic
  development of the area? Are public and

private initiatives in place?

- What community development corporations are part of the leadership in deciding new initiatives?
- What are the relationships among community development corporations, religious institutions, Urban League, United Way, family services agencies, neighborhood centers, universities, the housing authority, and state and local economic development departments?
- What pilot community projects were completed recently? What projects are planned or underway?
- What groups are addressing antidiscrimination, education reform, and welfare reform issues?
- What organizations are evaluating out comes of community-building projects?
- What organizations are providing technical assistance to community or neighborhood groups?
- How are policies and programs changing at the federal, state, or local level in housing, employment, economic development, and so on?
- Are the family services organizations serving primarily individual clients and families or do they also have capacity-building interventions in place?
- Is the state or local government piloting any projects in urban or rural communities?
- What changes in family services, housing, employment, crime and safety, or welfare are taking place as a result of the policy shift from the national to the state level?
- What is the relationship between social development (or community development) and economic development at the state and local levels?
- What is the approach to community work? Is it from an assets-based development perspective; from a needs-assessment, problem-solving perspective; or from a combination of perspectives?

Mental Health, Substance Abuse, and Employee Assistance

Work Settings

clubs or day programs for chronically mentally ill
community mental health centers
employee assistance firms or programs in companies or agencies
family services agencies
hospital units: inpatient, outpatient, eating disorders, dual diagnosis, stress, forensic, for example
managed care companies
military, family, mental health, or substance abuse services
private practice
psychiatric hospitals
substance abuse treatment programs: outpatient, inpatient, or therapeutic communities
women's services

Job Titles

adult outpatient counselor
care manager
case manager
chemical dependency counselor
clinic administrator
clinical case manager
clinical casework assistant
clinical consultant
clinical director
clinical social worker
community mental health services supervisor
community support worker
director for consumer affairs, mental health department
director of evaluation team
director of family development, child psychiatry unit
employee assistance program (EAP) counselor
mental health administrator
mental health outreach specialist
private practitioner
program coordinator

psychiatric disability case manager
psychiatric reviewer
psychiatric social worker
social work supervisor
social worker or program director of club house
substance abuse coordinator
substance abuse counselor
substance abuse treatment specialist
supervisor of supportive care
therapist
triage intake coordinator

Information to Gather

- What public, not-for-profit, or for-profit organizations provide mental health services: outpatient services, inpatient programs, managed care services, employee assistance programs, or correctional facilities?
- How does the state deliver public mental health services? Does the state own all of its mental health facilities or centers? Are state services organized by catchment or regional area? Is there a county mental health system?
- If you are interested in EAP work, what is the percentage breakdown of large and small companies in that community? Business needs will differ depending on the size of the organization. Do any companies have internal EAPs; which are outsourcing EAP services?
- What organizations or individuals are known for their expertise in addressing issues (for example, chronic mental illness, posttraumatic stress disorder, dual diagnosis, sexual abuse, eating disorders, substance abuse, domestic violence, or divorce)?
- Are public and private substance abuse services combined with mental health services? Might this change?
- What are the substance abuse treatment services offered (in therapeutic communities, outpatient programs, inpatient programs, services in the criminal justice system, EAPs, or managed care programs)? What models do they use? Are there links between mental health services and primary care or substance abuse treatment?
- Where do clinical social workers work? Are they in individual practice and have subcontracts for individual cases with managed care companies? Do private practitioners join the provider panels; which are open? Are they employees of not-for-profit, for-profit, or public organizations that are subcontractors with managed care companies?
- States are decreasing facilities and size of staff: How is this changing services and positions in the public and private sectors?
- What organizations have engaged the community in a partnership to develop community-based services?
- What is the profile of the community populations, cultures, and ethnic groups? What are the service needs of the population?
- Are consumers involved in all aspects of treatment, including program development: Are they on advisory committees?
- What is the status of funding for public or private mental health?
- What is the political climate? Is the tax base stable or being cut back?
- What are the state mandates or other legislation affecting mental health in this state?
- Who is the director or commissioner for the state, county, or local system? How long has the person been there? What is his or her professional reputation? How much turnover has there been in the position?
- What are the state's philosophy, mission, objectives, and history regarding mental health services?
- Rates for providers are dropping. What are providers doing in this area?

References

Brophy, P. C., & Shabecoff, A. (2001). *A guide to careers in community development.* Washington, DC: Island Press.

Gibelman, M. S. (2005). *What social workers do* (2nd ed.). Washington, DC: NASW Press.

Sample Cover Letters and Other Correspondence

The first four sample letters in this appendix correspond to resumes samples 4 and 5 in appendix 6. These are the letters of a fictional social work student, Lisa Denton, who has experience in pediatric medical social work, day treatment, and domestic violence. Lisa is thinking of returning to Dallas and is looking at several possibilities. Her letters emphasize those elements of her background specific to each audience. Letters 5–12 are additional samples for various other situations. Topics of the letters are as follows:

Sample 1:	Letter seeking advice
Sample 2:	Unsolicited letter
Sample 3:	Letter based on a referral
Sample 4:	Letter in response to an ad
Sample 5	Letter of application
Sample 6:	Letter requesting an information interview
Sample 7:	Thank you letter to a contact
Sample 8:	Letter following a telephone call
Sample 9:	Letter of application
Sample 10:	Letter following an application
Sample 11:	Thank you letter following a job interview
Sample 12:	Letter of acceptance.

Sample 1: Letter Seeking Advice

I am a graduate student at My University in Anytown with an interest in children and families at risk. At this time, I am exploring my career options for the future and a possible move to Dallas. I am writing to you for information and advice.

Providing therapy for youth and their families is my particular interest. However, because managed care has had a large impact on the field, I am wondering what types of therapeutic services are being offered in the Dallas–Fort Worth area. If I want to pursue a long-term career in clinical social work with youth and families in central Texas, what type of experience should I look for over the next several years? I would appreciate any thoughts you would be willing to share with me.

My clinical experience was at the Children's Center, Anytown, as a therapist intern for youth and families in the day treatment program. My course work in family therapy and practice, adolescent problems, and clinical interventions complements my training. In addition, I worked with families in crisis at Children's Hospital, Anytown. Before attending graduate school, I was coordinator of the children's program for the Women's Shelter in Dallas.

I would appreciate your advice, and will contact you soon.

Sample 2: Unsolicited Letter

I am seeking an opportunity to use my medical social work experience in pediatric health care and I would like to be considered for positions in your department. Dallas was my home for several years; I plan to return there in May when I complete my MSW degree.

My recent experience includes medical social work at Children's Hospital and day treatment at the Children's Center in Anytown. As a medical social work intern, I provided services on the neonatal and pediatric intensive care units and handled backup services for all other units in the hospital. I enjoyed the fast-paced team environment of a hospital and understand the complex ethical and managed care issues facing social workers today. At the day treatment program, I primarily provided therapy for youth at risk and their families. Previously, I coordinated an effective volunteer service and children's program for the Women's Shelter in Dallas. In all settings, I have been complimented for my work with families in crises.

Newton Children's Medical Center is my first choice in work settings. Several of my contacts in the Dallas area have said that your social work department is well integrated with all services in the center. They also indicated that your staff is respected in the community for its advocacy work on behalf of patients.

If possible, I would like to meet with you during my visit to Dallas the week of March 6; I will give you a call. My phone number is [area code and telephone number]. My resume is enclosed; thank you for your consideration.

Sample 3: Letter Based on a Referral

Susan Street, Director of the Family Center, suggested that I contact you regarding your opening for a social worker in day treatment. In May, I will be returning to Dallas and I've started looking for opportunities to work with at-risk children and families. I would like to learn more about this position and the Day Treatment Center.

In addition to an MSW education, I have training and experience in day treatment, pediatric social work, and womens and children's services. At the day treatment program for the Children's Center in Anytown, I handled assessments, participated in the treatment team, and provided therapy for youth at risk and their families. This experience expanded my skills in working with emotionally disturbed youth in a culturally diverse setting. Prior to my graduate work, I was the coordinator for an effective volunteer service and children's program for the Women's Shelter in Dallas. In all these settings, staff members have complimented me for my work with families and children in crises.

Susan Street highly recommended the Day Treatment Center. It is my understanding that your staff has initiated several programs that are considered models for working with culturally diverse populations.

Thank you for considering my application; my resume is enclosed. You can reach me at home [area code and telephone number] in the evenings or at work [area code and telephone number] on Tuesdays and Thursdays. I look forward to hearing from you.

Sample 4: Letter in Response to an Ad

I am responding to your announcement for a program coordinator in the January 22 issue of *NASW News*. In May, I will be returning to Dallas where I plan to continue my work with women and families in crises. The work of the Samuelson Women's Center is of particular interest to me.

Prior to my graduate work at the Deal School of Social Work, I served as the Volunteer Coordinator and Advocate for the Women's Shelter in Dallas. As the coordinator, I expanded the volunteer program and created a children's program. This experience included recruiting and supervising staff, working with board members on policies, co-authoring a grant application, and managing a budget. As a graduate student, I sought training opportunities to expand my clinical skills and knowledge of services. In all settings, I have been complimented for my work with families in crises.

I understand that Samuelson Women's Center is expanding and will need additional staff for a second shelter. During my tenure at the Women's Shelter, I enjoyed coordinating with Alice Sela, at that time with Samuelson's, on advocacy efforts. I learned a great deal about the field from the staff at Samuelson Women's Center; it would be exciting to continue my career with your organization.

If possible, I would like to meet with you during my visit to Dallas the week of March 6; I will contact you in the next two weeks. My phone number is [area code and telephone number]. Thank you for your consideration.

Sample 5: Letter of Application

Jana Smith, Specialist with University Extension, and Rochelle Jones, Dean for Extension, recommended that I contact you regarding openings that you have for the Community Development Specialist position. My interests lie in the area of rural community development. I would consider relocating for this rural assignment.

While completing my MSW education, I had the opportunity to work with Jana Smith and several of her University Extension colleagues in a statewide group, the Poverty Project, addressing rural poverty issues. Although I have graduated, I am currently assisting the group in a planning process to develop a project proposal to expand information about services and programs via the Internet to rural communities in [name the state]. My role with the group has been to research, to initiate contacts and relationships for collaboration, and to write and compile components for the project proposal. At the Community Development Group, I worked in a quasi-governmental setting forming successful relationships with community leaders. Assisting in developing, implementing, and evaluating the Initiatives Project in [name city] provided me the opportunity to use my skills in assessment, planning, and social and economic development for communities, and my experience with the King Business Association increased my knowledge of economic development.

In reviewing the mission and programs of University Extension, and in talking with several staff members, I am very interested in investigating how my skills might enhance the progress of University Extension. I would welcome the opportunity to discuss my background with you in person. Please call me at your convenience to discuss whether such a meeting would be possible and to confirm the appropriate next steps. I may be reached at [area code and telephone number].

Thank you for your consideration. I look forward to meeting you.

Sample 6: Letter Requesting an Information Interview*

I believe I have met you briefly on several occasions—at a breakfast sponsored by the social work school at State University, at a Lincoln Foundation function last summer, and at a Convergence, Inc., education committee meeting.

I am writing you in the hope of getting some advice about planning my next career move. I have had a unique experience as a full-time intern at Jackson Electric for the past 16 months; this internship is unusual for Jackson because I was accepted not as the usual MBA intern but as a social work intern. I have enjoyed my work at Jackson so much that I would like to continue working in the area of corporate philanthropy and community relations. I was wondering if you would be willing to meet with me to discuss the qualifications and experience necessary to work in this field.

I have attached a copy of my resume for your reference. I will give you a call in the next few days to get your response. If possible, I would like to schedule a brief informational interview with you or, if you are unable to meet with me, with someone you suggest.

*Note that such requests are usually made by telephone.

Sample 7: Thank You Letter to a Contact

Thank you so much for taking the time in February to talk with me about my job search. Your advice was helpful and appreciated.

As you suggested, I am in the process of contacting Natalie Jackson at Danes Hospital. I am also looking into the postmaster's program in eating disorders at State College. The program sounds very interesting.

I have enclosed a copy of my resume. If you think of other ideas or hear of any openings, I would appreciate it if you would keep me in mind.

Thank you again for your help.

Sample 8: Letter Following a Telephone Call

Thank you for taking the time to speak with me on Thursday, August 20. I am enthusiastic about the current and future job openings available in the Office of Family Assistance.

As indicated on the telephone, I have a Master of Social Work from One University in [name city]. I am interested in public policy issues regarding children and families. I believe that my experience in direct service with clients is a strong compliment to my interest in public policy and program development.

My experience with program planning and development has been quite successful and enjoyable. The most challenging task I have faced was to formulate a community development project in the Philippines. Through a combination of research, interviews, community meetings, and data analysis, the final project was accepted for funding through the Philippine Relief and Development Corporation.

My experience with local programs has been equally successful. While at Lutheran Family and Children's Services, I completed an intensive program evaluation and, through implementation of my recommended changes, increased the program success rate by 40 percent within a six-month period. I am very interested in contributing my enthusiasm and ideas to the development of federal social services programs.

As you suggested, I have enclosed a copy of my resume. I plan to call you within the next week to answer any questions you may have. If you wish to contact me sooner, my number is [area code and telephone number]. Thank you again for your time.

Sample 9: Letter of Application

Enclosed please find my resume in response to your recent announcement in the January 2003 issue of the *Advocate Voice*. This position sounds promising and I would welcome the opportunity to discuss it further with you.

I am currently employed by Advocates for Children, a statewide child advocacy organization which focuses on issues of family preservation, foster care, child abuse, substance abuse in families, child day care, and maternal and child health. As a Program Associate, I have lobbied for family leave and child care safety laws, and have conducted research and community education on state policy relating to substance-exposed children and day care.

My recent graduate studies at the World School of Social Work have included research and writing on children's policy, family poverty and policy, and the economics of social policy.

I would be most interested in learning more about your organization and your legislative advocacy program. I believe that my employment and academic experience would make me an asset to your organization. You can reach me at my office during the day at [area code and telephone number].

Thank you for your consideration. I look forward to hearing from you soon.

Sample 10: Letter Following an Application

After reading the article on the work of Catholic Family Services in the August 14 issue of the *Catholic Paper*, I decided to send you a second letter. I am again indicating interest in the part-time social work position in the program of drug prevention in the archdiocesan schools.

My practicum experiences while an MSW student at the University would be pertinent to this position. I have worked with children of various ages in school settings and have run groups on self-esteem and conflict resolution. At the center, I worked with at-risk teens and their families, individually and in groups, regarding addiction and other at-risk behavior.

I would welcome the opportunity to talk to you about this position. At present I am available at my part-time position at the Focus Center [area code and telephone number], Monday, Wednesday, and Friday. My home phone number is [area code and telephone number].

Again thank you for your consideration.

Sample 11: Thank You Letter Following a Job Interview

I would like to thank both you and Ms. Fox for taking time out of busy schedules to meet with me this past Tuesday to discuss the geriatric social worker position. After speaking with you and learning more about your facility, I feel strongly that the position available would be both interesting and challenging to me. I believe that my background and skills in working with older adults and their families can contribute to your comprehensive service.

Enclosed you will find a list of my references and a report which I wrote on long-term care. I hope you find these informative.

I look forward to hearing from you soon. Again, thank you.

Sample 12: Letter of Acceptance

I am writing to formally accept your job offer and to tell you once again how pleased I am to be coming to work at the Orange Center. After learning more about the center and its progressive services, I am excited about being able to contribute.

Per our conversation of January 12, 2004, I am accepting the social worker position you have offered me at Orange Center. I understand that my responsibilities will entail assessments and treatment planning with the interdisciplinary team at an annual salary of $39,000. As agreed, I will begin work on February 9, 2004. I look forward to receiving the contract and job description. The signed contract will be returned promptly.

Between January 26 and 29, I will be moving to Boston; I will call you with my phone number as soon as I arrive. Again, thank you for this opportunity.

Sample Resumes

The sample resumes included here are those of actual individuals; only the names have been changed. The samples demonstrate how experience and education might be presented in various resume formats.

The sample resumes illustrate the points made in chapter 3. For example, a paragraph format is used in samples 2 and 3 to save space. Sample 2 is a straightforward presentation of the experience of the fictional Andrew Teal. Note that both a current and a permanent address are listed, because he will be using the resume while he is in the process of moving (he could instead have indicated a moving date and new address in a letter, but that letter might not always be attached to the resume when it is circulating in an agency). The paragraphs about Andrew Teal's experience at Community Hospital and Stevens Foundation describe not only the skills he used but also the knowledge of issues he gained in these jobs. He has made an effort to understand the big picture, to see his work in context. The descriptions of an important asset—his leadership experience on campus—use quantities ("one of four," "netting $3,500") to express the selectivity or the level of responsibility involved. He could have listed each of his other work and volunteer positions in detail, but instead summarized them in two statements to keep the resume brief. These statements still convey the idea that he has work experience in several settings and additional volunteer experience with children. Sample 3 emphasizes Andrew's experience with children and families to support the objective he states at the top of his resume.

Samples 4 and 5 illustrate two different formats for resumes: chronological and functional. Both are written for the same fictional MSW student, Lisa Denton. These samples are straightforward, simple, one- or two-page presentations of the highlights of Lisa Denton's experience. If she wanted to create a resume specifically for positions in medical social work, she could describe her hospital experience in greater detail and her day treatment, shelter, and professional development work in less detail. She could eliminate the description of her work as research assistant completely, letting the title suffice. She could also add a specific objective—for example, "Seeking a medical social work position using skills in discharge planning, assessments, and crisis intervention." She could even add a second sentence to the objective, such as "Particularly interested in pediatric and teaching hospitals."

Sample 1: Chronological Format for a BSW Graduate with Prior Experience

Maria Gonzalez
Address
City, State Zip
Telephone & e-mail address

Objective To secure a position as a case manager in a service delivery setting. Interested in services for youths, families, and homeless people

Education Bachelor of Social Work, May 2002, Magna Cum Laude
University of South State, Town, State
Dean's List, Honors Convocation, 4.0 GPA in Major, 3.9 overall

Experience
Social Work Intern, 1/02—4/02
Social Services, Town, State
Introduced to probations, grant writing, volunteer programs, emergency shelter, and transitional-living programs, food and clothing services, FEMA and SHARE financial-aid assistance programs for families at risk of homelessness
• Conducted home visits; interviewed and built rapport with clients to assess needs
• Assisted clients in goal setting and conducted goal reviews
• Made appropriate referrals and followed up with clients and resources to evaluate the effectiveness of referrals
• Collaborated with employment counselor to overcome obstacles to clients' employment
• Participated in community case conferences to optimize services for a homeless population and reduce duplication
Resident Apartment Manager, 4/95—9/99
Management, Inc., Town, State
• Managed a 352-unit bond-financed property with a 12-member staff
• Interviewed, hired, trained, motivated, supported, and evaluated staff
• Collaborated with HUD to ensure guidelines were being followed
• Collaborated with retained attorney to ensure landlord complied with the law regarding contracts and compliance procedures
• Prepared annual budgets and monitored monthly expenses
• Assessed community functions, made recommendations, and implemented change
• Assessed community's place in the market to create and implement appropriate marketing strategies
• Promoted community spirit through organized activities and a monthly newsletter
• Established and maintained detailed record-keeping procedures
Volunteer Service
Senior Home Improvement Project, Town, State, Summers 1997—1999
• Worked effectively as a team member to completely paint individual senior citizen's homes in one day
The Center, Town, State, 9/99—2/00
• Consoled individuals over the telephone who had lost a loved one
Theatre Company, Town, State, 4/95—1/97
• Worked as a team member on set construction, props, lighting, sound, costumes, and special effects on 10 productions; required teamwork, quick problem-solving skills during performances, creativity with limited budgets, organizational and negotiation skills, and technical knowledge

Affiliations National Association of Social Workers Beta Sigma Phi
Skills American Sign Language (minimal)

Sample 2: Chronological Format for a BSW Student

JAMES TEAL

Present Address (until June 15, 2002)   Permanent Address
Address   Address
City, State Zip   City, State Zip
Telephone   Telephone & e-mail address

EDUCATION

Bachelor of Social Work, 2002, State College, Town, State
Dean's List, G.P.A. 3.2/4.0, Major G.P.A. 3.3

EXPERIENCE

Community Hospital, Town, State
Social Work Intern, January 2002—present
Work directly with chronically mentally ill individuals. Assist clients with daily living skills, social and recreational skills, and employment needs. Conduct home visits. Co-facilitate a support group; led two sessions independently. Observe supervisor in individual client sessions. Have developed a broad understanding of social policies, public and private services delivery, advocacy efforts, individual needs, and medical terminology related to this population. Complimented for efforts to integrate classroom knowledge and practice.

Stevens Foundation, Inc., Town, State
Trainer (paid position), September 1998—present
Teach independent living skills and provide support to people with developmental disabilities. As part of a team, provide assessments and evaluations. Serve as liaison with local employers. Assist in preparing new trainers. Served on a committee that successfully expanded employment sites. Familiar with issues facing families, agencies, and employers.

Camp Frost, Town, State
Lead Counselor (paid position), Summer 1998
Supervised a staff of four counselors serving 40 children in a residential camp.
Planned and monitored activities, safety, supplies, and maintenance. Hired and trained two new counselors.
Counselor (paid position), Summers 1996, 1997
Worked with a group of 10 children. Organized activities, taught swimming, led hikes, and provided support.
Intervened in crises; resolved disputes among campers.

1994—1996: Held part-time and summer jobs in hospital, retail store, and restaurant.

LEADERSHIP AND VOLUNTEER EXPERIENCE

Freshmen Orientation Leader, State College January—May 1998, August 1998
One of four students out of 20 applicants selected for the freshmen orientation committee. Planned a week-long series of events for 500 incoming students. Led a team of five volunteers, gave presentations to students and parents, and coordinated peer advising sessions.

Philanthropy Co-Chairperson for social fraternity, State College, September 1997—April 1998
Organized three fund raising events netting $3,500 to benefit three local nonprofits.

Other Volunteer Work includes tutoring and organizing activities for a children's program.

Sample 3: Combination/Target for a BSW Student

JAMES TEAL
2020 Newland Road, Apt. 203
Phoenix, Arizona 98765
686-0505-1234

OBJECTIVE: Seeking a position serving children and families in low-income neighborhoods.

SKILLS AND KNOWLEDGE
Oversaw planning for children's activities in an after school program and a camp.
Knowledgeable of child development and cultural diversity issues.
Hired, trained, and supervised counselors for a residential camp.

EDUCATION
Bachelor of Social Work, 2000, State College, Town, State
Dean's List: G.P.A. 3.2/4.0; Major: G.P.A. 3.3
Studies included child development, family issues, and social policy. Wrote papers on child abuse, low-income family issues, and teen violence.

RELATED EXPERIENCE
Camp Frost, Town, State
Lead Counselor (paid position), Summer 1999
Supervised a staff of four counselors serving 40 children in a residential camp. Planned and monitored activities, safety, supplies, and maintenance. Hired and trained two new counselors. Learned about the daily responsibilities of running a residential camp.
Counselor (paid position), Summers 1997, 1998
Worked with a group of 10 children. Organized activities, taught swimming, led hikes, and provided support. Intervened in crises; resolved disputes among campers.
State College Volunteer Corps, Town, State
Volunteer, Academic years 1997—2000
Tutored elementary school children in an after school program. Organized and supervised athletic activities.Provided support and encouragement to children in the program. Became familiar with the needs andconcerns of children living in a low-income community.

LEADERSHIP EXPERIENCE
Freshmen Orientation Leader, State College, January—May 1999, August 1999
One of four students out of 20 applicants selected for the freshmen orientation committee. Planned a week-long series of events for 500 incoming students. Led a team of five volunteers, gave presentations to students and parents, and coordinated peer advising sessions.
Philanthropy Co-Chairperson for social fraternity, State College, September 1998—April 1999
Organized three fundraising events netting $3,500 to benefit three local nonprofits.

ADDITIONAL EXPERIENCE
Community Hospital, Town, State
Social Work Intern, January 2000—present
  Assisted individuals with daily living skills, social and recreational skills, and employment needs. Conducted home visits and co-facilitated a support group. Observed supervisor in client sessions.
1995—2000
  Held part-time and summer jobs in a center for people with developmental disabilities, hospital, retail store and restaurant.

Sample 4: Chronological for MSW Student

LISA DENTON
1111 Ceaton Street
St. Louis, Missouri 63188
111-448-8882

PROFESSIONAL SUMMARY

MSW with experience and training in medical social work, children's day treatment, and domestic violence. Have experience in neonatal and pediatric intensive care units; individual, group and family therapy focused on at-risk youth; and advocacy for shelter clients. Coordinated volunteer and children's programs at a shelter, received a scholarship, elected Voices for Children vice president, and selected teaching assistant for a family therapy course.Certified in play therapy.

EDUCATION

Master of Social Work, My University, Town, State
Anticipated graduation: May 2001; Emphasis: Children and youth, health, and mental health care
Scholarship recipient, Student Council vice president, teaching assistant for family therapy
Bachelor of Arts in Psychology, 1997, Davis College, Dallas, Texas
Dean's List. Admitted to two honorary societies

PROFESSIONAL TRAINING

Hospital for Kids, Town, State
Medical Social Work Intern, September 2000—present
- Provided services on the neonatal and pediatric intensive care units
- Handled back-up services for all units, including the emergency room
- Completed assessments and discharge planning; dealt with crises
- Provided emotional support to families; led weekly parent support group

Children's Center Day Treatment Program, Town, State
Graduate Social Work Intern, January 1999—June 1999; Volunteer, July 1999—present
- Assessed needs of emotionally disturbed youth with severe behavior and learning problems.
- Provided individual, group, and family therapy.
- Expanded knowledge of community resources; made referrals.
- Worked with the recreation program; tutored pre-teens.

WORK AND VOLUNTEER EXPERIENCE

Family Center for Autism, Town, State
Respite Provider, May 2000–August 2000
- Provided respite care for youth with autism; gained knowledge about developmental disabilities

Women's Shelter, Town, State
Volunteer Coordinator, March 1998—August 1999
Advocate, August 1997—February 1998
- Recruited, trained, and supervised eight volunteers providing support for clients
- Designed and implemented a children's program staffed by volunteers.
- Provided support and advocacy for clients dealing with the legal system.

Crisis Intervention Center, Town, State
Hotline Volunteer, September 1997—August 1998

Davis College Psychology Department, Town, State
Research Assistant, Domestic Violence Project, September 1996—April 1997
- Conducted a literature review; collected data through interviews; entered data using SPSS

PROFESSIONAL DEVELOPMENT

Certificate in Play Therapy, Johnson Institute, Town, State
1998—2000 attended seminars on impact of domestic violence on children, divorce and children, crisis management, and fundraising

Sample 5: Functional for MSW Student

LISA DENTON
1111 Ceaton Street
St. Louis, Missouri 63188
111-448-8882

OBJECTIVE
Seeking a clinical social work position in a pediatric health or mental health
care setting working with children,adolescents, and families.

SKILLS
Direct Services
- Provided medical services on the neonatal and pediatric intensive care units
- Handled back-up services for all hospital units, including the emergency room
- Completed assessments, dealt with crises; provided emotional support to families
- Led weekly parent support group in a hospital setting
- Provided individual, group, and family therapy in a day treatment center
- Assessed needs of emotionally disturbed youth with severe behavior and learning problems
- Provided respite care for youths with autism
- Gained knowledge of various developmental disabilities
- Trained to handle crises and make appropriate referrals
- Provided support and advocacy for clients dealing with the legal system.

Program and Project Implementation
- Recruited, trained, and supervised eight volunteers for a women's shelter
- Designed and implemented a children's program staffed by volunteers
- Co-chaired a committee that held a successful orientation event for 130 students
- Collected data for a study through interviews; used the SPSS computer package.

EDUCATION
Master of Social Work, My University, Town, State
Anticipated graduation: May 2001
Emphasis: Children and youth, health, and mental health care
- Scholarship recipient; elected Student Council vice president; served on the curriculum committee
Bachelor of Arts in Psychology, 1997, Davis College, Town, State
Dean's list; admitted to two honorary societies

EXPERIENCE
- **Children's Hospital**, Town, State—Medical Social Work Intern, September 2000–present
- **Washington University School of Social Work**, Teaching Assistant for family therapy course, 2000
- **Children's Center Day Treatment Program**, Town, State
  Graduate Social Work Intern, January 1999–June 1999; Volunteer, July 1999–present
- **Family Center for Autism**, Town, State—Respite Provider, May 2000–August 2000
- **Women's Shelter**, Town, State
  Volunteer Coordinator, March 1998–August 1999; Advocate, August 1997–February 1998
- **Crisis Intervention Center**, Town, State—Hotline Volunteer, September 1997–August 1998
- **Davis College Psychology Department**, Town, State
  Research Assistant, Domestic Violence Project, September 1996–April 1997

PROFESSIONAL DEVELOPMENT
- Certificate in Play Therapy, Johnson Institute, Town, State, 1998
- 1998–2000 attended seminars on impact of domestic violence on children, fundraising, divorce and children, and crisis management

Sample 6: Combination-Target for Senior Manager

STEPHANIE LARSON
Address
City, State Zip
Telephone & e-mail address

PROFESSIONAL SUMMARY

Senior Manager, MSW, with a large not-for-profit organization: Possess keen skills in all aspects of fiscal management including budgets and contracting of services; adept at resolving conflicts and problems and encouraging positive relationships; dedicated to supporting and guiding staff in professional development; skilled at working with professional staff, board members, teen and adult volunteers.

COMMUNITY CENTER, City, State

Assistant Executive Director of Adult Services, 200X–present

Supervise four directors at two sites, includes programming, fiscal management, and human services

- Train for and develop interdepartmental cooperation and cohesiveness
- Develop business plans with department directors
- Serve on management program team of the agency
- Provide vision and out-of-the-box thinking
- Implement strategic plan for adult services
- Research and write grants
- Develop and implement trip programs for the over-55 population
- Serve on citywide committees dealing with transportation and nutrition concerns for theadult population
- Develop and implement the silent auction event for agency's annual fundraiser

Director of Camping and Outdoor Recreational Services, 198X–200X

Supervised 10 directors at four sites: program supervision, fiscal management, human resources, general operations, and camp and staff recruitment

- Developed and monitored budgets in excess of 1.65 million
- Served as management liaison between executive and departmental staff
- Provided information and feedback to board subcommittee and at board meetings
- Managed overall outdoors facility including sites for day and residential camps, outdoor pool complex, and family park for a community center with 10,000 members
- Attuned to assessing, developing, and implementing programs to meet the communities needs
- Developed program for teenage volunteers to perform community service
- Served as point person in coordinating entire agency programs and events for the community
- Conducted needs assessment and research for strategic plan concerning facilities and programs
- Developed alumni association as an affinity group to facilitate development efforts
- Played instrumental role in the formation of intergenerational programs: grandparents' day at camp, cooking and art classes, and lifetime university for adults

Director of Camp, 198X–198X

- Provided direct supervision of 140 staff members and over 450 campers
- Implemented the enrollment campaign, including development of new brochures, video, and other marketing material as well as conceptualized and created camp visits that resulted in a 30 percent increase in camper enrollment
- Enhanced the special needs camp program to include work–study and overnight options
- Supervised kitchen, medical, and operation managers
- Purchased services in areas of food, equipment, and recreational program supplies with a budget of approximately $500,000
- Created and implemented outdoor education adventure program for teens

Children and Teen Program Director, 198X–198X

- Developed and implemented classes and programs for children and youth
- Hired and supervised staff to run individual programs
- Developed elementary age vacation programs still in use today

Sample 6 continued on the following page

CITY SCHOOLS, 197X–198X, City, State
Learning Disabilities Tutor
- Provided support to middle school students in the areas of academics and socialization

EDUCATION   Master of Social Science Administration, Name of University, City, State
Bachelor of Science in Elementary/Special Education, Name of University, City, State

SERVICE
- American Camping Association—accreditation team (years)
- Camping Alliance—membership chairperson and secretary (years)
- American Camping Association—state camp representative (years)
- Network of Professionals—steering committee and membership chairperson (years)
- YMCA, City, State—led support group for women on separation and divorce (years);
  formal title: Scholarship recipient

Jerome Jacob Smart

EXPERIENCE

2001–Present   **Technology Development, Inc., Town, State**
Business Analyst–Business Lead
- Responsible for program requirements gathering, gap analysis and design creation, and documentation of software solutions for government level implementations
- Conduct consulting research into U.S. food stamps, TANF, Medicaid, Section 508, and HIPAA requirements for enhancements and future engagements

2000–2001   **Katwan Consulting, Town, State**
Consultant
- Consulting work as part of the Medicaid Administrative Claiming program administration engagement within the state
- Conducted sessions to train school district clinicians in Medicaid Administrative Claiming process

1999–2000   **Assistance Society, Town, State**
Supervisor of Licensing
- Coordinated training and education seminars for metropolitan foster parents
- Created and managed database system to monitor licensed and unlicensed foster parents
- Lead statewide effort to create uniform reporting for regional offices

1997–1999   **American Community Services, Town, State**
Supervisor of Counseling Department
- Created opportunities and programs to increase community activity among Asian Americans
- Developed and managed external contracts resulting in an increased revenue of 1,000 percent for the counseling department
- Regularly conducted cultural sensitivity seminars for practitioners

1995–1997   **Assistance Society, Town, State**
Treatment Foster Care, Social Worker
- Case management services for severely disturbed children and families
- Coordinated treatment foster home licensure process

1994–1995   **Women's Shelter, Town, State**
Director of Operations
- Managed hardware purchases
- Created access-based database to track clientele education

1995   **University of State, Town, State**
MSW, Children and youth concentration, 1995
- Scholarship recipient, 1994
  BSW, Children and youth Concentration, 1993
- Dean's list, scholarship recipient, Alpha Lambda Delta, Phi Eta Sigma

OTHER INFORMATION
- Licensed Clinical Social Worker [dates]
- Extensive knowledge in Medicaid billing and contracting
- E-business certified

Address   City, State Zip   Telephone   E-Mail Address

Sample 8: Combination Format for MSW Working in Policy

CAITLYN LAU GARCES
U.S. Citizen
Address
City, State Zip
Telephone & e-mail address

Objective: [fill in for specific situation.]

EDUCATION
Name of University, School of Arts and Sciences, City, State
Doctoral Program in Public Policy, August 199X–Present
Concentration: International Health and Development
Status: Qualifying exams passed in Month 200X, advanced candidacy expected June 2003

Name of University, School of Social Work, City, State
Master of Social Work, May 199X
Concentration: Community Development and Women's Issues
Specialization: Management

Name of University, College Name, City, State
Bachelor of Science in Psychology, May 199X
Overall GPA: 3.6–4.0
Major GPA: 3.7–4.0
Cum Laude with departmental honors

LANGUAGE SKILLS
- Tagalog (Filipino native language), no formal training received
- Japanese, 3 semesters, Name of University
- Chinese, 1 semester, Name of University

SKILLS
Research: Focus group interviews, survey research, data collection and analysis
Computer: Microsoft Word, Excel, PowerPoint, Corel Word Perfect, SAS, SPSS,
working knowledge of STATA
Management: Training in managing federal grants, contracts, and cooperative agreements

WORK EXPERIENCE
International Relations Officer, GS level, 08/200X–Present
U.S. Department of Labor (USDOL), Address, City, State Zip
Name of Program
Participated in a U.S. Government delegation in (international) meetings in Paris, France
- Represented the USDOL and traveled to the Philippines with a consultant to conduct a research mission on education needs of working children for project development
- Accompanied and prepared briefing materials for USDOL's Deputy Under-Secretary for International Affairs' trip to the Philippines
- Guest lectures on child labor at Name of University's introductory sociology classes and at USDOL's Bureau of Labor Statistics for International Visitors Program
- Coordinating statistical activities for child labor reports and program activities
- Writing, editing, and assisting in the publication process of annual child labor reports
- Overseeing 25 technical assistance programs on child labor surveys and research funded through the International Labor Organization's International Program on the Elimination of Child Labor
- Assisted U.S. Agency for International Development and International Institute for Tropical Agriculture write summary sheet on findings from child labor surveys conducted in West Africa to measure the extent and nature of child labor in the cocoa sector

Sample 8 continued on the following page

Continued from page 164

Survey Statistician, Presidential Management Internship Program, GS level, 11/199X–08/2000X
U.S. Department of Commerce
Address
City, State Zip
Name of Branch
- Participated in a detail with the Institute for Women's Policy Research and assisted with statistical programming for paper on women and pensions using the Survey of Income and
- Program Participation (paper cited in article in the Washington Post, date, "Title of Paper")
- Cleared and analyzed statistics on means-tested programs from data files in SIPP and the American Community Survey (ACS)
- Presented a miniseminar on women and poverty in the United States titled "Name of Seminar" to statisticians from developing countries at the U.S. Census Bureau's International Programs Center's summer seminar series
- Received two cash awards for outstanding performance in help with benchmarking of variables from the Survey of Program Dynamics and the Current Population Survey, and clearing data for ACS

Program Analyst, Presidential Management Internship Program, GS level, 07/199X–10/199X
U.S. Department of Health and Human Services, Name of Office
- Duties consisted of reviewing, analyzing, and responding to state proposals for Child Welfare Demonstration projects relating to the delivery of child welfare services in the areas of foster care, adoption assistance, independent living, and family preservation and support
- Prepared departmental clearance packages for approved demonstration projects
- Compiled and wrote the Paperwork Reduction Act packet for Name of Office submission for Child Welfare Demonstration project's information collection activities

Income Security Research Assistant, 01/199X–06/199X
National Policy Center (NPC)
Address, City, State
- Edited several testimonies on social security reform efforts for Director of Income Security and Executive Director of NPC
- Modeled and researched various reform efforts on child support policies for five states
- Attended congressional briefings and wrote summaries for NPC staff
- Coauthored with Name, "Title of Paper," April 199X

Junior Policy Analyst, 08/199X–12/199X
Citizens for Our State's Children
Address, City, State
- Assisted with research, compilation, editing, and publicity of State's Kids Count 1998 Data Book
- Wrote article for statewide newsletter on the privatization of federally funded social services

Certified Crisis Worker–Case Manager, 05/100X–12/199X
Life Crisis Services
Address, City, State
- Provided suicide prevention and crisis intervention counseling through 24-hour hotline
- Case managed elderly people and individuals living in high-crime, low-income areas—developed action plans to aid in locating information and referral services and for coordinating linkages with community resources
- Wrote letter to local community church on behalf of caller and secured $400 for case

Conference Co-Chair, 08/199X–03/199X
Name of University
Address, City, State
- Applied for grants and received funding for event totaling approximately $2,250
- Scheduled committee meetings and actively participated in decision making of content to be presented to students
- First known conference in New Orleans area to target female youths—goal was to affirm self-esteem, aspiration, and goal setting among participating girls

Sample 8 continued on the following page

Continued from page 165

CONFERENCE PRESENTATIONS AND PUBLICATION (SAMPLE LIST):

U.S. Department of Labor, 200X, "Title of Paper"

Washington, DC: Bureau of International Labor Affairs

- Authored statistical appendix and country reports for names of countries
- Edited and provided technical comments for all 143 countries and territories U.S. Department of Labor, 200X, "Title of Paper" Washington, DC: Bureau of International Labor Affairs
- Created graphs and detailed statistical tables, authored statistical appendix, and drafted country report for Ethiopia

Names of Coauthors, 200X, "Title of Paper"

Paper presented on June X, 200X, at IWPR's Conference, "Title of Paper"

AWARDS (SAMPLE LIST):

Public Policy Award, 200

"Title of Paper"—First place in doctoral student competition for Public Policy Student Association poster conference

Presidential Management Internship Program, 199X–200X

Women in Management Scholarship for Graduate Study in Social Work, 199X–199X

HONORS (SAMPLE LIST):

Mortar Board, National College Seniors Honor Society, 199X–199X

- President
- Awarded 199X Chapter of Excellence Award
- Omicron Delta Kappa, National Leadership Honor Society, 199X
- Psi Chi, National Honor Society in Psychology, 199X–199X
- Dean's List, four semesters

Sample 9: Chronological Format for an MSW with Community Developement and Evaluation Experience

ERICA DAVENPORT
Address
Town, State Zip
Telephone & e-mail address

EDUCATION
MSW, University of State, May 2001
BSW with honors, University of State, 1999

PROGRAM DEVELOPMENT AND EVALUATION EXPERIENCE
El Municipio Centro, Inc., Town, State
Special Projects Coordinator, May 2001–present
Develop new initiatives congruent with community needs and agency priorities, including financial literacy instruction, individual development accounts, Spanish and cultural competence instruction for professionals, and a leadership–policy analysis institute; work with program coordinators to develop new programs, identify funding sources, design implementation, and secure community participation

Crisis Services, Town, State
Spanish Hotline Developer, March 2000–May 2001
Write grants to develop Spanish hotline; meet with community leaders, develop promotional materials, conduct training, write and administer evaluation components, work with Latino immigrants in crisis, and supervise operation of hotline; learned about changing agency programs to meet changing community demographics

County Regional Prevention Center, Town, State
Prevention Services Intern, June–August 1999
Received external funding to enhance services for Spanish-speaking immigrants; wrote bilingual drug and violence prevention curriculum; collected data and wrote bilingual resource directory

Memory Book Project, The School District, Town, State
Program Developer and Facilitator, August 1998–May 1999
Received grant to research effects that intergenerational contact has on adolescents' attitudes about aging; supervised the program, and designed and performed evaluation

Intergenerational Program, Center for Outreach, University of State
Program Coordinator, May 1998–May 1999
Received funding to begin program linking older adults in the community to university students and area youth; supervised volunteers, facilitated special events, and developed elder programs in public schools

POLICY ANALYSIS AND POLITICAL EXPERIENCE
Center for Development, University, Town, State
Research Assistant and Social Work Intern, January 2000–May 2001
Research strategies to make higher education more accessible for low-income individuals; assist in planning national symposium on asset development policy; meet with stakeholders around the country to develop working document on providing state tax credits for corporate contribution to IDA matching funds; learned about state and federal policies to include low-income workers in the prosperity of the 1990s

Progressive Vote, Town, State
Campaign Organizer, June 2000–November 2000
Manage campaign for state representative; conduct voter registration drives, educate community about progressive issues, assist with fundraising and strategy planning, and recruit volunteers

Sample 9 continued on the following page

Continued from page 167

Older Adult Community Program, Town, State
Social Work Intern, January 2000–May 2000
- Researched state and federal policies impacting low-income older adults to write testimony for legislative hearings; worked with coalition on policy advocacy and lobbying

School of Social Welfare, University of State, Town, State
Long-Term Care Project Research Assistant, November 1997–August 1999
- Assisted in collecting, inputting, and analyzing data for community re-entry, outcomes, and expedited eligibility studies; used SPSS, Excel, and Microsoft Word to prepare data for publication

DIRECT PRACTICE WITH INDIVIDUALS IN POVERTY

Southside Community Services, Town, State
Bilingual Outreach Intern, September 1999–December 1999
- Recruited, trained, and supervised volunteers; supervised immigrant youth group and assisted with community programming for Latinos; wrote grant for domestic violence program; nominated for outstanding practicum student award

Adult Protective Services, Town, State
Social Work Intern, September 1998–April 1999
- Investigated allegations of abuse, neglect, and exploitation involving frail elders, persons with mental illness, and persons with developmental disabilities; participated in statewide task force, tracked relevant legislation, helped develop agency protocols, and assisted with public education

Our Café, Town, State
Shift Manager, and member of Steering–Fundraising Committee, January 1998–August 1999
- Served breakfast to homeless and in-need members of the community; supervised volunteer groups; fundraised and helped secure volunteers so that the café could open another day each week

HONORS AND AWARDS

Outstanding Field Student, May 2001
Truman Scholar, 1999 (National award for outstanding students in public service; one of 70 chosen)
Phi Beta Kappa, 1999
Impact Award for Professional Achievement, 1999 (State award for four outstanding social work students)
Undergraduate Research Award, 1998 (State award for 10 exceptional student research proposals)
National Merit Scholar, 1996

SPECIAL PROJECTS AND SELECT PAPERS
- "Service Learning and Senior Adults" for the Center for Development, April 2001
- "Needs Assessment and Community Dialogue: Preliminary Program Evaluation for Spanish-Language Crisis Line" for P. Smith, instructor, December 2000
- "Enhancing Low-income Families' Access to Higher Education: The Limitations of State College Savings Plans" for the Center for Development, December 2000
- "Intergenerational Programs to Meet Pressing Social Problems" for Dr. Minor, October 2000
- "Education Reform to Meet the Needs of Latino Immigrant Students in Semi-Rural Districts: An Analysis of Kansas' Current System" for Q. Moore, instructor, April 2000

OTHER SKILLS
- International proficiency certification in Spanish, SPSS statistical software, Microsoft Word, Powerpoint, and Excel; Access database (no programming experience); Web page design

Sample 10: Functional for Experienced MSW with Program Interests

JENNIFER BLACK, ACSW, LCSW
Address
City, State Zip
Telephone & e-mail address

SUMMARY OF QUALIFICATIONS

Ten years experience in program development and community organization entailing start-up, promotions, and fundraising; all positions have been in management or leadership capacities. More than 8 years social services experience in clinical and administrative functions including counseling, training, and supervision.

PROGRAM DEVELOPMENT–COMMUNITY ORGANIZATION SKILLS

- Successfully initiated Healthy Initiative, a comprehensive, multiagency partnership providing health services and wellness education to four day schools serving 700 students; program is currently allocated $100,000 budget by the hospital.
- Established first local intergenerational program at older adult housing project; identified appropriate facility and participants and organized activities for over five years.
- Planned elementary school fundraiser generating over $1,000 in sales of projects created by students; recruited parents and vendors to donate time and services.

CLINICAL SKILLS

- Provided clinical services to persons over 60 years of age as part of multidisciplinary team in a hospital setting; treatment included initial assessment, therapy, and discharge planning.
- Conducted short- and long-term therapy for older adults and facilitated support groups for family members regarding issues around aging.
- Supervised students working on Master of Social Work degrees.
- Solely staffed senior citizen employment office by canvassing local businesses.

LEADERSHIP SKILLS

- Recently appointed to Older Adult Committee; assist in decision making grant appropriations.
- Serving on Board of Directors, Academy; provide direction setting for school   policy.
- Member of Advisory Committee; recommend program enhancements and mediate difficulties.
- Selected by National Council of Jewish Women to interview citizens for oral history.

WORK HISTORY

Primary Clinician, Community Mental Health Clinic, City, State, 1997–1998
Clinical Therapist, Family and Children's Service, City, State, 1993–1996
Social Worker, Vocational Service, City, State, 1991–1993

EDUCATION

Master of Social Work, The University, City, State, 1989–1990
Bachelor of Science in Social Welfare, State University, City, State, 1985–1988

Sample 11: Combination for Executive Director

CARL JEFFERSON
Address
City, State Zip
Home telephone
Work telephone
e-mail address

Innovative social work and health care administrator with proven expertise in strategic planning, business development, continuum of care services, fund development, contract negotiations, and operations management for social service programs, medical center–research institute, home health services, physical medicine–rehabilitation, and physician medical groups. Outstanding record of improving profit by increasing volume, extending market penetration, developing new programs, and managing costs. Directed multiple departments with over 1,765 employees, improving patient outcomes and productivity.

PROFESSIONAL EXPERIENCE

January 2002–**THE HOSPITAL**, City, State
Present: Executive Director, Clinical Services

Responsibilities include operational oversight of social services, discharge planning, employee assistance program, outpatient case management, Neurosciences Institute, Neurosurgical Physician Practice, Neurology Laboratory, Physical Medicine, Continuum of Care services (Home Health), Respiratory–Pulmonary, and Orthopedic Institute. Additional responsibility for business development, contracting, marketing, and fund development. Supervise 175 employees, combined budgeted expenses of $12 million, revenue of $36 million.

- Created comprehensive movement disorders program (increased rehabilitation, skilled nursing unit, and out-patient therapy census 20 percent).
- Established community case management liaison service (grant funded).
- Reduced operating expenses with integration of new skill mix and elimination of purchased labor and overtime ($2 million).
- Developed Huntington's disease neurotransplant program (first in the United States).
- Created physician–social work practice partnership program (integration of social work and physician private practice).

October 1998–January 2002 **THE HOSPITAL**, City, State
Director Social Work Services, Neuroscience Institute

In this capacity, responsibilities included managerial oversight of social work services, discharge planning, community case management, The Neuroscience Institute, Neurology Lab, and Epilepsy Research Center. Supervised 45 employees, combined budgeted expenses of $6 million, revenue of $9 million. Main accomplishments:

- Obtained 14 grants for out-patient case management ($1.5 million).
- Established Epilepsy Research Center (physician recruitment).
- Developed community–physician–hospital continuum of care program (community outreach program, grant funded).
- Created Parkinson and Brain Tumor Information & Referral Centers (17 community support groups with three chapters).
- Provided leadership and coordination for continuum of care quality improvement team (95 percent JCAHO survey outcome).

August 1994–October 1998 **THE HOSPITAL**, City, State
Director Social Work Services

Responsibilities included management of social work and discharge planning, utilization review, employee assistance program, senior partner program, and respite care services. Supervised 15 employees. Provided clinical supervision of social work staff, coordinated department quality improvement program. Main accomplishments:

- Developed community outpatient case management program.
- Established computerized high-risk screening program, cost savings $1.9 million.
- Revitalized hospital and community respite program (community board).
- Created clinical social service revenue program.

- Improved productivity by 25 percent (high risk and intern program).
- Established two community–hospital partnerships to reduce LOS and improve quality of care
- (DE and psychiatric services).
- Developed hospital employee assistance program.
- Reduced average length of stay hospitalwide by 2.5 days (physician profiles, education).

April 1992–July 1994 **HOSPITAL HOME HEALTH CARE AGENCY**, City, State
Director Rehabilitation and Social Services

Responsibilities included management of rehabilitation services (physical therapy, occupational therapy, and speech therapy) and social services staff of 50 clinicians for three offices. Recruited, hired, and oriented qualified staff. Responsible for revenue of $2 million and quality assurance program. Main accomplishments:
- Established home health–university MSW internship program.
- Increased revenue by 50 percent through business development and departmental reengineering.

July 1989–April 1992 **THE HOSPITAL AND REHABILITATION CENTER**, City, State
Clinical Social Worker

Responsibilities included clinical social work (assessment and therapy) and discharge planning services to acute rehabilitation, and emergency department patients. Accomplishments:
- Developed rehabilitation support groups.
- Created community rehabilitation resource guide.

EDUCATION

MSW, State University, City, State
BA, Sociology, University, City, State
Licensed Clinical Social Worker

PROFESSIONAL ACTIVITIES

Adjunct Professor, University of StateMember:
- NASW
- Society for Social Work Administrators in Health Care
- Healthcare Consulting Services:
- Skilled nursing facilities
- Acute care hospitals

Sample 12: Combination-Target for MSW with Managed Care Experience

NICOLE STEVENS
Address
City, State Zip
Telephone & e-mail address

OBJECTIVE

Seeking a behavioral healthcare management position in a medium sized corporate healthcare setting in the geographic) area.

QUALIFICATIONS AND BACKGROUND

A Licensed Clinical Social Worker with more than six years experience in Behavioral Healthcare Management. Extensive expertise in developing and implementing client-specific managed care policies and programs; on-call policy development; contract negotiation; public speaking; clinical and administrative supervision; quality management; utilization and concurrent review; and pharmacological review including ECT.

ACHIEVEMENTS

- Developed national leadership consultation program for the senior executives of select clients. Result: Established a national network of highly specialized professionals to provide client-specific services.
- Conceptualized a care management program that identified beneficiaries who had reached 70 percent of their life time benefit. Result: Intensive planning between patients, their families, and provider(s) maximized the remaining benefits and transition into community resources with minimal stress.
- Designed client-specific clinical criteria and policies to be used for six (type) accounts. Result: Improved satisfaction and compliance among beneficiaries and management. Able to address client-specific needs and blend "medical necessity" protocols with the client culture. This criteria is used in the national sales and marketing division, and has identified a niche market.
- Public speaking, including presentations at workshops and symposia, to mental health practitioners and clients on managed behavioral healthcare issues. Result: Company is seen as a leader in client-specific behavioral healthcare programs.
- Troubleshooting with third-party payors to reduce pending claims. Designed a numerical coding system, allowing case managers to authorize care using a code number, ensuring a consistent interpretation by commercial carriers, increasing claims processing to within two weeks.
- Supervised and managed daily operations of six clinical and seven support staff members. Result: Customer satisfaction at 90 percent; quality assurance protocols were maintained; computer training and troubleshooting; policy implementation.
- Negotiation of contracts with specialized individual providers and facilities. Result: Special rates and cost savings to the client while meeting managed care goals.
- Risk management program developed and implemented. Result: Decreased lawsuits by 60 percent in one year; increased stable labor force by 72 percent; improved insurability by commercial carriers, thus reducing placement in risk pool.

CAREER EXPERIENCE

Health Plans, City, State, *Psychiatric Disability Case Manager*, 2001–Present
Health, Inc., City, State, *Senior Clinical Case Manager*, Team Leader, 1997–2001
Aetna Health Plans, City, *State, Psychiatric Reviewer*, 1995–1997
The Children's Center, City, *State, Senior Clinician*, 1993–1995
Medi-Kleen Corp., City, State, *Risk Manager/Operations Manager*, 1986–1993
Private Clinical Practitioner, 1997–Present

PROFESSIONAL AFFILIATIONS

National Association of Social Workers, State Chapter
- Board of Directors, elected 2002–Present • Executive Committee, appointed by President: Policy, Development, and Budgeting, 2001–Present • Member, Managed Care Committee, 1999–Present

EDUCATION

University, Master of Social Work, 1987; University of State, Bachelor of Arts in Psychology, 1985

COMPUTER SKILLS

Microsoft Works for Windows; Word; Excel; ACCESS

Sample 13: Chronological Format for Experienced MSW Graduate with Direct Service and Policy Experience (Includes Keyword Summary for Electronic Scanning)

MELISSA JONES
Address
City, State
Telephone & e-mail address
Keywords:
child protective services supervisor; child welfare policy specialist; guidelines for states; MSW University of Cayne; policy analysis; regulation development; social policy development; U.S. Department of Health and Human Services

EDUCATION
Master of Social Work, University of Cayne School of Social Work, Town, State, 1989
Bachelor of Science degree in Social Work and Psychology, Prince College, City, State, 1986

EXPERIENCE
U.S. Department of Health and Human Services, Washington, DC

Child Welfare Policy Specialist (March 2000–Present)
   Develop regulations, policies, procedures, and guidance materials for the use of state and federal staff related to child welfare services programs; provide consultation to regional, central office, and state staff as well as other federal agencies in program areas related to child welfare; represent the Division of Name, as requested, with respect to public child welfare services in group and individual conferences with other divisions, bureaus, and federal agencies

County Department of Social Services, Town, State
December 1991–March 2000

Child Protective Services Supervisor (January 1998–Present)
   Supervise Sexual Abuse Treatment Services Unit staff of five, provide clinical and casework consultation regarding the treatment of sexual abuse victims and their families

Foster Care Supervisor (March 1994–January 1998)
   Supervised a unit of seven foster care workers, provided casework and clinical consultation regarding family reunification and adoption preparation, provided policy and procedures training for new staff, managed the foster care supportive services budget, served as Foster Care Review Board liaison to coordinate monthly case reviews, monitored and reviewed cases for compliance with federal and state regulations, reviewed and edited all written documents such as court reports and case plans, handled crisis in worker's absence, and supervised MSW student

Social Worker (December 1991–March 1994)
   Managed a caseload in both foster care–adoption services and independent living–adolescent foster care services; handled individual and family casework, home and school visits, counseling with foster parents, written court reports, and court appearances; supervised BSW student

Correctional Center for Women, Town, State

Social Worker (December 1990–December 1991)
   Conducted initial admission and reentry to the community groups with incarcerated women, written psychosocial assessments completed upon admission through inmate and family interviews, developed group protocols for ongoing and specialized population groups, crisis intervention with inmates, completed daily written group process reports and individual evaluations for each group member at termination, participated in multidisciplinary team meetings, and developed interagency contacts and agreements for referrals for inmates at release

Sample 13 continued on the following page

Continued from page 173

Barrons House, Town, State

Social Worker (August 1989–December 1990

   Provided individual, group, and family counseling with emotionally disturbed adolescents in group home setting, formulated treatment plans, organized preadmission interviews, led treatment team meetings, and monthly evaluations on each resident, provided supervision to child care staff, acted as administer on duty once a month

Regional Institute for Children and Adolescents, Town, State

Mental Health Associate (August 1988–August 1989)

   Handled individual counseling and crisis intervention with emotionally disturbed adolescents in a residential treatment facility, led group meetings, participated in planning and implementing the adolescent independent living program

City Hospital, Adolescent Clinic, Town, State

Graduate Social Work Intern (January 1987–December 1987)

   Provided individual counseling, casework, psychosocial assessment, group counseling, co-led family therapy, home, and school visits; provided services to pregnant adolescents and sexual assault victims

CERTIFICATION

State Licensed Certified Social Worker

Sample 14: Curriculum Vita

DEA JONES
Address
City, State Zip
Home telephone
Work telephone
e-mail address

EDUCATION
PhD Social Work Candidate
School of Social Work
Name University, City, State
Dissertation topic: Effects of Poverty Wages on Health
Advisor: Name

Master of Science in Social Work, 199X
Administration and Planning Concentration
University of State, City, State

Bachelor of Arts: Major in Sociology, Minor in History, 198X
University of State, City, State

TEACHING INTERESTS
Analysis of Practice
Child and Family Policy and Advocacy
Evaluation of Programs and Services
Social Welfare Policy, Policy Practice

RESEARCH INTERESTS
Health Care Policy and Health Status Research
Homelessness
Poverty Wages and the Working Poor
Program Evaluation and Policy Practice

HONORS
198X–198X Liberal Arts Scholarship, University of State, City
198X Name Honor Society, University of State, City
198X Phi Theta Kappa, City Community College, City, State

PROFESSIONAL EXPERIENCE
Teaching Experience
Name of University, Town, State—MSW Program
199X–199X, Instructor, Evaluation of Programs and Services
    Coinstructor: Name
199X, Coinstructor, Analysis of Practice
    Coinstructor: Name
199X Lab Instructor, Statistics
    Course Instructor: Name
    Name of University, Town, State—BSW Program
199X Teaching Assistant, Social Policy Course
    Course Instructor: Name

Research Experience
199X–199X, Development Corporation, Town, State
    Program Evaluation Consultant
    Survey development, interview training, statistical consultant

Sample 14 continued on the following page

Continued from page 175

199X–199X, Name of University, Town, State
   Research Assistant for Administrative Dean's Office
   Data entry and statistical analysis for academic advisor evaluation survey
199X–199X, Name of University, Town, State
   Research Assistant for Career Services
   Project coordination, SAS programming, design, and statistical analysis for reaccreditation and alumni surveys
199X–199X, Salvation Army Transitional Housing Project, Town, State
   Research Assistant for Name, Associate Professor
   Computer programming, manual preparation, statistical analysis

PRACTICE EXPERIENCE
198X–199X, Name of Agency, City, State
     Director of Homeless Services
         Worked with homeless women and children in locating temporary and permanent housing; experienced in crisis intervention, resource development, and referral, volunteer training, and program planning; managed budget
198X–199X, Name of Agency, City, State
     Social Work Intern
         Worked with individuals with mental retardation in groups and individually, and with their families as a liaison between the institution, client, and family to advocate for client needs

PUBLICATIONS (SAMPLE LIST)
Journal Article
Name, Name, Name (199X), "Title of Article," *Title of Journal*, volume, page numbers

Papers under Review
Title, author(s)

PRESENTATIONS (SAMPLE LIST)
199X Appalachian Leadership Initiative on Cancer
- Guest Speaker: "Challenges and Benefits of Community Development"
199X HUD Southeast Regional Conference
- Panel: "Building Partnerships to Build Communities"
199X Tennessee Conference on Social Welfare
- Workshop: "Advocacy and Community Organizing for Human Service Providers"
199X Council on Social Work Education, 41st Annual Program Meeting
- "Predictors of Permanent Versus Temporary Housing for Homeless Families"
199X American Public Health Association Annual Meeting, City, State

UNIVERSITY AND CIVIC SERVICE
- 199X Academic Adviser and Field Liaison, Name University
- 199X Graduate Student Committee, Name University
- 198X–198X Volunteer instructor for English as a Second Language classes
- 198X–198X Volunteer reader for the blind with the commission
- 198X Volunteer for the physically handicapped

AFFILIATIONS
- Council on Social Work Education
- National Association of Social Workers
- Society for Social Work Research

SPECIAL SKILLS AND TALENTS
- Bilingual in English and Spanish: Have translated in both medical and educational environments; extensive travel in rural and urban Latin America
- Computer skills: SAS statistical package, SPSS statistical package, Excel spreadsheet, Lisrel structural equation modeling, Rbase, Microsoft Word, Word Perfect, QuatroPro
- Research Skills: Worked on several research projects in both academic settings and in community; have worked as a research assistant, consultant, and taught statistics, research methods, and program evaluation

Sample Interview Questions

Questions that have been asked in interviews for social work and related positions listed below were generated from discussions with employers and job candidates. It is important to note that some employers are using the behavioral interview format. Behavioral interview questions are often phrased as follows: "Tell me about a time when . . . ."

The focus is on specific situations. Preparing responses, which should include examples from your experiences, to the following questions will enable you to respond effectively regardless of the interview format used. Tailor your responses to the specific position for which you are interviewing. Note that you will sometimes encounter vague questions—several of which are included here. At the end of this appendix is a sample list of questions that would be appropriate for you to ask in an interview.

Generic Questions
- What are your career goals?
- Are you where you thought you would be in your career?
- How does the work in this organization fit your professional mission?
- What is your experience with diverse staff members? What did you find difficult? Easy?
- What is your experience with diverse ethnic groups?
- Why do you think you can work well with people who are [ethnic group]?
- How do you work?
- Tell me about a time when you had to juggle your regular responsibilities and deal with a sudden priority.
- How do you evaluate your work?
- What would most intimidate you?
- What would you dislike most in a position?
- What do you need to hear about this organization and position that will tell you this would be a good match for you?
- What is your knowledge of regulations [Medicare or Medicaid, for example]?
- What issues might you have with [adoption, for example]?
- I am getting the impression that you really do not know what it is like [to work in that community with the drug situation or to be poor, for example]. Do you have a comment?
- What is the biggest obstacle you found in working with [a particular issue or population]?
- What did you not like about your work?
- How did your coworkers describe you? How would your supervisor describe you?
- What kinds of people rub you the wrong way?
- Describe a situation in which you feel you could have done a better job with a [project, patient, or client, for example]?
- How do you plan?
- What qualities do you feel are most important in a supervisor?
- What do you do to cope in a fast-paced work setting?

- What makes you think you would be good at this job?
- What do you think will work and why [in a particular situation]?
- How do you take care of yourself?
- Why do you want this job? Why do you want to work for this organization?
- Is this job still something you are interested in now that you have heard about it?
- Tell me about yourself.
- Why do you want to leave your present position?
- What do you see as the most difficult aspects of work in this field [or with this population]?
- What do you want to be doing in five years?
- What are your qualifications?
- Why should I hire you?
- How would you approach [a particular problem or situation]?
- What are your clinical strengths; what are your administrative strengths?
- What are your weaknesses?
- What did you learn from your field-training experiences?
- What has been your greatest accomplishment?
- Tell me what you know about our agency [or this position or program].
- How do you see yourself in the role of [school social worker, advocate, clinical supervisor, or legislative aide, for example]?
- Talk about your view of [hospice, family life education, or community development, for example].
- What experience or training have you had in the area of [a particular field or function]?
- How do you deal with anger, hostility, or stress?
- Describe the process you go through in developing a [case plan, budget, workshop, contract, or marketing plan, for example].
- What kinds of things are important to you in a job? What has been satisfying?
- What kinds of things do you like or not like in a job? What has been a hassle in your work?
- What do you have to offer as a [clinician or administrator, for example]?
- Why are you in social work? Why did you study social work?
- What brought you into social work?
- How is social work different from what you expected?
- What would your friends say about you?
- What could you offer to this job?
- How would you handle a situation in which you had a disagreement with a coworker?
- Have you ever been perceived as not doing something correctly, and how did you handle it?
- What are your questions?
- In what areas do you prefer not to be involved?
- What about this position is most attractive to you? What are the disadvantages or concerns you have about this job?
- What was the most adverse situation you have had to deal with in your professional life? How did you deal with it? What was the outcome?
- Have you made any mistakes in your career? If so, what were they? How did you fix them?
- What was the most difficult ethical decision you have had to make and what was the outcome?
- If we hired you next week, what unfinished business would you leave in your current work?
- Walk me through a challenge you faced.

Direct Practice Questions

- Delivery of services has been changing for several years away from long-term services delivered in offices to intensive services delivered in homes, schools, and other settings. What skills can you bring to these services?
- What is your understanding of service delivery in [a particular field or region]?
- What is your experience with targeted case management?
- Tell me about a time you were in a disagreement over a treatment plan.
- Describe your favorite and least favorite clients.
- What is your experience in working with clients who are different from yourself?
- Why were you successful working with clients who are different from yourself, and why were you unsuccessful?
- How do you assess for suicide risk?
- What are your technical skills [or diagnostic skills or treatment skills]?
- Tell me about a time when you advocated for more services for a client, but funding or policies did not allow you to provide the services you thought were appropriate.
- Why do you think you can work with [for example, parents, older adults, substance abusers, clients with low incomes, survivors of rape or incest] when you haven't been there yourself? What could hinder your work with this population?
- How is practice different from what you expected?
- What do you think produces change?
- What is your philosophy on a [particular issue or treatment]?
- What is your theory base? What is your theoretical approach? How has your theoretical approach changed?
- Describe one of your cases. Describe a particularly challenging case for you.
- What types of client issues have you dealt with?
- Give some examples of treatment choices you made and explain why you made those choices.
- With what client issues are you most comfortable working?
- What has been your experience with agency paperwork and how do you feel about it?
- What does [family therapy, for example] mean to you?
- What are your expectations of both individual and group supervision?
- How do you protect your personal boundaries when responsibilities demand your time, attention, and energy?
- How do you think court intervention might be useful in a case?
- What other populations have you worked with?
- Clinically, what is the most difficult experience you have had?
- Identify some boundary issues that may confront someone in this position and describe the way you would handle them.
- How do you like working with diversity, such as client populations, issues?
- What does diversity mean to you?
- What is your experience with grieving and how have you dealt with it?
- Tell us about a time when you had a conflict with a client and another when you had a conflict with a coworker.
- Have you had to do your work in a cubicle? How did that work for you?
- How will you deal with the dual-relationship issues of working in a small community?

Policy Questions

- Many people want to impact policies, yet don't have an understanding of how to do it. If you wanted to work in policy, why did you go into social work rather than public policy immediately (or a public policy graduate program)?
- If a policy is up for reauthorization, what is the process you would use for affecting policy reform?
- Where do you see yourself in five years?
- How would you approach working with people from diverse backgrounds who may have points of view different from yours? Do you enjoy this?
- How would you handle a situation where a legislator vehemently disagrees with you and becomes argumentative? What would you see as your goal in this situation and how would you accomplish it?
- Which one of your experiences do you feel is most relevant to the work we do here and why?
- How comfortable are you working with quantitative data and research?
- How comfortable are you working with advocacy work, for example, talking with staff on Capitol Hill and other government officials?
- What issues are you particularly interested in working on?
- What is your experience with building coalitions?
- If you developed a coalition, whom did you decide to include?
- Tell us about a time when your efforts to build a coalition failed. What was the purpose, what approach did you use, why did it fail, and what did you do then? Looking back how would you do things differently?
- How have you created opportunities for your coalition to dialogue with elected officials, particularly in public forums?
- What is your experience working in collaboration?
- How do you handle shifting priorities and working in a fast-paced, pressured environment? What is your experience with writing quickly, under pressure?
- What do you do to keep track of a lot of information at once?
- Tell me about a team work experience you've had, what you learned, and what you might do differently in the future.
- What are the pitfalls of extrapolating data, particularly from the local to the national level?
- Give an example of a situation in which you had to set aside your beliefs on a particular issue and work toward a politically and financially feasible goal?
- Have you been involved in projects or efforts that took more than a year? How did you maintain your enthusiasm and organize your work?
- Have you been involved in an effort that failed? Did you attempt to resurrect it? Why or why not? Did you make changes the second time?
- What is your experience in working with people with opposite viewpoints on policy?
- What is your experience with writing fact sheets, option papers, and sound bites?
- What is your experience with legislative advocacy? What is your experience with policy advocacy?
- Who is in your congressional delegation? Who are your state representatives?
- If you do not have frontline experience, how will you be an effective [program manager or policy analyst, for example]?
- How does your particular policy interest fit into the big picture?
- What experience do you have in analyzing the opposition's viewpoint?

Program Development Questions

- How would you start up this project [program or initiative]?
- How would you communicate a new program to the rest of the agency that may not be willing to add work to their regular routine?
- How would you present your ideas or results to other staff members? What methods would you use to get your points across?
- How comfortable are you with speaking in public or to a group?
- What is the extent of your knowledge about computers and the Internet? What experience do you have working with PowerPoint, Excel spreadsheets, Word, and so forth?
- What knowledge do you have of the city or community where this position is located?
- How would you go about locating community resources in a neighborhood in which you have no relationship?
- What experience have you had working in program development?
- What is your leadership style?
- What type of environment do you work best in [that is, autonomous, teams, and so forth]?

Administrative Questions

Note that questions for executive and higher level management positions will be much more specialized and specific to the organization than those listed below.

- Since this is a newly created position, how would you proceed?
- What projects [or programs] have you run? What challenges did you face?
- What is your experience with preparing and monitoring a budget?
- What kinds of financial information do you need to make decisions?
- Tell us about your experience with grants (including identifying funders, writing proposals, success rates, size, collaborations, evaluation plans, and implementation).
- What is your experience with directing fundraising operations and capital campaigns?
- What is your experience with for-profit services that are part of not-for-profit organizations?
- How do you work under pressure?
- What was the tensest situation you experienced, and how did you handle it?
- Tell me about your research skills.
- What is your experience in working with people from other disciplines? What did you bring to the discussion?
- Tell me about your involvement in collaborative efforts.
- Tell me about a time when you had responsibility for a complex project. How did you ensure that it was completed?
- How do you approach negotiation? What are some examples?
- As the new CEO of an agency, what steps would you take to assess its strengths, weaknesses, and opportunities?
- How would you handle the press if a negative situation developed in the agency and became public knowledge?
- How would you develop and maintain the commitment and motivation of the staff [or board]?
- How have you approached strategic planning with boards?
- What criteria should the board use in evaluating your performance?

- What are the primary issues facing this type of agency?
- What is your approach to evaluation of [services, operations, programs]? How would you approach that here?
- How would you approach the process of making key contacts in this community?
- What would your priorities be in the first three months of this position?
- Based on what you know about our organization, what ideas do you have for future developments of the program?
- Tell me how your approach to managing an organization has changed from the way it was 10 years ago.
- Explain your management style.
- Describe an innovative way you resolved a major problem that resulted in a change in how the organization did business.
- Describe your management style specifically as it relates to setting direction, creating an environment, and changing organizational cultures in a complex organization.
- Highlight your experiences in forming partnerships and coalitions with diverse community groups.
- Describe your experience in setting priorities and allocating and managing resources, including budgets and staff.
- Describe your experience and identify specific strategies you used to provide quality assurance and continuous quality improvement.
- How would you describe your supervisory style?
- How would you address tension in a group?
- What are examples of work you have accomplished by facilitating [or organizing] the work of others?
- If you had a staff member who isn't following through on something he or she had promised to do or change, what would you do?
- How would you resolve a problem between two staff members who disagree on the handling of a [case, project, team, initiative]?
- Give a specific example of your experience in resolving staff conflict.
- Describe your experience in managing a diverse workforce.
- Tell me about a time when you found it difficult to work with a team.
- How would you build a team under you?

Teaching and Scholarship Questions
- What are your teaching interests?
- What are you looking for in a work environment? What do you think you can contribute to this work environment? What have you contributed in other work environments?
- What texts would you use to teach a course on [a particular subject]?
- What can you teach? What theoretical perspective would guide the course?
- How would you go about teaching [a particular subject]? What is your teaching philosophy?
- How would you describe yourself as a teacher?
- Do you know how our curriculum differs from other programs?
- Why are you interested in our school? What contributions can you make to this school? How will you increase the school's standing in the profession?

- What is your dissertation topic and how does it contribute to the knowledge of the profession?
- In five years, what contribution do you want to have made in this field?
- How did you collect your data? Tell us of an experience with quantitative and qualitative methodology. Was your analysis primarily [quantitative or qualitative]? How did you use the other to supplement the findings?

Research Questions
- What are your research interests?
- Tell us about your research experience. What skills did you gain from those experiences? What contributions did you make to the work?
- Tell us about [a particular] project. What was your role? How was it accomplished? What were the results?
- Do you like to work collaboratively or independently?
- How did you collect your data?
- What are the implications of your project for policy and practice?
- What computer applications have you used?
- Do you have experience with data collection and, if so, what kind?
- Have you worked with secondary data sets and, if so, what was the experience?
- Do you have survey design experience and, if so, what have you done?
- What is your background, both academic and in practice, in statistics?
- Are you comfortable with writing reports or articles? What kind of reports or articles have you written? Has any of your work been published? What writing samples can you provide?
- Do you have experience in grant writing and, if so, what kind [federal, state, or foundation] and were any of your grants successful?
- Are you familiar with the institutional review boards and policies related to these boards?

Sample Information to Collect Regarding a Position
These questions build on questions listed in chapter 2 "Gather Information on Specific Organizations" and chapter 6 "Making a Decision." Note that not all of these questions are ones you would actually ask in an interview.

Generic Questions
- How committed is this organization to evaluation of practice or services and the use of evidence-based practices when possible?
- What are the opportunities for advancement?
- What is the management style [of the supervisor, management in general]?
- How would you describe the culture of the organization?
- How does staff describe the work environment?
- What are the responsibilities and scope of the position? Why is the position open?
- Where does this position fit in the organizational structure? Is it in a social work department?

- Is the organization a single entity or part of a local, regional, or national system? If the agency is part of a parent company or umbrella organization, what is that relationship? If it is part of a larger organization, how easily do people transfer to other positions in the system?
- What are the strengths and weaknesses of the organization?
- What is the organization's philosophy? For example, in a children's facility, is the focus on developing empathy in children or on behavior modification?
- What structures support the philosophy? If you are told that staff members work as a team, ask how often they meet. You can also ask, "How does that work [or work out]?" Look for inconsistencies.
- How does the agency encourage excellence in staff? How is staff morale?
- Take a tour. How well is the building maintained? Are the workspace and resources adequate?

ADMINISTRATION QUESTIONS

- Who is the organization's constituency? Who are you accountable to? [Be clear about whether it is a membership organization, or funded primarily by foundations, or receives government funding, and so forth.]
- Does your organization work in coalition with other advocacy organizations? If so, which ones?
- How do decisions get made about the organization's position on issues and legislation? How are priorities set?
- How would you say other people view the organization? For example in policy, how do Capitol Hill staff and others in the advocacy community view the organization? Is the organization considered progressive, liberal, or conservative?
- Who is on the board, and what struggles do board members face?
- What is the relationship of the board to the staff?
- What are the goals of the board? Where do they want to take the agency? Does the agency have a strategic plan?
- What are the agency's funding sources, and how successful has the agency been in securing new sources?
- What is the budget and how does it compare to similar organizations?
- If this agency uses public funds, what are its relationships with public agencies?
- Who are the key people in the organization that ensure its success or make it work?
- What accounting procedures are in place? Is there a financial plan?
- What is this agency's reputation among the public, its peers, its funders, its clients?
- Is the organization contracting, expanding, rebuilding, or stabilizing?
- What is the organizational structure? Is it centralized or decentralized? How long has this structure been in place?
- How strong is the leadership? What disciplines do they represent? What are their roles inside and outside the organization?

DIRECT PRACTICE QUESTIONS

- What types of supervision are available? Is consultation available?
- What are the characteristics of the population, and how severe are their problems?
- What practice theories are used in this organization?

- What is the organization's approach to working with clients who threaten staff?
- What is the typical caseload? When a coworker is swamped, can another worker be asked to open a case?
- Is the staff on call, and how is that handled?
- How stable is the staff? Or, what is the turnover rate?
- What are the requirements of the position, that is, the hours worked, any evenings or weekends?
- How much autonomy does a person have in this position?
- With what other staff members will the person in this position work [for example, marketing department director]?

Teaching Questions
- What are the committee responsibilities for junior and senior faculty?
- What are the advising responsibilities for faculty and what is the advising system?
- Do faculty design each of their courses and select the texts or is that done by a committee or by a lead teacher?
- What is the expected course load for junior faculty and senior faculty?
- What are the supports for research: school and university staffs, offices, committees? What is the role of each?
- How many grants went out and were received last year?
- What is in place to support the career development of junior faculty? Is there a formal mentoring system and how does that work? Do junior faculty apply for career grants? What funding sources are available in the school and university for attending conferences?
- Are there summer salaries and how does that work?
- What resources are available: teaching assistants, research assistants, computers, secretarial support?

Online Job Information and Career Services

There are a wide variety of career services available online, including
- career and job-hunting information
- discussion groups
- job listings
- organization information
- resume databases

Social Work and Other Career Services

The Web sites listed below are good jumping-off points if you are looking for job announcements and researching organizations or if you just want to learn more about using the Internet for career purposes. Many of these sites have links to other Web sites listing jobs and to sites of specific organizations. Note that a number of the associations hold conferences or training programs that you may also want to explore.

Alliance for Children and Families
http://www.alliance1.org
Alliance offers jobs online.

American Association of Homes & Services for Aging
http://www.aahsa.org
This Web site includes an online search for member organizations as well as state association partners.

America's Job Bank
http://www.ajb.dni.us
This site offers searches by job category and zip code. Social-work-related searches include community and social services and health care.

Association for Advanced Training in the Behavioral Sciences
http://www.aatbs.com
Provides information on independent study programs for the social work licensing exams. Registered members may take practice exams online and participate in Internet classes.

Association of Jewish Family and Children's Agencies
http://www.ajfca.org
An online membership directory and job database are available. The *Professional Opportunities Bulletin*, a monthly publication, also lists open positions. Also see http://www.jewishjobfinder.com

Career Search
http://www.careersearch.net
This is a comprehensive job-search database to which many universities subscribe. Contact your career center to see if it is offered. The program allows users to research information on metropolitan areas, salary information, and specific organizations.

Catholic Charities USA
http://www.catholiccharitiesusa.org
There is an online search for social services affiliates and a jobs section at http://www.catholiccharitiesinfo.org

Charity Channel: Career Search Online

http://www.charitychannel.com/careersearch

This site is geared toward job searches in the non-for-profit sector. You can search positions by title, location, organization, and multiple other criteria. International searches are also available.

Child Welfare League of America

http://www.cwla.org

The Web site offers an online job bank and a listing of member organizations.

Children's Defense Fund

http://www.childrensdefense.org

Online services include job postings. There is also a volunteer hotline at 202-662-3797 and an employment hotline at 202-662-3680.

Chronicle of Philanthropy

http://www.philanthropy.com

The publication's Web site offers job listings, including fundraising, executive, program, and administrative positions. It is also a source of information on current developments and trends in not-for-profit organizations. Positions are also printed in their publication.

Community Career Center

http://www.nonprofitjobs.org

This site provides jobs and information on community-based development and human services.

Council for Health and Human Services Ministries

http://www.chhsm.org

This site has links to member social services organizations.

Council on Social Work Education

http://www.cswe.org

The Web site provides job listings in academia as well as links to multiple national and inter-national social work organizations.

The Everett Jewish Job Finder

http://www.jewishjobfinder.com

This site is a central job-posting site for all organizations that are part of the Jewish community.

Family Support America

http://www.familysupportamerica.org

This Web site has a directory of family support programs across the United States.

Federal Jobs Digest

http://www.jobsfed.com

This is a free database of federal employment opportunities, updated daily.

Flip Dog

http://www.flipdog.com

This is a general job search site with multiple social work listings.

Gateway to International Development and Environmental Jobs

http://www.devnetjobs.org

International job listings are posted on this site. Users may subscribe to weekly job e-mails.

Government Jobs

http://www.govtjobs.com

This is a Web site geared toward jobs in the public sector. It offers job listings as well as job resource information for individual states.

Guide to Careers in Child and Family Policy

http://www.igpa.uiuc.edu/cfp

This is a comprehensive site offering multiple resources to individuals interested in child and family policy. Resources include job, internship, and fellowship listings; academic programs; and contact information for various agencies.

Guidestar: The National Database of Non-Profit Organizations
http://www.guidestar.org
This site offers a searchable database of over 850,000 not-for-profit organizations.

Hospital Web
http://neuro-www.mgh.harvard.edu/hospital-web.html
This site offers links to medical centers by state and country.

HS People
http://www.hspeople.com
This is a career search site for health and human services, not-for-profit, and mental health jobs.

Idealist.org: Action without Borders
http://www.idealist.org
This site offers a search engine for organizations, job openings, volunteer opportunities, and multiple other resources. You can sign up for e-mail updates.

Immigration & Refugee Services of America
http://www.refugeesusa.org
A directory of affiliates is online.

InterAction (American Council for Voluntary International Action)
http://www.interaction.org
This site has information about the work of this coalition of nonprofit organizations, which focuses on international efforts such as relief and social development.

International Career Employment Weekly
http://www.internationaljobs.org/contents.html
This is a newspaper that can be accessed in print, by e-mail, or online.

Internet Career Connection
http://www.iccweb.com
This site offers multiple job search options by keyword, industry, state, or city. Provides links to career resources and publications as well as information on career mentors in multiple fields.

Jewish Community Centers Association
http://www.jcca.org
Personnel services to member centers and individuals seeking positions with Jewish community centers are offered. An online job search of openings is also available.

Job Hunt.Org
http://www.job-hunt.org
This site offers links to job sites in all 50 states as well as advice on the Internet job search process.

JobWeb
http://www.jobweb.com
This site has a searchable job and employer directory, job-search and industry information, and career planning resources.

Lutheran Services in America
http://www.lutheranservices.org
This site has an online directory of links to social services organizations by state.

Medhunters.com
http://www.medhunters.com
This site provides social work job listings, licensing information, links to professional organizations, job relocation tools, and information on social work academic programs.

Medical and Health Care Jobs
http://www.nationjob.com/medical
This job database allows you to search by field, position, location, education, duration, salary, or internship. Another service does the job searching for you for free. There are Specialty Pages for particular employment categories. A directory of all companies is available, or you can search for a company based upon criteria.

Medline Plus

http://www.nlm.nih.gov/medlineplus/directories.html

This site, a service of the U.S. National Library of Medicine and the National Institutes of Health, includes links to general medical centers and specialized health services.

Mental Health Corporation of America

http://www.mhca.com

The Web site includes links to its member organizations and employment ads.

MonsterTrak

http://www.jobtrak.com

College students can post a resume and access jobs if their colleges are members.

National Alliance for Hispanic Health

http://www.hispanichealth.org

This Web site includes links to man social services in the United States.

National Alzheimer's Association

http://www.alz.org

This site offers links to state chapters.

National Assembly of Health and Human Service Organizations

http://www.nassembly.org

This site offers online links to membership organizations as well as an online directory of internships in youth development and job listings at member organizations.

National Association of Area Agencies on Aging

http://www.n4a.org

This Web site includes job listings and links to area agencies on aging across the United States.

National Association of Child Advocates

http://www.childadvocacy.org

The Web site features postings of job openings at member organizations.

National Association of Community Action Agencies

http://www.communityactionpartnership.com

This group publishes jobs online.

National Association of Social Workers

http://www.socialworkers.org

The Web site of the NASW national office provides links to related sites, including state chapters. Members may use JobLink, which allows users to post and send resumes, receive e-mail alerts of job openings, and search nationwide job listings. Jobs are also printed in the *NASW News* publication.

National Conference of State Legislatures

http://www.ncsl.org

Job openings in state legislatures are listed at the Web site. An online directory of state legislators and legislative staff is also available.

National Congress for Community Economic Development

http://www.ncced.org

Job openings are listed online.

National Council on Alcoholism and Drug Dependence

http://www.ncadd.org

The council offers an online affiliate directory, or you may call 1-800-NCA-CALL to find the closest affiliate.

National Council for Community Behavioral Healthcare

http://www.nccbh.org

Job openings are listed online.

The New Social Worker Online

http://www.socialworker.com

This is the Web site of *The New Social Worker*, a professional development publication for social work students and recent graduates. The site offers a message board, jobs page, and a free online newsletter.

Opportunities in Public Affairs

http://www.opajobs.com

This site lists jobs in public relations, government affairs, and legislation in not-for-profit, corporation and federal agencies in the Washington, DC, area.

Opportunity NOCS

http://www.opportunitynocs.org

This site lists nonprofit career opportunities. Search by state, position title, or organization. Listings are available for 20 states. Registered users may post their resumes online.

PRAXIS (Resources for Social and Economic Development)

http://www.caster.ssw.upenn.edu/~restes/praxis.html

This site has links to international organizations, employment opportunities, and other Web sites related to international social development.

The Riley Guide

http://www.rileyguide.com

This site offers guidance through multiple stages of the job search process. There are guidelines for posting a resume online. Lists employment opportunities and job resources on the Internet; there is a category for the social sciences.

Social Service.com

http://www.socialservice.com

Offers free e-mail notification of job postings in your state, as well as a searchable job database.

Social Work Access Network

http://www.sc.edu/swan

SWAN has links to many resources of interest to social work job hunters, including national organizations, global organizations, U.S. government departments, schools of social work, listservs, and newsgroups.

Social Work.Com

http://www.socialwork.com

This site provides job listings in social work, case management, mental health, and counseling both in the United States and abroad. Registered users receive e-mail listings of job openings.

Social Work Examination Services

http://www.socialworklicense.com

The site offers information on licensing review and study guide publications. It provides links to other specific social work career sites.

Social Work Job Bank

http://www.socialworkjobbank.com

This site offers job listings through multiple search options. Registered users may also post their resumes.

Social Work p.r.n.

http://www.socialworkprn.com

This site has links to its affiliates and primarily temporary jobs in social work.

Social Work Search.com

http://www.socialworksearch.com

This site is a gateway to multiple social work links ranging from licensing to education to employment opportunities.

Social Work and Social Services Jobs Online

http://www.gwbweb.wustl.edu/jobs

The SWSSJO is a social-work-specific career resource. It includes a job database, links to other databases, and links to career resources.

Travelers Aid International

http://www.travelersaid.org

Web site visitors may access a directory of its member agencies.

United Jewish Communities

http://www.ujc.org

A nationwide recruiting event is held each spring where candidates can interview with Jewish Federations from across the country; jobs are online.

United Neighborhood Centers of America

http://www.unca.org

This Web site lists nationwide member organizations.

United Way of America

http://www.national.unitedway.org

The Web site includes links to United Way affiliates and lists job openings at member organizations across the country.

USA Jobs

http://www.usajobs.opm.gov

This is the U.S. Government's official site for jobs and employment information, provided by the U.S. Office of Personnel Management.

What Color Is Your Parachute

http://www.jobhuntersbible.com

This guide outlines uses of the Internet for job hunting and provides links to related sites. There is also an extensive library of frequently updated job articles.

YMCA

http://www.ymca.net/index.isp

The Web site lists jobs at the national level and links to member agencies nationwide.

Special Opportunites: Fellowships, Internships, Training, and Loan Forgiveness Programs

Postgraduate and predegree training opportunities are described in this appendix. These programs are very competitive, and many of them serve as springboards for exciting careers. Before applying for these programs, ask for the names of current program participants and consult with them on the quality of the experience and strategies for making a successful application. Always address the interest of the program in every aspect of your application, and ask several people with knowledge of the subject to critique your essays. Many programs pay a salary or stipend, but some charge participants.

POSTGRADUATE DEGREE OPPORTUNITIES: ADMINISTRATIVE & POLICY
AFL–CIO ORGANIZING INSTITUTE
815 16th Street, NW
Washington, DC 20006
202-637-5000
Fax: 202-637-5058
http://www.aflcio.org

The Organizing Institute combines classroom, field training, and job placement. It is a three-step program in which participants are recruited, trained, and then placed in union-organizing positions across the country. The first step is a three-day training program. If completed successfully, the trainee moves on to a paid, 14-day orientation and three-month field-training program. Finally, if all steps are completed successfully, participants are recommended for job placement in local and national unions. Placement rates are higher than 95 percent among graduates.
Requirements: Each stage has a set of selective criteria; the three-day training program looks for applicants with strong social justice values and aspirations.
Where: The three-day training program occurs in cities throughout the country; see the Web site for annual training dates.
When: Starting dates vary, see the Web site for training dates.
Stipend: Housing and food are provided for the three-day training. Participants are paid a weekly stipend of $450 during the field training; housing, transportation, and health insurance are also provided. If placed in a job, starting annual pay averages between $23,000 and $32,000 plus benefits.
Deadline: None—there is open enrollment for the nationwide training

AMERICAN & WORLD AFFAIRS FELLOW PROGRAM
Fellows Program Coordinator
World Without Wars Council
1730 Martin Luther King Jr. Way
Berkeley, CA 94709
510-845-1992
Fax: 510-845-5721
http://www.wwwc.org

This program provides experience in working with nongovernmental organizations (NGOs). Fellows are exposed to the ways in which NGOs function in the international arena. Students learn through seminars, work experience, individual study, and skills training.
Requirements: Completion of master's degree; some bachelor-level graduates will be considered
Where: San Francisco Bay area
When: September–June
Stipend: Varies
Deadline: June

CALIFORNIA SENATE FELLOWS
6000 J Street
Sacramento, CA 95819
916-278-6906
Fax: 916-278-5199
E-mail: calstudies@csus.edu
http://www.csus.edu/calst/programs/senate_fellows.html

This fellowship places participants as legislative aides and committee consultants. Fellows will research issues, analyze legislation, and develop legislative proposals.
Requirements: Degree from a four-year college or university
Where: Sacramento, CA
When: Eleven months, beginning in October
Stipend: Monthly stipend of $1,882 plus health and dental benefits; 12 units of graduate credit
Deadline: February

CARE
151 Ellis Street NE
Atlanta, Georgia 30303-2440
800-521-CARE
http://www.careusa.org

This is a two-year fellowship geared toward individuals interested in international aid and relief. Fellows gain experience in project design and evaluation, budgeting, human resource management, and strategic planning.
Where: Various international placements
When: This is a two-year placement.

CONGRESSIONAL FELLOWS PROGRAM
Congressional Black Caucus
1720 Massachusetts Avenue, NW
Washington, DC 20002
202-263-2800
Fax: 202-547-3806
http://cbcfinc.org/Congressional_Fellows.html

This fellowship is designed to give participants the opportunity to work on congressional committees and to learn the various elements of the legislative process. Students provide scholarly research before Congress.

Requirements: Graduate students completing their coursework or public policy professionals with five years of experience or college faculty
Where: Washington, DC
When: September–May
Stipend: $25,000 for nine months
Deadline: April

CONGRESSIONAL RESEARCH SERVICE INTERNSHIP
Congressional Research Service
Library of Congress
James Madison Memorial Building
101 Independence Avenue, SE
Room LM-205
Washington, DC 20540-7000
202-707-7641
Fax: 202-707-1833

This is a volunteer position in which participants perform research and reference work for congressional inquiries on public policy. Volunteers will gain research, analysis, and reference experience and skills. CRS is a department of the Library of Congress, which supplies information services exclusively to members of Congress and their staffs.

Requirements: Good research and writing skills; open to undergraduates, graduate students, postgraduates, faculty, and other professionals; computer knowledge and statistical skills are desirable
Where: Washington, DC
When: Appointments vary from three months to one year; hours are determined by the needs of the applicant and assigned division.
Stipend: None, though students may be able to acquire college credit
Deadline: None; applications should be submitted four to eight weeks in advance of proposed starting date

CORO FELLOWS PROGRAM IN PUBLIC AFFAIRS
http://www.coro.org

Coro National Office	Coro Midwestern Center	Coro Eastern Center
1010 West 39th Street	911 Washington, Suite 510	42 Broadway, Suite 18-2735
Kansas City, MO 64111	St. Louis, MO 63101	New York, NY 10004
816-931-0751	314-621-3040	212-248-2935
Fax: 816-756-0924	Fax: 314-621-1874	Fax: 212-248-2970

Coro Northern California
580 California Street
7th Floor
San Francisco, CA 94104
415-986-0521
Fax: 415-986-5522

Coro Southern California
811 Wilshire Blvd, Suite 1025
Los Angeles, CA 90017-2624
213-623-1234
Fax: 213-680-0079

This professional program focuses on the structure and functions of government agencies, political campaigns, community-based organizations, labor unions, and businesses. The program is an intensive array of field assignments, projects, and seminars, with the aim of understanding how people function and organize themselves to meet social, political, economic, and religious needs in society.
Requirements: Must be bright, self-motivated risk taker with a commitment to public service
Where: New York, Pittsburgh, St. Louis, San Francisco, Los Angeles
When: September–May
Stipend: There is no financial compensation for this program; tuition is $3,500 (some financial assistance for living expenses is available, based on need)
Deadline: January

EMERGING LEADERS PROGRAM
U.S. Department of Health and Human Services
200 Independence Avenue, SW
Washington, DC 20201
E-mail: Emerging.Leaders@hhs.gov
http://www.hhs.gov/jobs/elp/about.html

This program is designed to create future leaders of the U.S. Department of Health and Human Services. Students rotate through various divisions, each assignment lasting from 60 to 90 days. All participants work closely with a mentor throughout the program.
Requirements: Completion of bachelor or master's degree
Where: Washington, DC, Baltimore, Atlanta
When: This is a two-year program beginning in July.
Stipend: Salary at government pay scale GS7 or GS9, depending on experience
Deadline: April

EXECUTIVE FELLOWSHIP PROGRAM
Center for California Studies
6000 J Street
Sacramento, CA 95819-6081
916-278-6906
Fax: 916-278-5199
E-mail: calstudies@csus.edu
http://www.wwwc.org

Fellows gain knowledge in policy development and implementation and executive–legislative relations. Placements are in offices throughout the executive branch; past placements have included the health and welfare agency, department of social services, and governor's office.
Requirements: Completion of four-year degree
Where: Sacramento, CA
When: September–August
Stipend: $1,882 plus 12 credits to California State University's Graduate Program in Public Policy and Administration
Deadline: February

FELLOWSHIP IN PUBLIC POLICY
Congressional Hispanic Caucus Institute
504 C Street, NE
Washington, DC 20002
202-543-1771
Fax: 202-546-2143
http://www.chci.org

This is a fellowship program for people of Hispanic origin to study and participate in public policy at the national level. Fellows have the opportunity to work in the area of their choice such as international affairs, economic development, education policy, housing, or local government.
Requirements: College graduation within one year of application and active participation in public service; applicants must be of Hispanic origin
Where: Washington, DC
When: August–May
Stipend: Monthly stipend of approximately $2,000 with round-trip airfare provided to Washington, DC; participants also receive health insurance
Deadline: February

GOVERNOR'S POLICY FELLOWS PROGRAM
Maryland Higher Education Commission
16 Francis Street
Annapolis, MD 21401
410-974-2971

This fellowship program offers an opportunity to work with policy-making officials in the executive branch of Maryland state government. The program is tailored to fellows' needs and professional aspirations.

Requirements: Recent graduation from a master's or doctoral program in policy or administration
Where: Location varies
When: Two-year commitment
Stipend: Salaried position of $32,500; does not include health insurance or other benefits
Deadline: February

JAMES H. DUNN, JR., MEMORIAL FELLOWSHIP PROGRAM
107 William G. Stratton Building
Springfield, IL 62706
217-782-5213
Fax: 217-524-1677
http://www100.state.il.us/gov/govsteam/internships.cfm

This is a one-year fellowship designed to give participants firsthand experience in the operations of state government, including the budget, legislative, and scheduling offices. The goal of the program is to give practical experience in state government for fellows with aspirations toward policy-making positions.

Requirements: Bachelor degree and demonstrated commitment to excellence in community or public service areas
Where: Majority of positions in Springfield, IL, with some openings in Chicago and Washington, DC
When: August–July
Stipend: $27,900 plus benefits
Deadline: January 31

JESSE MARVIN UNRUH ASSEMBLY FELLOWSHIP PROGRAM
California State University
Center for California Studies
6000 J Street
Sacramento, CA 95819
916-278-6906
Fax: 916-278-5199
http://www.csus.edu/calst/Programs/jesse_unruh.html

This fellowship allows participants the opportunity to directly participate in the legislative process as a full-time professional legislative staff member. Fellows perform a variety of tasks ranging from drafting legislation to speech writing to policy research in the capitol offices of assembly members.

Requirements: Bachelor degree (no preferred major); people with advanced degrees and those in midcareer are encouraged to apply
Where: Sacramento, CA
When: October–August
Stipend: $1,882 per month plus benefits
Deadline: February

THE JOSEPH P. KENNEDY, JR., FOUNDATION PUBLIC POLICY FELLOWSHIP

1325 G Street NW
Suite 500
Washington, DC 20005
202-393-1250
Fax: 202-393-1250
http://www.jpkf.org

This fellowship is designed to give professionals in the field of mental retardation exposure to public policy. Fellows work with a congressional committee or federal department.

Requirements: Experience in state-level advocacy, social services, or community development; evidence of dedication to the disability field
Where: Washington, DC
When: 1 year, begins January
Stipend: Annual stipend plus relocation expenses
Deadline: August

THE MILLENDER FELLOWSHIP

Associate Vice President for Academic Programs
Wayne State University
4116 Faculty Administration Building
656 W. Kirby
Detroit, MI 48202
313-577-2424
http://www.millenderfund.org/fellowship.html

This fellowship is designed to assist minorities in achieving public service careers. Fellows are assigned to high-level responsibilities with executives of public, private, and not-for-profit organizations in the Detroit area.

Requirements: Master's degree or equivalent experience in the public sector
Where: Detroit
When: August–May
Stipend: $30,000 plus benefits
Deadline: March

NEW VOICES FELLOWSHIP
1825 Connecticut Avenue, NW
Washington, DC 20009
202-884-8051
E-mail: newvoice@aed.org
http://www.newvoices.aed.org/home.html

This program is geared toward individuals entering the field of human rights and international cooperation. Eligible program areas include international human rights, women's rights, racial justice, migrant and refugee rights, peace and security, foreign policy, and international economic policy. Individuals may approach an organization of interest to apply for funding. Applications are completed jointly by the organization and prospective fellow.

Requirements: See Web site for detailed description of eligible organizations
Where: Varies
When: Two-year placement
Stipend: Annual salary plus up to $6,000 of loan repayment per year, or $4,000 for other approved expenses; also receive up to $1,500 for professional development
Deadline: January

POLICY FELLOWSHIP
Society for Research in Child Development
750 First Street, NE
Washington, DC 20002-4242
202-336-5926
Fax: 202-336-5953
E-mail: SRCD@apa.org
http://www.srcd.org/policyfellowships.html

Two fellowships are offered, the Congressional and the Executive Branch Fellowship. Fellows further develop their research skills to influence public policy. Placements are in federal agencies or congressional offices.

Requirements: Doctoral degree; demonstrated expertise in child development research; membership in society
Where: Washington, DC
When: September–August
Stipend: Annual stipend depending on experience plus moving expenses
Deadline: December

THE POLIKOFF–GAUTREAUX FELLOWSHIP
Business and Professional People for the Public Interest
25 East Washington Street
Suite 1515
Chicago, IL 60602
312-641-5570
Fax: 312-641-5454
E-mail: info@bpichicago.org
http://www.bpichicago.org

Fellows will develop skills for a career in public interest advocacy. Activities may include research, drafting motions, and organizing public housing residents.
Requirements: Graduate degree in public policy or related field
Where: Chicago
When: One year
Stipend: $37,500 plus full benefits
Deadline: October 31

PRESIDENTIAL MANAGEMENT INTERN PROGRAM
U.S. Office of Personnel Management
Philadelphia Service Center
William J Green, Jr., Federal Building
600 Arch Street
Philadelphia, PA 19106
215-861-3027
Fax: 215-861-3030
http://www.pmi.opm.gov

This is a management-training program aimed at attracting high caliber graduates to the federal government. The program focuses on analysis and management of public policy.
Requirements: Master's or doctoral degree; must be nominated by academic institution
Where: Washington, DC
When: Two years, usually beginning between June and September
Stipend: Regular GS-9 level employee
Deadline: Academic departments select nominees in the early fall; finalists are announced in the spring.

RALPH I. GOLDMAN FELLOWSHIP IN INTERNATIONAL JEWISH
COMMUNAL SERVICE
American Jewish Joint Distribution Committee
711 Third Avenue
New York, NY 10017
212-687-6200
E-mail: service@jdcny.org

This is a fellowship program that focuses on international Jewish communal affairs and international
social welfare. The program provides one year of overseas work and study. Fellowships are tailored to
the needs identified by AJJDC as well as the individual talents of the fellow.
Requirements: Master's degree; program is geared toward individuals in the early stages of their career
Where: Varies
When: September–August
Stipend: Yearly stipend plus benefits
Deadline: November

SOCIAL WORK CONGRESSIONAL FELLOWS PROGRAM
Council on Social Work Education
1725 Duke Street
Suite 500
Alexandria, VA 22314-3457
703-683-8080
Fax: 703-683-8099
http://www.cswe.org/programs/Swcfp/SWCFP.htm

Fellows serve as legislative assistants on the staff of members of Congress or a congressional
committee. The program is intended to increase effectiveness of social work knowledge and values
in government.
Requirements: Must be member of CSWE, NASW, National Association of Deans and Directors of
Schools of Social Work, or BPD; accredited degree in social work; two years of post-social-work-
degree experience
Where: Washington, DC
When: 11 months, beginning in January
Stipend: $31,000
Deadline: January

SUPREME COURT FELLOWS PROGRAM

Supreme Court of the United States
Washington, DC 20543
202-479-3415
http://www.fellows.supremecourtus.gov

Fellows will serve at the Supreme Court, the Federal Judicial Center, the Administrative Office of the United States Courts, or the U.S. Sentencing Commission.
Requirements: Postgraduate degree, two or more years of professional experience, familiarity with the judicial system
Where: Washington, DC
When: One year, beginning in August or September
Stipend: GS-15/3 level ($98,198)
Deadline: November

TOM JOE PUBLIC POLICY FELLOWS PROGRAM

Center for the Study of Social Policy
1575 Eye Street, NW
Suite 500
Washington, DC 20005
202-371-1565
Fax: 202-371-1472
http://www.cssp.org

This fellowship is geared toward individuals with an interest in public policy related to children and families, income support, education reform, and family support. Fellows will assist staff in the areas of child welfare reform, local decision making, policy analysis, and advocacy and technical assistance to communities. Participants will also develop a specific project to be completed throughout the fellowship year.
Requirements: Interest in public policy career; priority given to individuals with a master's degree in social work, management, policy analysis, or community development; or individuals with relevant direct services experience
Where: Washington, DC
When: One year, beginning in January
Stipend: Salary commensurate with experience and health insurance; some fellows may qualify for relocation costs
Deadline: November 30

UNITED WAY COMMUNITY FELLOWS PROGRAM
United Way
701 North Fairfax Street
Alexandria, VA 22314
703-836-7100
Fax: 703-683-7851
E-mail: execsearch@uwa.unitedway.org
http://www.national.unitedway.org/jobs/fellows.cfm

This program is designed to provide experience in various departments of the United Way. Following completion of the program, fellows may apply for open positions in the organization.
Requirements: Recent graduate
Where: Students are placed in United Way location in major metropolitan area; placement varies
When: February–January
Stipend: Salary and benefits plus partial relocation costs
Deadline: November

URBAN FELLOWS PROGRAM
NYC Department of Citywide Administrative Services
1 Centre Street
Room 2425
New York, NY 10007
212-669-3695
http:///www.nyc.gov/html/dcas/html/urbanfellows.html

This is a nine-month fellowship for students interested in government work. Students will work in the mayor's office and city agencies.
Requirements: Recent college graduate or graduate student
Where: New York City
When: September–May
Stipend: $25,000 plus health insurance
Deadline: January

THE WELLSTONE FELLOWSHIP
Families USA
1334 G Street, NW
Washington, DC 20005
202-628-3030
Fax: 202-347-2417
http://www.familiesusa.org

This fellowship focuses on health care issues for communities of color at the national and state levels.
Requirements: College degree
Where: Washington, DC
When: September–August
Stipend: mid-$30,000s plus health care benefits
Deadline: February

WHITE HOUSE FELLOWS PROGRAM
1900 East Street, NW
Room B431
Washington, DC 20415
202-606-1818
http://www.whitehouse.gov/fellows
This is a very competitive program that offers firsthand look at the process of governing the nation. Fellows work in the Executive Office of the President or a related office. Opportunities include working with the vice president, traveling to meet foreign dignitaries, and taking part in other official meetings.
Requirements: Must be U.S. citizen and cannot be federal employee
Where: Washington, DC
When: September–August
Stipend: Regular GS-14 level employee ($83,482)
Deadline: February

POSTGRADUATE DEGREE OPPORTUNITIES: CLINICAL
ADVANCED CLINICAL SOCIAL WORK FELLOWSHIP
Cedars-Sinai Medical Center Fellowship
Thalians Mental Health Center
8730 Alden Drive
E-33
Los Angeles, CA 90048-3811
310-855-3567

This program offers 1,600 hours of supervised clinical experience plus seminars and conferences. Wide range of clients and social problems are addressed with dynamic therapeutic approaches to individual and family evaluation and treatment.
Requirements: MSW degree
Where: Los Angeles
When: One year, starts in September
Stipend: Contact agency
Deadline: Check with program

POST-CLINICAL SOCIAL WORK FELLOWSHIP PROGRAM
Yale School of Child Development
230 S. Frontage Road
P.O. Box 207900
New Haven, CT 06520
203-785-5930

This fellowship offers advanced clinical training in evaluating and treating emotionally disturbed children, adolescents, and families. Each fellow is required to carry 18 to 20 cases of children and parents in the outpatient clinic. After a year of such intensive learning and supervision, the fellow is qualified to provide quality clinical services to children and families.
Requirements: MSW degree
Where: New Haven, CN
When: July 1–June 30
Stipend: $13,000 full or $7,000 partial

POST-DOCTORAL FELLOWSHIP IN ADOLESCENT HEALTH CARE
Baylor College of Medicine
Teen Health Clinics
One Baylor Plaza
Houston, TX 77030
713-873-3603

This fellowship is designed to help students refine their research skills in adolescent health—with a focus on the health care needs of young fathers and the mental health needs of pregnant and parenting teens.
Requirements: PhD in social work
Where: Houston, TX
When: January–December
Stipend: $35,000

POST-GRADUATE CLINICAL SOCIAL WORK FELLOWSHIP
Children's Psychiatric Hospital
1001 Yale Blvd., NE
Albuquerque, NM 87131-5631
505-272-2944
http://www.hsc.unm.edu/som/psychiatry/clinical/socialwork.html

This fellowship is designed to enhance clinical skills through work with children, adolescents, and families.
Requirements: MSW degree; graduate emphasis in clinical social work with course work in child development and family therapy preferred; applicants with two years' postgraduate professional experience with children and families given primary consideration; apply online

Where: Albuquerque, NM
When: July–June
Stipend: $17,500
Deadline: February

POST-GRADUATE SOCIAL WORK FELLOWSHIPS
University of Michigan Health System Fellowships
http://www.med.umich.edu/psych/socialw/postgrad2003.htm

DEPARTMENT OF PSYCHIATRY: ADULT AMBULATORY DIVISION
University of Michigan Medical Center
Riverview Building
900 Wall Street
Ann Arbor, MI 48109
734-764-0267
Fellows will complete psychiatric evaluations and provide psychosocial treatment. They will also participate in training seminars, research, and other educational experiences.
Requirements: Completion of MSW degree; preference to individuals interested and experienced in evaluation and treatment of depressive disorders

DEPARTMENT OF PSYCHIATRY: CHILD AND ADOLESCENT DIVISION
University of Michigan Medical Center
1500 E. Medical Center Drive
Ann Arbor, MI 48109
734-764-0267

Fellows will complete psychiatric evaluations and provide psychosocial treatment. They will also participate in training seminars, research, and other educational experiences.
Requirements: Completion of MSW degree; preference to individuals interested and experienced in evaluation and treatment of pediatric obsessive–compulsive disorders and other anxiety disorders

DEPARTMENT OF SOCIAL WORK: SEXUAL HEALTH COUNSELING SERVICE
734-764-3140

This fellowship is for individuals interested in sexual health and sex therapy, and who plan to work toward Association of Sex Educators, Counselors, and Therapists certification.
Requirements: Recent completion of MSW degree
Where: Ann Arbor, MI
When: 1 year, beginning in January
Stipend: $21,000, medical benefit, and three weeks vacation

POST-GRADUATE SOCIAL WORK FELLOWSHIP
The Danielsen Institute
185 Bay State Road
Boston, MA 02215
617-353-3047
http://www.bu.edu/danielsen/index.html

This fellowship is for new MSW graduates with interest in integrating spiritual and religious issues with advanced training in psychotherapy–clinical social work practice. Training includes a community component. The primary theoretical orientation is psychodynamic. Hours and supervision will count toward licensure; one must pass the LCSW exam in the State of Massachusetts prior to starting. A degree in theology or experience is required.
When: September 1–August 31
Stipend: $30,000 plus benefits
Deadline: February

POST-MASTER'S SOCIAL WORK INTERNSHIP & SOCIAL SERVICES
POST-MSW INTERNSHIP
University Health Services
University of California, Berkeley
Tang Center
2222 Bancroft Way
Berkeley, CA 94720-4300
Contact for Social Work Internship: 510-643-2904
Fax: 510- 642-2368
Contact for Social Services Internship: 510-642-6074
Fax: 510-642-0211

These internships offer comprehensive training in mental health services to a diverse student body. The intern participates in crisis intervention, assessment and referral, brief psychotherapy, group counseling, outreach, and consultation.
Requirements: MSW degree from accredited institution; coursework in personality development, psychopathology, and theories and techniques of psychotherapy; two years of supervised clinical experience
When: August–August
Stipend: $18,000
Deadline: March

TRAINING PROGRAM FOR CLINICAL SOCIAL WORKERS
Reiss–Davis Child Study Center
3200 Motor Avenue
Los Angeles, CA 90034
213-204-1666
http://www.vistadelmar.org/main.html

Fellowship program combines psychodynamic and developmental theory with opportunities to work with children and parents performing long- and short-term therapy. Apply to the director of training.

Requirements: MSW degree
Where: Los Angeles
When: Two-year commitment
Stipend: Check with program
Deadline: Check with program

STUDENT OPPORTUNITIES
AMERICAN ENTERPRISE INSTITUTE FOR PUBLIC POLICY RESEARCH INTERNSHIPS
1150 17th Street, NW
No. 1100
Washington, DC 20036
202-862-5800
Fax: 202-862-7178
http://www.aei.org

AEI provides approximately 40 internship opportunities year-round in the areas of economic policy, foreign and defense studies, social and political studies, public relations, the *American Enterprise Magazine*, communications, seminars, and conferences, publications, publications marketing, information systems, marketing, and accounting. Students are paired with a leading scholar in their area of interest to serve as a mentor.

Requirements: Applicants should view Web site for specific openings
Where: Washington, DC
When: Positions are available year-round; hours are flexible
Stipend: None, positions are on a volunteer basis
Deadline: Summer: April 1; fall: September 15; winter: December 1

CENTER ON BUDGET AND POLICY PRIORITIES INTERNSHIP PROGRAM
820 First Street NE
Suite 510
Washington, DC 20002
202-408-1095 ext. 386
Fax: 202-408-1056
http://www.cbpp.org/internship.html

Various internship opportunities are available at the Center on Budget and Policy Priorities. They are designed to give students exposure to public policy issues affecting low-income families and individuals. Internship areas include: media, federal legislation, health policy, housing policy, income security policy, international budget project, food stamps, national budget and tax policy, outreach campaigns, state budget and tax policy, and state low-income initiatives.

Requirements: Open to undergraduate and graduate students as well as recent graduates
Where: Washington, DC
When: Internships are offered in fall, spring, and summer semesters.
Stipend: $10 per hour for interns with a master's degree, $9 per hour for graduate students, $8 perhour for interns with a bachelor degree, and $7.50 per hour for undergraduate students
Deadline: Varies by semester, see Web site

CENTER FOR LAW & SOCIAL POLICY SUMMER INTERNSHIP

Center for Law and Social Policy
1015 15th Street, NW
Suite 400
Washington, DC 20005
202-906-8038
Fax: 202-842-2885
e-mail: ahouse@clasp.org
http://www.clasp.org

Summer interns assist and research projects in child support enforcement, welfare reform, workforce development, job creation, child welfare, couples and marriage policy, and teen parents and reproductive health issues in welfare reform. CLASP is a national public policy organization that conducts policy research, analysis, and advocacy efforts.
Requirements: Enrollment in a graduate program
Where: Washington, DC
When: Summer
Stipend: $2,600 per month
Deadline: January

CENTURY INSTITUTE SUMMER INTERNSHIP

http://www.centuryinstitute.org

This is a two-week summer program designed to expose students to the progressive tradition of public policy. Students will participate in such activities as debates, case studies, and writing speeches and policy memos.
Requirements: Undergraduate students with sophomore or junior standing
Where: Williams College, Williamstown, MA
When: Summer
Stipend: $650
Deadline: April

CIVIL RIGHTS SUMMER

1629 K Street, NW
Suite 1010
Washington, DC 20006
202-466-6058
Fax: 202-466-3435
http://www.civilrights.org/programs/san

This internship is for students interested in social justice. Students will learn about such topics as advocacy, grassroots organizing, leadership, and the legislative process.

Requirements: Sophomore or junior status at an accredited institution

Where: The first week of training is held at Harvard University; remainder of program in Washington, DC

When: June–August

Stipend: $120 per week and a $1500 scholarship at the end of the program; travel costs and housing included

Deadline: February

CONGRESSIONAL FELLOWSHIPS ON WOMEN AND PUBLIC POLICY

1750 New York Avenue, NW
Suite 350
Washington, DC 20006
202-628-0444
Fax: 202-628-0458
http://www.wrei.org

The fellowship, offered by the Women's Research and Education Institute, is aimed at giving practical policy-making experience and college credit. The program is designed to encourage more effective participation by women in policy making and to increase understanding of how policies affect women and men differently.

Requirements: Current enrollment or completion of graduate program within the past two years; proven commitment to equality for women.

Where: Washington, DC

When: January–August

Stipend: Monthly stipend of $1,300 plus $1,500 to be applied to tuition costs

Deadline: June

DIVERSITY IN CONGRESS PROGRAM
The Washington Center
2301 M Street, NW
5th Floor
Washington, DC 20037
http://www.twc.edu

This internship is designed for minority students interested in public service and a career in government. Students will work in a congressional office.
Requirements: Must be enrolled at an accredited college or university with at least sophomore standing and minimum 2.5 GPA
Where: Washington, DC
When: One semester with year-round start dates; see Web site for detailed schedule
Stipend: Students receive a minimum $2,000 to be applied toward housing costs; additional financial assistance may also be available.
Deadline: None

EMBASSY AND DIPLOMATIC SCHOLARS
1776 Massachusetts Avenue, NW
Suite 201
Washington, DC 20036
202-833-8580
Fax: 202-833-8581
E-mail: info@ielnet.org
http://www.ielnet.org

This internship is designed for students with interests in international affairs. Interns have placements with embassies, the U.S. Department of State, and international not-for-profit agencies. Students also participate in coursework geared toward developing skills of diplomacy and international relations.
Requirements: Minimum of sophomore standing; recent college graduates and graduates students are encouraged to apply
Where: Washington, DC
When: Year-round with one semester placements
Stipend: None, students may explore financial aid through their academic institution; some scholarships are also available based on need
Deadline: Varies by semester

THE EVERETT PUBLIC SERVICE INTERNSHIP PROGRAM
http://www.everettinternships.org

These summer internships for undergraduate and graduate students are offered by 58 organizations, including the Advocacy Institute, Asian Americans for Equality, Center on Budget and Policy Priorities, and Child Welfare League of America. For a listing of all participating organizations, visit the Web site.

Requirements: Completion of at least two semesters of college; graduate or undergraduate student
Where: Organizations in New York and Washington, DC
When: 10 weeks over the summer; specific start dates are negotiated between student and organization
Stipend: $225 per week
Deadline: Varies by organization, usually March or April

FRANK HORTON FELLOWSHIP PROGRAM & DANIEL K. INOUYE
FELLOWSHIP PROGRAM
The Interface Group, Ltd.
2445 M Street, NW
Suite 250
Washington, DC 20037
202-296-9200
Fax: 202-296-9236
http://www.apaics.org

This fellowship is for individuals interested in public policy and work with Asian American and Pacific Islander communities. Fellows will be placed in the office of a congressional member, a congressional committee, or a federal agency.
Requirements: Bachelor or master's degree from accredited institution; minimum 3.3-4.0 GPA
Where: Washington, DC
When: June–March
Stipend: $15,000
Deadline: February

GALBRAITH SCHOLARS
Harvard University
John F. Kennedy School of Government
79 John F. Kennedy Street
Cambridge, MA 02138
617-496-0109
Fax: 617-496-9053
E-mail: inequality@harvard.edu
http://www.ksg.harvard.edu/inequality

This summer program is geared toward undergraduates with an interest in social policy and inequality. The main goal of the program is to encourage minority and impoverished students to pursue doctoral study in this area.
Requirements: Junior or senior status at an accredited institution
Where: Harvard University
When: One week in June
Stipend: All expenses will be covered for travel, hotel, and activity expenses
Deadline: April

INTERNSHIPS IN CONGRESS
The Washington Center
2301 M Street, NW
5th Floor
Washington, DC 20037
http://www.twc.edu

This internship is intended to help interns acquire Capitol Hill experience, develop contacts, and expand knowledge on public issues and the legislative process. Interns will attend hearings, write press releases, maintain constituency relations, research issues, and draft legislative histories.
Requirements: Must be enrolled at an accredited college or university with at least sophomore standing and minimum 2.5 GPA
Where: Washington, DC
When: One semester with year-round start dates; see Web site for detailed schedule
Stipend: None; some financial assistance is available
Deadline: None; some agencies require background checks, so additional processing time should be allowed; see Web site for listings

MEDICAL SOCIAL SERVICES GRADUATE RESIDENCY PROGRAM
Mayo School of Health Sciences
200 First Street, SW
Rochester, MN 55905
800-626-9041
Fax: 507-284-0656
http://www.mayo.edu

This is a three-month residency program geared toward medical social workers. Students participate in practicum at the Mayo clinic and affiliated hospitals. Students will conduct psychosocial assessments, discharge planning, facilitate support groups, link patients with community resources, and participate in multidisciplinary team conferences.
Requirements: Enrollment in an MSW program with prior field work; recommend all coursework be completed prior to the residency
Where: Rochester, MN
When: Offered throughout the year; students participate for three months
Stipend: Yes
Deadline: Summer session: January 15; fall session: May 15; spring session: October 15

MIDWEST ACADEMY SUMMER INTERNSHIP PROGRAM
Midwest Academy
28 E. Jackson Street, No. 605
Chicago, IL 60604
312-427-2304
Fax: 312-427-2307
E-mail: mwacademy1@aol.com
http://www.midwestacademy.com

This is a training institute for community organizers offering a summer internship program for students in intensive training and assignments in community organizing campaigns.

Requirements: Enrollment in an accredited institution; preference is given to juniors and seniors
Where: The first week of training is held in Chicago; students are then placed in Chicago and other locations throughout the country
When: June–August
Stipend: $2,500
Deadline: February

MINORITY FELLOWSHIP PROGRAM
Council on Social Work Education
1725 Duke Street
Suite 500
Alexandria, VA 22314
703-683-8080
Fax: 703-683-8099
http://www.cswe.org

There are two fellowships available for students interested in doctoral programs: the Mental Health and Substance Abuse Clinical Fellowship Program and the Underrepresented Mental Health Minority Research Fellowship Program. The fellowships aim to increase the enrollment of ethnic minorities in doctoral programs.

Requirements: Completion of MSW, concurrent enrollment in full-time doctoral program
Where: Doctoral programs with faculty involved in funded mental health research
When: Awards are renewable, up to three years
Stipend: $1,513 per month
Deadline: February

MINORITY LEADERS FELLOWSHIP PROGRAM
The Washington Center
2301 M Street, NW
5th Floor
Washington, DC 20037
http://www.twc.edu

This internship is intended to help students acquire Capitol Hill experience, develop contacts, and expand knowledge on public issues and the legislative process.

Requirements: Enrollment in an accredited college or university; a competitive program in which most recipients have a minimum GPA of 3.2; U.S. citizenship required; must be a person of Asian American, African American, Pacific Islander, or Native American descent
Where: Washington, DC
When: One semester with year-round start dates
Stipend: Availability varies
Deadline: None

NATIONAL ASSOCIATION OF SOCIAL WORKERS FELLOWSHIPS & SCHOLARSHIPS
NASW Foundation
750 First Street, NE
Suite 700
Washington, DC 20002
http://www.naswfoundation.org

Four different opportunities are offered by the NASW Foundation. The Jane B. Aron Doctoral Fellowship is awarded to individuals working on their dissertation in the field of health care policy and practice. The Eileen Blackey Doctoral Fellowship is for individuals working on a dissertation in welfare policy and practice. Two opportunities are also available for MSW candidates: the Consuelo W. Gosnell Memorial MSW Scholarship is for candidates committed to working with American Indian or Alaskan natives and Latino or Hispanic populations; the Verne LaMarr Lyons Memorial MSW Scholarship is awarded to individuals with experience in health and mental health practice with African Americans.
Requirements: NASW membership, relevant experience, and demonstrated commitment to the field of study of each fellowship or scholarship
Deadline: December

NATIONAL PARTNERSHIP FOR WOMEN AND FAMILIES INTERNSHIP PROGRAM
1875 Connecticut Avenue, NW
Suite 650
Washington, DC 20009
http://www.nationalpartnership.org

Various internships are offered through the National Partnership. Specific internship areas include: Action Council and Membership Intern, Annual Luncheon Intern, Information Systems Intern, Work and Family Intern, Workplace Fairness Intern, and Communications Program.
Requirements: Undergraduate student
Where: Washington, DC
When: Year-round one-semester internships available
Stipend: None, but students may be eligible for school credit
Deadline: Spring: November 15; summer: March 1; fall: July 15

NEW YORK STATE SENATE FELLOWSHIPS
Senate Student Programs
State Capitol
Room 500A
Albany, NY 12247
518-455-2611

Fellows are placed in senators' offices in order to gain first-hand knowledge and experience in the area of their fellowship. The three fellowship areas are legislature, journalism, and public service.

Requirements: Current enrollment in a master's or doctoral program; applicant must be a New York State resident or be enrolled in a college or university of New York State

Where: Albany, NY

When: September–July

Stipend: $22,575 plus health insurance

NONPROFIT LEADERS INTERNSHIP PROGRAM
The Washington Center
2301 M Street, NW
5th Floor
Washington, DC 20037
http://www.twc.edu

This internship is designed to develop leadership in the not-for-profit sector. Students will organize community development initiatives, research and write reports, develop fundraising efforts, plan events, and engage in advocacy efforts.

Requirements: Must be enrolled at an accredited college or university with at least sophomore standing and a minimum GPA of 2.5

Where: Washington, DC

When: One semester with year-round start dates; see Web site for detailed schedule

Stipend: Students receive a minimum $1,000 stipend to be applied toward housing costs; additional financial assistance may also be available.

Deadline: None

SOMERS AGING AND LONG-TERM CARE RESEARCH INTERNSHIP
National Academy of Social Insurance
1776 Massachusetts Avenue, NW
Suite 615
Washington, DC 20036
202-452-8097
http://www.nasi.org

This internship focuses on aging and long-term care research. Interns have worked on research projects at the National Academy on an Aging Society, the Health Insurance Association of America, the Agency for Health Care Policy and Research, Congressional Research Service, and the Institute for the Future of Aging Services.

Requirements: Enrollment in graduate school or upper level undergraduates

Where: Washington, DC

When: June–September

Stipend: $2,000

Deadline: March

U.S. DEPARTMENT OF STATE INTERNSHIP PROGRAM
Recruitment Division
U.S. Department of State
2401 E Street, NW
5H
Washington, DC 20522
703-875-7490
http://www.careers.state.gov

This internship program attracts students from a variety of academic backgrounds, including social work. Interns will gain firsthand knowledge of foreign service and civil service career opportunities. Assignments vary based on academic background and area of interest.
Requirements: Junior, senior, or graduate level students; bilingual candidates are encouraged to apply
Where: Half the internships are in Washington, DC; the other half are overseas
When: Varies based on placement
Stipend: Most internships are unpaid
Deadline: Varies based on placement

WASHINGTON INTERNSHIP PROGRAM
National Academy of Social Insurance
1776 Massachusetts Avenue NW
Suite 615
Washington, DC 20036
202-452-8097
http://www.nasi.org

This internship focuses on furthering knowledge and understanding of policy issues centered on social security and health care financing. Internship includes working with leading experts in the field, seminars, discussion, and individual projects. Interns have worked in House and Senate committees, the Congressional Budget Office, the General Accounting Office, the Social Security Administration, the Urban Institute, AARP, the Brookings Institution, and other sites.
Requirements: Enrollment in graduate school or upper level undergraduates
Where: Washington, DC
When: June–September
Stipend: $2,000
Deadline: March

WOMEN IN PUBLIC POLICY INTERNSHIP
The Washington Center
2301 M Street, NW
5th Floor
Washington, DC 20037
http://www.twc.edu

This internship is designed for women interested in careers in public policy. Students will research policy, draft grant proposals, serve as advocates for battered women, and write marketing materials for women-owned businesses.

Requirements: Must be enrolled at an accredited college or university with at least sophomore standing and a minimum GPA of 2.5

Where: Washington, DC

When: One semester with year-round start dates; see Web site for detailed schedule

Stipend: Students receive a minimum $1,000 stipend to be applied toward housing costs; additional financial assistance may also be available

Deadline: None

LOAN FORGIVENESS AND REPAYMENT PROGRAMS
AMERICORPS/VISTA

1201 New York Avenue, NW
Washington, DC 20525
202-606-5000
http://www.americorps.org

Following a year of community service, volunteers are given a $4,725 award that may be used for loan repayment or tuition.

LOAN CANCELLATION FOR FEDERAL PERKINS LOAN

Individuals working for early intervention services or services for high-risk children from low-income communities may be eligible. Only those who took out loans in 1992 or after are eligible. Check your university financial aid office and employer's personnel office for details.

MARYLAND GOVERNMENT EMPLOYEES

Maryland State Scholarship Administration
16 Francis Street
Annapolis, MD 21401
410-974-2971 ext. 146

State and local government employees in the state of Maryland who earn less than $40,000 gross annually may be eligible for a loan assistance–repayment program to study law, nursing, physical and occupational therapy, social work, or education.

NATIONAL HEALTH SERVICE CORPS LOAN REPAYMENT PROGRAM
1-800-221-9393
http://www.nhsc.bhpr.hrsa.gov

Licensed clinical social workers provide services for two years in areas with a shortage of health professionals in exchange for loan repayment. The assignment can be extended beyond two years. Limited positions are available nationwide.

Requirements: State licensure or certification in the state where you plan to serve; U.S. citizenship
Benefits: A competitive salary and benefits package is offered, in addition to loan repayment.

PEACE CORPS
1111 20th Street, NW
Washington, DC 20526
800-424-8580
http://www.peacecorps.org

Requirements: Students must have received a loan disbursement on or after July 1, 1987.
Benefits: For the first and second years of service, 15 percent per year of volunteer's total Perkins loan obligation, including interest, will be cancelled; loan deferment may be available for some Stafford loans during service, but no cancellation is available.

TEACH FOR AMERICA
315 West 36th Street
New York, NY 10018
800-832-1230
Fax: 212-279-2081
http://www.teachforamerica.org

Corp members serve as teachers in underserved communities throughout the nation.
Benefits: Participants are eligible to receive $4,725 for each year of service ($9,459 over two years) that can be used to pay back student loans or toward future education costs; members are also eligible for loan forbearance

VETERANS ADMINISTRATION
http://www.va.gov
A loan repayment benefit is available to social workers hired in a limited number of locations where it is difficult to recruit employees.

Sample Skills By Function

Listed here are skills related to the following functions: community development and community organizing, consulting, direct practice, management, policy, research, supervision, and teaching. Also listed are skills common to several functions and some general performance skills. Skills specific to presentations, writing, and information management are listed separately.

No list is exclusive. Use these lists to generate ideas about your skills. If you use one of the phrases listed here, be sure you "own" that skill—think of at least one example that demonstrates that skill. Edit the items to fit your language and experience or the language of your field of practice. Each skill is described actively—that is, each phrase begins with a present tense verb. You will convert these to past tense verbs for descriptions of previous experience. You may wish to change verbs to noun phrases—"analyze data" can become "data analysis." Some of these phrases would not be used in written communication but would serve you well in a face-to-face interview.

Cross-Cutting Functions

When stating a skill that cuts across functions, try to give it more meaning by attaching it to a specific knowledge area (for example, "conduct needs assessments for low-income housing, transportation, and employment for three communities").

- advise clients, patients, and families on accessing services
- advocate for particular groups, consumers, clients, and patients
- analyze class differences regarding service access and policies
- articulate connections across disciplines
- assess and respond to ethical issues
- build consensus
- conduct assets and needs assessments
- demonstrate a high tolerance for frustration
- demonstrate realistic expectations of self and others
- demonstrate a sense of professional mission
- educate and collaborate with people from other disciplines
- evaluate practice
- facilitate groups: clients, consumers, families, staff, task forces, collaborations
- follow protocols
- function as part of a multidisciplinary team
- guide and monitor volunteers
- identify group dynamics
- identify and resolve ethical issues
- incorporate knowledge of theory with research and practice experience

- maintain confidentiality in oral and written communications
- manage crises
- mentor and monitor volunteers
- navigate a bureaucracy
- network with local, regional, and national organizations
- think from a generalist perspective—think clearly about problems
- tie immediate work, problems, and solutions to a long-term vision
- use comprehensive systems thinking

Community Development and Community Organizing
- acquire and develop abandoned and vacant space
- acquire financing for a community project
- build consensus with community coalitions, grassroots groups, collaborations, and so forth
- communicate with diverse neighborhood residents
- compile a community resource list
- connect residents with other resources in the community for starting businesses
- construct a community map
- coordinate and train volunteer groups for staff projects
- counsel home owners and small business owners about the loan acquisition process
- demonstrate effects on the social development of the community and economy
- demonstrate effects of social development on the community and economy
- design a campaign strategy for social change
- develop community, neighborhood, and social networks
- develop policies and plans that integrate social and economic development efforts
- educate community members on intent of outside groups
- educate corporate staff and other groups on how their messages are received in the community
- engage community members in leadership training; identify local leaders
- establish a plan of incremental goals that can sustain a long-term collaborative effort
- evaluate the assets of the community: individual, organizational, and physical
- evaluate physical assets of a community: land, buildings, transportation, and so forth
- evaluate target community's, population's strengths, interests, needs, and so forth
- examine formal and informal service delivery systems
- facilitate a community-building effort
- facilitate the shaping of a vision for the community
- foster a commitment among organizations and individuals to improving the community
- function as a liaison with the business community and local institutions
- gain acceptance in the community
- identify barriers to starting businesses and making improvements in the community
- identify tactics: media events, public hearings, elections, and so forth
- identify and work with potential sources of capital and credit, investors
- manage conflict among community groups
- manage varying interests of coalition and collaboration members
- provide technical assistance and training to neighborhoods and community groups
- staff a community organization, coalition, collaboration, or neighborhood association

- start community development banks, microloan funds, community development loan funds, or community development credit unions
- work effectively within a local political system
- work with groups: chamber of commerce, small business owners, neighborhood associations, religious institutions, recreation programs, and so forth

Consulting
- analyze client resources, strengths, problems, and needs
- deliver products and reports by deadline
- determine fees
- develop a network
- direct, troubleshoot implementation and evaluate solutions
- draft and negotiate contracts
- educate client staff on issues, terminology, and so forth
- establish rapport with clients
- facilitate discussions with clients on problem clarification, solution options
- identify and investigate potential clients
- identify and package specific services to offer
- identify potential and future consulting needs of clients
- prepare marketing plan
- research, develop, and recommend solutions
- train or collaborate with client staff to implement new solutions

Direct Practice
- analyze social support networks
- assess for substance abuse, nutrition status, support systems, physical functioning, financial situation, safety, and so forth
- assist clients, consumers, and families with developing coping skills
- assist clients in processing information and issues
- base interventions on evidence-based practice or best practices
- build effective client relationships
- collaborate with a treatment team
- complete detailed assessments of clients
- conduct intake interviews
- conduct psychosocial assessments and social histories
- construct genograms and family maps
- contract with clients or consumers
- deal with client resistance
- design treatment to achieve short-term outcomes in a cost-conscious context
- determine client eligibility
- develop and implement intervention plans, treatment plans, care plans, and discharge plans
- educate clients, consumers, and patients about health risks, preretirement planning, chemical dependency issues, medical compliance, compensation for sensory deficits, and so forth

- educate and train family members, care providers, and staff
- evaluate practice
- facilitate family team meetings and partner with community
- follow up treatment
- identify and intervene with clients who are at risk
- identify outcomes measures
- identify, evaluate, and compile list of or develop links with references to community resources
- intervene with angry, violent, or suicidal clients
- interview clients, consumers, patients, and families
- lead a treatment team
- manage permanency planning, family group conferencing, or victim–offender dialogues
- measure caregiver strain or stress
- monitor changing functional levels
- organize and run a support group or educational group
- provide case consultation
- provide case management
- provide culturally appropriate services
- recruit, select, train, and prepare foster or adoptive parents, guardians, respite care providers
- set and collect fees
- shape the context with diagnostic expertise
- understand an individual in context
- use different treatment approaches: brief therapy, family therapy, play therapy, solution focused therapy, etc.
- use DSM criteria

Management
- access and work with the media
- analyze an annual report
- analyze unit costs
- anticipate and deal with change
- assess risk, liability, and legal issues
- change an organization's culture
- collaborate with board members in strategic planning and directing the organization
- communicate with outside groups: funders, governments, consumer groups, media, and so forth
- conduct feasibility studies
- coordinate multicommittee events and projects
- create and facilitate interorganizational entities: partnerships, networks, collaborations, and so forth
- create a vision for the organization
- design and evaluate services that meet varying funders requirements
- design services, programs, and projects that produce measurable outcomes
- develop a board: select, train, direct
- develop a high profile in the community
- develop and monitor budgets

- develop a network of contacts
- develop and oversee a marketing plan
- develop policies and procedures
- develop quality assurance measures
- evaluate programs, projects, services, and agency structures
- formulate and direct a fundraising strategy: special events, capital campaigns, annual funds, volunteer programs, and grant writing
- formulate and follow a project work plan
- formulate and implement public relations strategies
- identify tangible results that measure outcomes for objectives
- implement a system for collecting and reporting outcome measures
- interpret federal, state, and local policies and regulations
- make the difficult decisions regarding agency priorities
- manage a complex composition of funding sources and reporting requirements
- manage change
- manage large volumes of information: organization statistics, outside data, and so on
- manage multiple departments and programs
- move a pilot project to a mainline service
- negotiate and secure contracts
- organize committees, groups, and special events
- prepare cost–benefit analyses, budgets
- provide data and testimony for law and policymakers
- reconcile conflicting values: among multidisciplinary teams, agency and funders, agency and regulators
- recruit, supervise, evaluate, promote, and terminate managers, supervisors, staff
- recruit, train, organize, and motivate volunteers
- represent the organization in public arenas
- secure financing
- set agendas, organize, and run meetings
- stay current on policy and service delivery trends
- understand financial impacts on services
- weigh alternatives: service delivery, staffing, funding, and so forth

Policy
- access and use governmental publications and data sets
- advocate for particular aspects of policies and regulations
- analyze community strengths, assets, resources, and needs
- analyze federal policy impacts at local and state levels and state policy impacts at local level
- analyze and interpret statutes, regulations, policies, and programs
- analyze policy in political and financial terms
- appreciate the complexity of the larger system
- approach policy with a win–win situation rather than all or nothing
- articulate connections across disciplines
- articulate opposite viewpoints

- articulate political feasibility and funding realities
- build consensus and coalitions; develop relationships
- convey a compelling picture of what might be done
- define agendas
- develop legislative strategy
- formulate policy recommendations
- get beyond passion and process to make the difficult decisions and complete tasks
- handle the frequent and extensive critiquing, editing, and rewriting of one's work
- identify common ground to advance the agenda
- lobby for or against legislation
- locate, explain, and apply relevant statistical data
- prepare action alerts and legislative fact sheets
- prepare and deliver testimony to legislative committees
- prepare proposals for technical amendments to a law
- present options and defend positions orally
- see connections across the big picture rather than focus on a single issue
- take a long-term view
- think agilely about public policy
- think from a generalist perspective; think well about a lot of problems
- tolerate very frustrating political situations
- understand current public policy issues
- understand the language of other players and opponents
- use data accurately; understand pitfalls of extrapolating data from local to national level
- work in political and bureaucratic environments
- write in a quick, concise, clear style

Research
- analyze data using quantitative and qualitative techniques
- analyze an issue
- assess and document intervention outcomes
- clarify, define problems and issues
- collect, clean, code, input, analyze, and manage data
- conceptualize areas of knowledge
- conduct structured and unstructured interviews
- conduct surveys
- coordinate research and evaluation projects
- create graphic presentations of data
- critique and assess data, articles, reports
- design, conduct needs assessments, feasibility studies, program evaluation, clinical practice evaluation
- design, improve, and critique questionnaires
- design research study
- develop data profiles
- develop measures

- develop research proposals, write grants
- frame questions
- generate hypotheses
- interpret quantitative and qualitative empirical results
- locate, review, and summarize literature
- run general statistical packages—SAS, SPSS—and specific packages for structural equation modeling, network analysis, cluster analysis, and qualitative analysis
- secure and analyze consumer feedback
- use descriptive, inferential, multivariate statistics
- work with institutional review boards to satisfy criteria for protection of human subjects

Supervision

- collect organization and services statistics
- consult with and inform management about progress, crises situations, personnel issues, staff, client, community assets, and needs
- critique oral assignments: case, project presentations, public speeches, in-service training
- differentiate tasks and supervision for professional, paraprofessional, student, and volunteer staff
- draft and make recommendations on content for job descriptions
- edit written assignments: documentation, reports, treatment plans, proposals, grants, assessments, articles
- evaluate staff work: interventions, treatment plans, documentation, projects, programs
- fine-tune services, procedures, and staff performance to meet outcome objectives
- handle staff development: identify training preferences and needs and provide training
- interpret organization objectives, policies, procedures, and outside trends and issues affecting the agency
- make decisions: crisis situations, ethical dilemmas, reduced or expanded resources, changing demands, etc.
- manage the conflicting needs of management, staff, and clients, consumers, and communities
- match staff abilities with work assignments
- motivate and direct staff performance
- organize, delegate, and schedule work
- orient new employees
- review resumes and interview job candidates and make recommendations on hiring
- serve as liaison between staff and management
- set performance expectations
- suggest changes in services, policies, and procedures

Teaching

- analyze student learning difficulties and recommend action
- command knowledge of the subject area
- compare courses for overlap and continuity
- create electronic assignments
- create syllabi

- define parameters of a course
- design assignments that develop critical thinking, practice, and creative skills
- design course lab components: videotaping, community projects, and so forth
- design distance learning courses
- evaluate learning, assign grades, assign credit
- evaluate teaching techniques and seek outside consultation on teaching style
- facilitate discussions and debates
- facilitate self-directed, independent learning
- identify appropriate theoretical and practice literature
- incorporate at-risk population and cultural diversity material in courses
- incorporate technology and presentation options in teaching
- manage disagreement and conflict
- manage a range of student abilities, knowledge, learning styles, and special needs
- orchestrate co-teaching units
- provide constructive criticism
- select course readings, books, and visiting speakers
- think conceptually about educational curriculum design
- write exams that measure levels of learning and evaluate knowledge and skill mastery

Presentation

- conduct informative, educational presentations: public forums, workshops, seminars, and so forth
- conduct in-service training
- debate issues effectively
- defend an opinion or argument
- deliver an extemporaneous speech or presentation
- facilitate town meetings, focus groups, neighborhood meetings
- interview effectively: listening, reframing, reflecting, attending
- lobby in person, by telephone, and by mail
- make case presentations
- persuade different audiences on the same topic
- persuade diverse groups: neighborhood associations, small and large businesses, local and state governments, school systems, health care providers, funders, social services agencies
- present in front of a camera: videotaping or live coverage
- present testimony to legislative bodies
- provide court testimony
- respond to impromptu questions: points of information, controversial issues
- serve as liaison between agencies, organizations, and the community
- serve as a point person handling questions about issues and projects
- serve as a spokesperson with media and other audiences
- speak to large and small audiences
- use effective interpersonal communication: active listening, open-ended questions
- use multimedia technology for presentations: computer, audio, and visual
- use negotiation techniques
- use parliamentary procedure accurately
- "work" a room

Writing

- create training or education materials
- edit written material quickly, provide constructive criticism
- prepare briefings on issues, meetings, legislation, and so forth, for an executive or leader
- prepare case plans with interdisciplinary teams
- prepare talking points on an issue for leaders or groups
- script an executive or leader to conduct a meeting or event (written and verbal step-by-step preparation)
- summarize a large volume of information
- write affidavits, documentation, case notes, executive summaries, reports, mission statements, sound bites, treatment plans, minutes, legislation, regulations, press releases, brochures, newsletters, letters, journal articles, op-ed pieces, business plans, project reports, memos, direct mail pieces, marketing plans, option papers, proposals
- write appropriate material for Internet, video, audio, CD-ROM, and multimedia projects
- write in particular styles: grants, academic, persuasive, promotional, journalistic (features and news), technical, legal, regulatory
- write quickly, concisely, and clearly
- write in styles appropriate to a leader, the purpose of a project, the culture of the organization, or the situation
- write technical material and reports using statistics and financial data

Information Management and Computer Technology

- address issues of confidentiality and information management
- consult with users to develop information systems
- develop and maintain an office intranet
- develop management information systems
- link systems across organizations
- manage a listserv discussion group or newsgroup on social or clinical issues
- produce computerized presentations
- provide services through remote access links
- serve as a webmaster: design and maintain pages, create interactive sites
- train staff and managers to input and retrieve data
- use computer packages: word-processing programs, databases, spreadsheets, desktop publishing, and statistical packages
- use computer software to record, access, analyze, and report information
- use computers and telecommunications in case management, treatment, and reimbursement
- use decision support tools

Work Characteristics or General Performance Skills

You will often hear people use work characteristics to describe their skills, for example, organized, detail oriented, assertive, on time, dependable, and thorough. Remember that your specific professional skills are much more vivid and powerful statements of your skills than general work characteristics. Let your professional skills and examples of your experience speak for your work habits. The same can be said for general performance skills. If you need to use a phrase like any of those listed below, tie it to an example: "I have taken initiative on several projects including the resident leadership training program and the intergenerational program which I established."

- act calm and professional in strained situations and relationships
- anticipate and think ahead
- assert ideas, positions, and needs
- identify, analyze, and solve problems
- pick up on cues, read the social context
- take initiative
- work effectively in a team environment
- work with individuals of varied cultural or ethnic and socioeconomic backgrounds
- work with unpredictable schedules

Additional Readings

Bobo, K., Kendall, J., & Max, S. (1991). *Organizing for social change: A manual for activists in the 1990s.* Washington, DC: Seven Locks Press.

Brophy, P., & Shabecoff, A. (2001). *A guide to careers in community development.* Washington, DC: Island Press.

Council on Social Work Education. (1996). *Strategic action plan: Social work and managed care.* Alexandria, VA: Author.

Doelling, C., & Paulsrud, D. (1994). *Preparing for careers in child welfare at the national level: A report on meeting with leaders in Washington, DC.* Unpublished project collaboration report, George Warren Brown School of Social Work, St. Louis.

King, R. M. (2000). *From making a profit to making a difference: How to launch your new career in nonprofits.* River Forest, IL: Planning/Communications.

Kretzman, J., & Mcknight, J. (1993). *Building communities from the inside out.* Chicago: ACTA Publications.

Midgely, J. (1995). *Social development: The developmental perspective in social welfare.* London: Sage Publications.

Perlmutter, F. (1990). *Changing hats: From social work practice to administration.* Washington, DC: NASW Press.

Selznik, P. (1957). *Leadership in administration.* Evanston, IL: Row.

Sxiridoff, M., & Ryan, W. (1996). *Prospects and strategies for community centered family services.* Milwaukee: Family Service America.

Selecting Master's and Doctoral Programs

Planning for Graduate Study at the Master's Level
Identify Your Career Goals
- Why do you want a master's degree?
- Must you have the master's degree to do the work you want to do?
- What other disciplines have you considered? Why do you want a master's degree in social work rather than a degree in policy, gerontology, management, law, or psychology?
- What specific knowledge and skills do you want to develop in a master's program?
- Are you ready for the self-discipline, self-direction, and time management that graduate school requires?

Identify Potential Programs
You will find links to master's degree programs on the Council on Social Work Education Web site at http://www.cswe.org. What is most important to you in selecting a program?
- academic and career advising—within the program, centralized at the institution
- characteristics of the student body
- cost and financial aid
- curriculum offerings—range of courses, concentrations, specializations, electives, skills training, generalist versus specialist training
- distance learning
- employment—success of alumni, career services
- faculty—specialties, publications, research interests, teaching emphasis
- interdisciplinary training through electives or joint degree programs
- learning resources—library, computers, multimedia resources
- location—urban, rural, near family and friends, region, safety, transportation, housing, costs
- physical facilities—skill labs, classrooms, student center, athletic facilities, parking
- practica offerings—settings available, block/concurrent, self-selected, out-of-town/country
- quality of the host institution
- reputation—in the community, among other schools of social work
- schedule—summer, evening, weekend programs
- special program aspects—training centers, research centers, community projects
- student–faculty ratio

Questions to Consider
Talk with faculty and doctoral students. Where else did they consider applying and why? How selective is the program? Get information about the following aspects of the program from its Web site and staff:
- Is the program accredited by the Council on Social Work Education? This will be important when you want to secure a state licensure.
- Ask for contact information for current students and recent alumni. Ask them what they like and dislike about the program. Do the alumni feel prepared for their work and future directions they might take?

- Inquire about the average GPA and test scores for applicants at each school.
- Find out whether you need additional course work or experience.
- How well have graduates done in the job market? Does the school collect employment data on new graduates? How long did it take new graduates to find jobs during the last two years? What types of positions, practice, settings, and salaries characterize the job search experience of last year's class?
- Can you see a profile of alumni? How many are in management, private practice, your interest area? What are the alumni of particular curriculum tracks doing five and 10 years later?
- What percentage of students receive scholarships? How are financial aid awards determined? What percentage of the students work while going to school?
- What is the expected cost? Will you need to borrow money to attend this school? How much will you need to borrow and what would be your monthly loan costs after you graduate?
- What choices do you have for practica? Ask to see a list.
- What tradeoffs will you have to make by selecting this program?
- Look at the bios/vitae of faculty who teach in your interest area.

Planning Your Academic Experience
- Think of yourself first as a professional who works in the community and second as a student who is expanding her or his knowledge and skills.
- Set goals for what you want to accomplish and learn in courses and in field work. Do not rely on faculty and field instructors to plan your education. Explore the field well enough that you can design a plan that complements the required curriculum.
- Look carefully at the skills lists in appendix 10; discuss them with social workers and others in your field. What skills and knowledge could you demonstrate by the time you leave the program, a field placement, or set of courses? What field work and course projects will you be able to show in the form of a portfolio?
- Determine what courses you may need for licensure or certifications.

Planning For Graduate Study at the Doctoral Level
This material is based on suggestions from chairs of doctoral programs, an associate dean of graduate school, and recent PhD graduates.
Identify Your Career Goals
- What do you want to do? Do you want to do research, teach, or practice?
- Do you have enough experience to define the problem you want to address in your work?
- What type of teaching, research, clinical practice do you want to do?
- What setting do you want to be in—a university, research organization, policy think tank, consulting firm, agency, or private practice? Do you need a doctorate to advance this work?
- Do you want to stay in the social work discipline? Do you want to explore other disciplines?
- For what career directions will the degree programs you are considering prepare you?
- Be realistic about your potential and your weaknesses.
- If you are considering a PhD as an additional credential for practice, explore this carefully. The payoff may not be there.
- Do you have the time in your life to devote to a doctoral program?
- Identify strong social work researchers in your interest area and investigate their schools.

Also keep in mind the following advice from faculty:

- If you want to teach practice courses, you will need two years paid post-MSW experience before you complete your doctoral degree. This is an accreditation requirement of the Council on Social Work Education for schools with faculty teaching practice courses. Some schools of social work hire only faculty candidates who have this experience.
- Get your license. It is a plus and alleviates questions about your practice experience. Of course you may benefit personally from having a license.
- You need to take debts from your previous education into consideration. How much debt would you incur if you chose to pursue a doctoral degree?

Interests in Research

- Do you consider the doctoral program to be an extension of the MSW program? Study at doctoral level is qualitatively—not just quantitatively—different from the MSW level. The types of thinking, tasks, expectations for learning, time required, dedication, and commitment are different.
- Are you interested in and do you have a facility for doing research? Do you have a fear of statistics? Are you comfortable with computers? Do you have an inquiring mind and an interest in theory? Can you translate theory into hypotheses? Do you find that type of thinking exciting?
- If spending a couple of hours browsing through a social work library is your idea of a good time, you will probably enjoy a doctoral program.

Selection of Programs

The Group for the Advancement of Doctoral Education includes links to doctoral degree programs at http://www.socwk.utah.edu/gade/index.html. Note that as you research doctoral programs, you are in a sense looking at potential employers if you plan to work at a university.

- Talk with chairs of programs regarding program fit.
- For what purpose is the program designed—research, teaching, clinical work?
- How is the program designed? How many courses are required? Are there electives? Can you take courses outside your department? Is interdisciplinary training encouraged?
- Is the conceptual training of the students as strong as the methodological training in research? Do students learn the conceptual foundation of statistical techniques and how to formulate questions?
- What opportunities do doctoral students have to conduct research? What specific course work and training is there including grant writing?
- Are there teaching opportunities? What specific course work and training is available including course design?
- Are there PhD faculty in the program who share your research or practice interests? Are they conducting research in your area? Is that research funded?
- What have faculty published and in what journals? If faculty are publishing research articles, it is likely that the research training is going to be strong.
- How often do doctoral students publish with faculty?
- Is there an opportunity for mentorship?
- Where are recent graduates working? Where do faculty expect them to find employment? You will be employed at the same level or below the rank of the program if you are looking at faculty positions. It is unlikely that the program from which you graduate would hire you.

- Talk with faculty and doctoral students. Where else did they consider applying and why?
- How selective is the program? Inquire about the average GPA and test scores for applicants at each school.
- Find out whether you need additional course work or experience.
- What is the average length of time for completion of the program? What percentage of the students does not finish?
- Are there part-time and full-time students?
- What is the expected cost?
- How strong is the host institution? What is the relationship of the program to the institution?
- Does the PhD program have its own resources and an identity separate from the MSW program?
- What is the formal or informal ranking of the program?
- How well regarded is the program?
- In what part of the development cycle is the program?
- What is the size of the program, the number of students? What are the sizes of the classes?
- How long has the program existed?

Environment for PhD Students
- Does the school value its PhD students? How much autonomy do students have?
- How safe is the campus at night?
- How supportive are the services and environment for PhD graduates? Consider funding for attending conferences, office space, computer access, special purchasing arrangements, housing for graduate students, affordability of the community, and financial-aid services.

Financial Aid
- Learn about funding sources including the government.
- At least in the past, you could, at a minimum, expect a tuition waiver and fellowship or assistantship. However, in the current funding climate, you might expect less scholarship funding.
- Decisions are made on grades, recommendations, and GREs.
- If you have only partial funding, you need to do very well to get a chance of better funding for the second year.
- Investigate funding from sources other than your specific department.
- External funding gives you a better shot at better universities, as it provides admissions leverage.
- Often the deadline for external funding is 1½ years before you want to start.
- You need to plan for financial aid for a dissertation separately.

Application Process
Generally you want to apply to schools in three categories:
- two schools that are a reach for admission
- two schools with a 50–50 chance of admission
- two schools with a high probability of admission.

Ask your former instructors and chairs of doctoral programs to help you realistically assess your chances for admission into particular programs. Find the best social work researchers in your particular field of interest, call them, talk with them about their work, and apply to their schools.

Application Preparation

- Do you have references who can speak to your ability to do doctoral work?
- Do all your transcripts speak to your ability to do doctoral work?
- Address the issue of any poor grades in your statement.
- Have at least one writing sample of 10–15 pages.

Graduate Record Exam and Master of Arts in Teaching

Keep this information in mind:

- The scores are good for five years.
- If you take the GRE during school, you will probably do better.
- It is best to take the GREs six months before you apply. If you are required to take an area exam in addition to the GRE, take it on a different day.
- Prepare for the math, verbal, and analytical sections. Preparation will make a difference.
- Check the school's policy regarding acceptance of a second set of scores if you are thinking of repeating a test.

Planning Your Career as a PhD Student

Once you are accepted to a program, you start the beginning process for tenure if your goal is an academic career. Develop strong relationships with faculty. Manage your time carefully: set goals to research, publish, present, and teach. Project a time line and try to adhere to it. Plan all term papers, projects and written coursework to apply to the subject of your dissertation.

Specialty Certifications from the National Association of Social Workers

In addition to the ACSW, QCSW, and DCSW credentials, the National Association of Social Workers offers specialty certifications in many areas of practice.

NASW credentials and specialty certifications are developed only by social workers. These credentials and specialty certifications do not a replace a required license.

There are currently seven specialty certifications available from NASW:

Certified Advanced Children, Youth, and Family Social Worker (C-ACYFSW), which requires two years of children, youth, and family social work practice

Certified Children, Youth, and Family Social Workers (C-CYFSW), which is exclusively for BSWs, requires two years of children, youth, and family social work practice

Certified Social Worker in Health Care (C-SWHC), which requires two years of health social work practice

Certified Clinical Alcohol, Tobacco, and Other Drugs Social Worker (C-CATODSW), which requires two years of full-time substance abuse specific practice

Certified School Social Work Specialist (C-SSWS), which requires two academic years of school-based social work practice

Certified Advanced Social Work Case Manager (C-ASWCM), which requires one year of social work case management practice

Certified Social Work Case Manager (C-SWCM), exclusively for BSWs, which requires one year of social work case management practice

Index

Individuals with Disabilities, 129

Tax benefits, 88

Teach for America, 220

Teaching and scholarship questions, 184–186

Teaching experience, 34–35

Teaching interests, 34

Teaching skills, 227–228

Technology and job trends, 98

Telephone call(s), 62, 66. *See also* Contacting people for advice
  keeping them brief, 21
  letter following, 140–141
  making cold calls, 8, 18

Telephone interviews, 78–79

Temporary work, 62

Tenure, applying for, 33

Thank-you letter
  to a contact, 140
  following interview, 83

Tom Joe Public Policy Fellows Program, 203

Training, professional, 29, 30, 35–36

Training Program for Clinical Social Workers, 208–209

Training programs, 118, 193–220

Transferring skills and knowledge, 9

Transitions. *See* Career transition(s)

Travelers Aid International, 191

U

United Jewish Communities, 192

United Neighborhood Centers of America, 192

United Way Community Fellows Program, 204

United Way of America, 192

University of Michigan Medical Center, Postgraduate Social Work Fellowships
  Department of Psychiatry: Adult Ambulatory Division, 207
  Department of Psychiatry: Child and Adolescent Division, 207
  Department of Social Work: Sexual Health Counseling Service, 207

University work, 34

Urban Fellows Program, 204

U.S. Department of State Internship Program, 218

USA Jobs, 192

V

Veterans Administration, 220

Victim services, 134, 143–144

Visa status, 36

Visibility, 100

Visits, keeping them brief, 21

Volunteer work, 62
  in résumés, 29, 30

W

Washington Internship Program, 218

Web sties, 61. *See also* Online directories
  scanning, 16

The Wellstone Fellowship, 204–205

What Color Is Your Parachute, 192

White House Fellows Program, 205

Women in Public Policy Internship, 218–219

Work characteristics, 229–230

Work preferences
  current, 5
  examining your, 4–5, 131–132

Work settings, 139–146

Writing exercises during interview process, 81

Writing skills, 109, 229

Y

YMCA, 192

Youth outreach services, 80

Youth services, 134, 141–145

About the Author

Carol Nesslein Doelling, MS, is director of career services at the George Warren Brown School of Social Work (GWB) at Washington University in St. Louis. She provides comprehensive career services for social work students and alumni, recruitment services for employers, and information on the social work job market to faculty.

Ms. Doelling developed the Job Market for MSW Graduates (with Barbara Matz, EdD), an annual report on the job-search experience of new MSWs nationwide. Later, she created Social Work and Social Services Jobs Online (with Violet Horvath, PhD, MSW), a career Web site especially for social workers. She has presented at annual meetings of Career Development and Social Work Education, the Council on Social Work Education (CSWE), and the National Association of Social Workers (NASW) and its chapter affiliates.

She cofounded and hosted the first Career Development and Social Work Education conference. In 2003, she chaired the 11th conference, which was an Invitational Meeting on Recruitment, Retention, and Succession. The meeting, held at Washington University, brought together social work career specialists, executives from large service providers and national networks of social services, and representatives from NASW and CSWE .

MORE RESOURCES FROM NASW PRESS

Social Work Career Development: *A Handbook for Job Hunting and Career Planning, 2nd Edition,* by Carol Nesslein Doelling. Updated to respond to changes in the job market and the profession since the best-selling first edition, this unique handbook addresses in detail the career management and job search needs of social workers across job functions, fields, or degree levels, including self-assessment exercises, strategies for researching the job market and networking, details on resumes, curriculum vitae, and portfolios; tips on selecting master's and doctoral programs, and much more.

ISBN: 0-87101-363-0. 2004. Item #3630. $49.99.

What Social Workers Do, 2nd Edition, by Margaret Gibelman. A much-awaited sequel to Gibelman's best-selling book, this second edition provides a panoramic look at social work and offers practical information about the current status of various service areas. It makes extensive use of case studies and demonstrates the connection between what appear to be diverse specializations by highlighting the intersection between practice functions, practice settings, and practice areas.

ISBN: 0-87101-364-9. 2004. Item #3649. $49.99.

Changing Hats while Managing Change: *From Social Work Practice to Administration, 2nd Edition,* by Felice Davidson Perlmutter and Wendy P. Crook. A unique and useful guide for practitioners who want to broaden their repertoire of professional choices and are either moving up the administrative ladder or considering making a career move in that direction. In user-friendly language, *Changing Hats* addresses the major challenges that face social workers in these complex times and presents a picture of the various roles and responsibilities of administration, illustrating them with lively case studies.

ISBN: 0-87101-361-4. 2004. Item #3614. $44.99.

A Dream and a Plan: *A Woman's Path to Leadership in Human Services,* by Lorrie Greenhouse Gardella and Karen S. Haynes. The helping professions are rich with women who have the imagination and aspiration to be successful leaders, but lack confidence or opportunity. Written from an inclusive, multicultural perspective, this empowering book offers practical guidance on pursuing career advancement, overcoming barriers, and cultivating mentorship. A pragmatic and motivating text for social workers, students, and human services providers, as well as for experienced managers.

ISBN: 0-87101-359-2. 2004. Item #3592. $34.99.

Lessons from Abroad: *Adapting International Social Welfare Innovations,* by M.C. Hokenstad and James Midgley, Editors. Regarded as among the world's leaders in formulating social work policy and practice, U.S. social workers have much to learn from colleagues in other nations. The third in an NASW Press series on international social work edited by Hokenstad and Midgley, this book examines how domestic policies and practice can be enhanced by documenting, analyzing and judiciously adapting innovative approaches emanating from other countries.

ISBN: 0-87101-360-6. 2004. Item #3606. $44.99.

Prudent Practice: *A Guide for Managing Malpractice Risk,* by Mary Kay Houston-Vega and Elane M. Nuehring with Elisabeth R. Daguio. Today, practice is more specialized and licensing regulations, professional standards, and statutes are more complex. The best defense in our increasingly litigious society remains competent, ethically conscientious practice. *Prudent Practice* offers practitioners a complete practice guide to increasing competence and managing the risk of malpractice. Included in the book and on CD-ROM are 25 sample forms and five sample fact sheets to distribute to clients.

ISBN: 0-87101-267-7. 1996. Item #2677. $45.99.

(Order form and information on reverse side)

ORDER FORM

Qty.	Title	Item #	Price	Total
___	Social Work Career Development, 2nd Edition	3630	$49.99	_____
___	What Social Workers Do, 2nd Edition	3649	$49.99	_____
___	Changing Hats while Managing Change, 2nd Edition	3614	$44.99	_____
___	A Dream and a Plan	3592	$34.99	_____
___	Lessons from Abroad	3606	$44.99	_____
___	Prudent Practice	2677	$45.99	_____

POSTAGE AND HANDLING
Minimum postage and handling fee is $4.95. Orders that do not include appropriate postage and handling will be returned.

DOMESTIC: Please add 12% to orders under $100 for postage and handling. For orders over $100 add 7% of order.

CANADA: Please add 17% postage and handling.

OTHER INTERNATIONAL: Please add 22% postage and handling.

Subtotal	_____
Postage and Handling	_____
DC residents add 6% sales tax	_____
MD residents add 5% sales tax	_____
NC residents add 4.5% sales tax	_____
NJ residents add 6% sales tax	_____
Total	_____

❏ **Check** or **money order** (payable to NASW Press) for $ _____.

❏ **Credit card**
   ❏ Visa   ❏ MasterCard   ❏ American Express

_____ _____

Credit Card Number   Expiration Date

Signature _____

Name _____

Address _____

City _____ State/Province _____

Country _____ Zip _____

Phone _____ E-mail _____

NASW Member # (if applicable) _____

(Please make checks payable to NASW Press. Prices are subject to change.)

NASW PRESS
P. O. Box 431
Annapolis JCT, MD 20701
USA

Credit card orders call
1-800-227-3590
(In the Metro Wash., DC, area, call 301-317-8688)
Or fax your order to 301-206-7989
Or order online at www.naswpress.org

CPCD04